DAY by DAY
with the SAINTS

Patrick R. Moran

Our Sunday Visitor Publishing
Huntington, Indiana 46750

ACKNOWLEDGMENT: Scripture quotations in this work are taken from the Revised Standard Version Bible, Catholic Edition, © 1965 and 1966 by the Division of Christian Education and the National Council of the Churches of Christ in the U.S.A., and are used by the permission of the copyright holder.

International Standard Book Number:
0-87973-714-x

Library of Congress Catalog Number:
85-80353

Cover Design by James McIlrath

Printed in the United States of America

714

Contents

Day by Day

Thanks be to You,
My Lord Jesus Christ,
for all the blessings and benefits
which You have given me,
for all the pains and insults
You have borne for me.

O Most merciful Friend,
my Brother and Redeemer,
may I know You more clearly,
love You more dearly,
and follow You more nearly,
day by day, day by day.
Amen.

— St. Richard of Wyche (1197-1253)

Editor's Preface

When the Church revised the calendar of saints' feastdays in 1969, she did in fact reduce the number of feasts that had to be celebrated throughout the world. Pope Paul VI gave these reasons for the change: "So that the Advent-Christmas period and the Lent-Easter period could focus almost entirely on our Lord's birth, death and resurrection." Also, " to emphasize the importance of those saints who were known and venerated locally."

At the same time, Pope Paul VI wanted us all to remember that the Church is universal and not merely local or national. It is a brotherhood of believers in Christ of people of every race, color and nation.

This is what we call the Communion of Saints. The preface of the Mass on the feast of All Saints expresses the idea with this prayer: "Father. . . around Your throne the saints, our brothers and sisters sing Your praise forever. Their glory fills us with joy and their communion with us in Your Church gives us inspiration and strength, as we hasten on our pilgrimage of faith, eager to meet them."

Day by Day with the Saints provides readers with a look at 385 feastdays. Some of the saints were canonized as recent as 1984. Popular writers and "guest editors" of *My Daily Visitor* supplied 221 inspirational reflections on the lives of the saints, while I researched and wrote the remaining 164 daily entries.

The 87 writers all emphasize that there is a saint for everyone and a saint for all seasons. These 385 reflections are edited in a popular biographic, historic and contemporary style, allowing easy reading for young and old. Each day concludes with a prayer, a thought, or an activity to stimulate spiritual meditation.

Day by Day with the Saints is an ideal addition to previous books: *Day by Day with Mary* and *Day by Day with My Daily Visitor*. A beautiful prayer by St. Richard Wyche will provide readers with a spiritual reminder "day by day."

— **Patrick R. Moran**

JANUARY

January 1
Solemnity of Mary, Mother of God
The General Roman Calendar promulgated by Pope Paul VI on February 14, 1969, reinstated the Marian character of this commemoration on the octave day of Christmas. New Year's Day was formerly observed as the feast of the Circumcision of our Lord.

We honor Mary as the Mother of Jesus Christ, the Incarnate Word of God. We recognize her unique and exalted role in the redemption her Son brought to men. Because we love Mary, we strive to imitate her virtues of faith, purity, humility and conformity to the will of God. The more we know and love Mary, the more surely will we know and love her Son and better understand His mission in the world. The more we know and love Jesus, the better we shall appreciate His Mother's place in God's plan for the redemption of mankind.

Mary, the Mother of God, is called by many titles because she is the universal patron of every Christian man, woman and child who has ever sought to follow more closely the vocation to which they are called by Christ. We can find the truth about Mary in the salutation: "Hail, Holy Queen, Mother of Mercy: Hail, our life, our sweetness, and our hope!"

— Thomas M. Brew, S.J.

TODAY: Include Mary in my New Year's resolution, to promote a personal devotion to Mary, the Mother of God and our Mother.

January 2
St. Basil the Great (c. 329-379)
Father of Monasticism in the East
St. Gregory Nazianzen (c. 330-390)
The Theologian

Byzantine saints are not very well known by most Catholics. They lived in a far different age, in a strange and different civ-

1

ilization. The Byzantine Empire was the first Christian nation, and most of the great events of the early Church took place there: the first Councils, the first great Doctors of the Church, the first great theological developments. Saints Basil and Gregory bear witness to the rich diversity of the Church. Their lives and their teachings are part of our Catholic heritage. St. Basil is the great father of monasticism, and St. Gregory is one of the great masters of mystical theology. They served God in their own age with the best tools they could find, and left their mark upon their century and upon their times.

St. Basil stood up to the emperor, lashing at him for his inhumanity and lack of Christian principle. "No one," said the emperor, "has ever spoken to me like that." "Apparently," said St. Basil, "you have never met a Catholic bishop." This rare kind of courage, born of faith, was badly needed in those early days when the Church was in danger of being crushed by hostile forces. In Saints Basil and Gregory, the Faith found worthy champions.

— **Blase Schauer, O.P.**

TODAY: In the example of those saints of old, we should say: "Lord what would you have me do?"

January 3
St. Genevieve (422-512)
Patron of Paris

Her childhood was much like that of the other shepherd children of Nanterre (France), spending much of the day tending the sheep grazing on Mount Valerien. Unlike the other children, Genevieve had already begun a life of prayer and "committed herself to serving God." When she was eight years old she met the saintly Bishop Germain, who blessed the little girl and encouraged her virtuous living. It was Bishop Germain who foretold: "Genevieve will lead a holy life and guide countless pilgrims to God." The bishop then gave her a medal engraved with a cross, as a sign of her virginity and complete dedication to God.

She gave of herself, as St. Paul wrote, "a living sacrifice, holy and acceptable to God" (Romans 12:1). The daughter of Severus and Gerontia took the veil of the religious life when she

2

was 15 years old. From that age she spent herself in acts of charity and penance. Hers was an austere lifestyle that included abstinence from meat. Genevieve was also blessed with the power of visions and the gift of prophecy; however, she almost drowned because of these charisms and her unfailing belief in God.

Today's saint is also credited with the saving of Paris from the sword of the Huns when Attila invaded Gaul. She encouraged the Parisians to remain firm and steadfast, to watch the enemy, to fast and do penance, and to trust in God for their welfare. In 1129 St. Genevieve interceded again for the welfare of the city during the "burning fever" epidemic which had killed 14,000. While her relics were carried in procession through the streets, many victims were miraculously cured and the plague ceased.

> TODAY: That modern youth may turn more to the lifestyle of the little shepherd girl praying in the meadows, to combat the glitter and glamor of today's high style.

January 4
St. Elizabeth Ann Seton (1774-1821)
First American-Born Saint

Today we celebrate the feast of the first American-born saint, St. Elizabeth Ann (Bayley) Seton. She lived in Baltimore and was a wife, mother of five children, widow, teacher, and founder of the first American religious order — the Sisters of Charity. Even a casual look at the life of Elizabeth Seton impresses us, not with what she did, but with what she suffered through, not with what she accomplished but with what she endured. Her life became an almost continual separation from those who were closest to her, at times through death and at other times through the circumstances which life imposed. Her life became a living example of the phrase — love means letting go.

We may come close to the best we can say about Elizabeth Seton by stating she endured out of love. We may also come close to the best we can hope for ourselves by saying the same thing — to endure out of love.

— Rev. Edward O'Heron

January 5
St. John Nepomucene Neumann (1811-1860)
Canonized by Pope Paul VI, June 19, 1977

In 1836, about 15 years after the death of St. Elizabeth Ann Seton, John Neumann came to the United States from Bohemia (Czechoslovakia) and was ordained a priest for the Diocese of New York by Bishop John Dubois. For the next 16 years he labored, as a diocesan priest and then as a Redemptorist, in upstate New York, Ohio, Maryland and Pennsylvania. Then in 1852 he became the fourth Bishop of Philadelphia. There he died on January 5, 1860.

The bare facts of his heroic life clothe a deep and inspiring spiritual life. He had come from a thoroughly Catholic culture to one that was anti-Catholic in many ways. He was determined to help save the Faith of the many Catholic immigrants and to build up the body of Christ, His Church. His devotion to the Pope as the visible head of Christ's Church was totally admirable. It is part of the legacy that he and many of the pioneering bishops of this country have left to us today. Devotion to the successor of St. Peter is a distinguishing mark of American Catholicism.

— Msgr. Charles Dollen

TODAY: Let there be a resurgence of the Forty Hours devotion in our parishes like that espoused by St. John Neumann.

January 6
St. Melanius (c. 530)
Bishop and Confessor

Trivial Pursuit is a modern pastime enabling one to examine those little-known facts about still lesser-known persons, places or things. Today's saint is an ideal candidate. His only identity in the *New Catholic Encyclopedia* is a three word line — Bishop of Rennes.

4

A 1926 revision of *Butler's Lives of the Saints* sheds some light on Melanius, Bishop of Rennes. He was born in Placs in Brittany and for some years lived a monastic life, serving in the Diocese of Vannes. Upon the death of St. Amandus, Bishop of Rennes, Melanius was elevated to the bishopric. Humility and prayer enhanced the virtues of the bishop, and he is reported to have performed numerous miracles. His chief contribution to the Church was his canons calling for the Council of Orleans in 511. Because of Bishop Melanius's zealous prayer life, idolatry was eradicated in the Diocese of Rennes.

We may well thank God that there are saints for all occasions and even the lesser-knowns.

> *TODAY: I will ask God to help me to be honest with myself about myself.*

January 7
St. Raymond Penyafort (1175-1275)
Patron of Students of Canon Law

This is a Dominican saint, one of those rare people who became legends in their own lifetimes. The legends about St. Raymond have him sailing on cloaks across the waters of the Mediterranean, but the reality is more sobering. He was an astute canon lawyer, a lover of languages, and it was he who inspired St. Thomas Aquinas to write one of his greatest works, the *Summa Contra Gentiles*, a handbook for the Christian missionary facing the Moslems.

What contributed to the legends was the fact that he seemed immortal; it seemed he would never die. He was over 100 years old when he did die, and had lived through one of the most exciting centuries in the history of the Church: the 13th century. It is good to know that even the saints suffered sometimes from too great a reputation, and it must have been very difficult to face people when they heard stories that you had sailed miraculously across the water on a cloak. But St. Raymond seems to have had a delightful sense of humor, took these stories in good stride, and simply continued to serve God in his own unique and inimitable way.

— Blase Schauer, O.P.

5

January 8
St. Apollinaris (c. 175)
Bishop, Martyr, "The Apologist"

Throughout history, God has given us signs of His presence through lives of saints, and holy men and women, who remind us of God's place in the world. One of these "signs" in the first ages of the Church was Bishop Apollinaris of Phrygia (central Turkey), who wrote and preached in defense of the Church's doctrines. This early Christian teacher rebuked the militant heretics of that time. According to St. Jerome, the bishop wrote many treatises dealing with the philosophy upon which the sects and their heresies were founded.

Apollinaris earned the title "The Apologist" for his apologia (apology) in defense of the Christian religion addressed to Emperor Marcus Aurelius. The emperor was reminded that a crucial military victory occurred because of the "miraculous" prayers by the Christian soldiers, members of the "Thundering Legion." Marcus Aurelius, "out of gratitude to his Christian soldiers, published an edict forbidding, under pain of death, the denunciation of Christians on account of their religion."

History records the edict certainly did not remove the anti-Christian laws of the land, and persecution continued. It is ironic that today's saint died a martyr's death while teaching the law of God to enemies of the early Church.

> *TODAY: Do we stand up for our religious beliefs? How do we rebuke those modern heresies? Study the Faith and live it to the full.*

January 9
St. Peter of Sebaste (d. c. 391)
Bishop and Confessor

What a wonderful experience it would be to interview an entire family of saints. Heritage and family "roots" have become

6

very important factors. As Christians our "roots" are in Christ, as were those of our ancestors of the early Church.

Today's saint was the youngest of 10 children born to St. Basil the Elder and St. Emmelia. The parents were banished to the deserts of Pontus (Turkey), while Peter was left to the care of his sister Macrina. Her only aim was "to instruct him in the maxims of religion and piety." Peter later succeeded his brother Basil to the abbacy of a monastery founded by his mother. Imbued with the spirit of charity and self-denial, Peter gave food to the starving people facing a disastrous famine. He was consecrated Bishop of Sebaste in the year 380 in order to root out Arianism, rampant in Armenia at that time.

Peter's family tree reads like the calendar of saints, for his grandmother was St. Macrina the Elder; his father, St. Basil the Elder; his mother, St. Emmelia; his sister, St. Macrina; his brother, St. Basil, and another brother St. Gregory of Nyssa. With such roots it is certain the remaining unnamed children were reared in the charisms of the Faith.

> TODAY: As parents, let our counsels be founded on piety, charity and sanctity that Christian "roots" may be sustained in our family.

January 10
St. William (d. 1209)
Confessor, Archbishop of Bourges

Thomas Merton, an American Trappist monk, in one of his books provided us with a simple formula for sainthood. He wrote: "The simplest and most effective way to sanctity is to disappear into the background of ordinary routine."

St. William seems to have adopted that formula for himself as "he learned from his infancy to despise the world, to abhor its pleasures and to tremble at its dangers." Mortification, purity of heart and soul, prayer were his daily lot as a Cistercian Abbot at Pontigny, France. When he was chosen Archbishop of Bourges, he was overcome with grief. William, already lost in the "background of ordinary routine," accepted the archbishopric only out of obedience to Pope Innocent III, and to his religious superior, the Abbot of Citeaux.

Even as Archbishop William treated the penances of others

7

as his own, he also helped others by providing bodily and spiritual nourishment. He was much in demand as a confessor. St. William converted many Albigensians from their philosophical heresy before his death. William was canonized by Pope Honorius III in 1218.

> *TODAY: O heavenly patron, please help me chart a spiritual journey toward a saintly lifestyle.*

January 11
St. Theodosius, the Cenobiarch (c. 423-529)
Archimandrite of the Religious Monks of Jerusalem

Theodosius, a saint with a most unusual name, was also a most unusual person, living for l06 years. The *New Catholic Encyclopedia* refers to him as Theodosius of Palestine.

Today's saint was influenced by St. Simeon Stylites, the famous and colorful religious ascetic who lived on a pillar (platform) in the Syrian desert for 36 years. Theodosius, in his quest for the religious life, visited all the holy shrines of Jerusalem as a penitent and a prayerful pilgrim. He then chose the monastic life rather than a hermitage. The first lesson he taught his monks was "that the continual remembrance of death is the foundation of religious perfection." In order to make a lasting impression on the holy men, Theodosius dug a pit or grave which would be the common burial place for the whole community. His monastery, near Bethlehem, is likened to "a city of saints in the midst of a desert, and in it reigned — regularity, silence, charity and peace." The monastery also cared for the sick, the aged and feeble and the mentally handicapped.

Theodosius was banished from his monastery by the Emperor Anastasius because of his refusal to sign a "heretical profession of faith, in which the divine and human natures in Christ were confounded into one." After the emperor's death, Theodosius returned to Cathismus (monastery) where he served 11 years prior to his death.

> *TODAY: Not all of us can be solitaries and go off to the desert and wilderness for a life of total prayer. But I can have a life of prayer and dedication to my apostolate.*

8

January 12
St. Marguerite Bourgeoys (1620-1700)
Founder of Sisters of the Congregation of Notre Dame

In his homily at the canonization of St. Marguerite Bourgeoys, October 31, 1982, Pope John Paul II said: "Come and behold all the works God has done. . . . We are celebrating what the Holy Spirit has accomplished in (her)." In order to understand the vocation of today's saint, it is best to dwell on the Gospel of Mark (12:30-31), ". . . you shall love the Lord your God with all your heart, and with all your soul, and with all your mind, and with all your strength. . . . You shall love your neighbor as yourself. There is no other commandment greater than this."

Marguerite Bourgeoys was born in Troyes, France, in 1620. From the age of 20 she spent her life in serving the needy and caring for the poor families of her community. She left the "cultural center of France" in 1653 for the "rugged wilderness" of Canada, then a French possession. Jeanne Mance, founder of Hotel Dieu Hospital, accompanied Marguerite to the fort at Ville Marie, now known as Montreal. "Life here has been very sad," Jeanne Mance had forewarned. However, Marguerite consoled young families in their trials. She taught the women to cook and to sew, and how to care for the family in the wilderness. She converted the governor's stable into a schoolhouse where she taught the French and also Indian children to read, write, count. For 47 years Marguerite also "taught them about God and His special love for each of them." The people of Montreal, today, refer to its newest saint as "Mother of the Colony."

> TODAY: I will begin to put into practice with increasingly greater commitment the commandment of love of God and neighbor.

January 13
St. Hilary (315-368)
Doctor of the Church

When God entrusted His word to the Church, He guaranteed that error would not destroy it. But every century brings a new infection of heresy, and Christians rise anew to save the truth.

In the fourth century, the identity of Christ was called into question. Is He God or only man? A dozen shades of doctrine appeared, and later it was sneered that Christianity was split over nothing.

St. Hilary, the Bishop of Poitiers, defended the unvarying Christian doctrine: Christ is true God and true Man. The saint, twice exiled for his teaching, is hailed as one of that small band of intellectual heroes whom the Church calls "Doctor." He has special meaning today for Catholics in a world which makes Faith a man-made package. He wrote that Faith is in danger as soon as "definitions of the Lord's teaching are enacted by a human judge, a prince." Or, we might add, by a council of professors or churches.

— **Most Rev. Paul J. Hallinan**

TODAY: By your own example strive to lead others to the true Faith.

January 14
St. Felix of Nola (d. 260)
Priest, Confessor

The saints are the Christian heroes for all time. They are the role-models for those of the 20th century. Their lives project lessons teaching us more about our Christian Faith, holiness and our relationship with God.

Today's hero is St. Felix, a native of the village of Nola in Italy. He was a son of Hermias, a retired soldier. Like many saints, he gave away any personal fortunes to help the poor as a service to God. From history we learn that he was "ordained a reader of the Word, exorcist and priest." He assisted Bishop Maximus and the Church at Nola, near the city of Naples. During the persecution of the Church by the Emperor Decius in 250, Felix was tortured and imprisoned for his Faith. According to legend, Felix was told by an angel to go to the aid of the elderly Maximus, who was gravely ill. "The confessor, seeing his chains fall off and the jail doors open, followed the angel-guide to the aging bishop." Following the death of the emperor, peace was somewhat restored to the Church, and "Felix was received into the city as an angel sent from heaven."

Felix refused the bishopric upon the death of Maximus,

10

and suggested that Quintus should head the see. Felix refused any of the "return of the spoils" of the family estate; rather, he rented "a bit of barren land upon which he could subsist." St. Felix died "in a good old age." His lifelong philosophy in treating wealth and earthly riches is found in his words: "In poverty we should be the more secure of possessing Christ."

> TODAY: *What does it profit a man if he gains the whole world, yet suffers the loss of his own soul?*

January 15
St. Paul the Hermit (d. 342)
First Christian Hermit

In the fourth age of the Church, many holy men "went into the desert" in their search for solitude and a place for heavenly contemplation. Paul of Egypt is the first in a long succession of the Church's "Fathers and Saints of the Desert." Fleeing persecution at the age of 22, Paul lived in a cave in the Theban desert for 90 years, and died at the age of 113. In *The Lives of the Saints*, we read that the Prophet Elias and St. John the Baptist had "sanctified the desert." Jesus Christ was also the model of a hermitic state, demonstrated by His 40 days praying and fasting in the wilderness. We learn that Paul the Hermit's solitude was invaded, through divine intervention, with a meeting of St. Anthony of Egypt.

According to tradition, the two hermits were talking and a raven flew toward them and dropped a loaf of bread at their feet. St. Paul said, "Our good God has sent us dinner. In this manner I have received half a loaf every day these 60 years past; now you have come to see me, Christ has doubled His provision for His servants." Shortly after receiving the "bread from heaven," Paul prepared for his death by asking Anthony to shroud him with the cloak given by St. Athanasius. It was during Anthony's journey to the monastery for the cloak that Paul died. We learn that Anthony returned to the hermit's cave to bury Paul, during which St. Anthony sang hymns and psalms according to the burial custom of the Church.

> TODAY: *Reflect on the longevity of this saintly hermit. ". . . At the close of a man's life his deeds will be revealed. Call no one happy before his death. . . ."*

11

January 16
St. Marcellus I (d. 310)
His Pontificate lasted one year, seven months and 20 days

Hilary was a theologian, Paul a recluse, Marcellus a good administrator. When Marcellus became Pope in 308, the Christians were just recovering from the blows of Diocletian's persecution. The Church was disorganized and, worst of all, torn by many factions. Those who had remained loyal during the trouble objected to those who had fallen away and now wanted to come back. The new Pope briskly brought order into the chaos. But he made enemies, like most good leaders. He insisted that those who had betrayed the Faith had to do penance. For this he was captured and sent into exile, where he died.

In the Gospel of his feast, we read our Lord's invitation: "If any man would come after me, let him deny himself and take up his cross and follow me" (Matthew 16:24). The short-lived Pope wanted to follow Christ.

— Most Rev. Paul J. Hallinan

TODAY: How consoling it is for us to know that day by day we have some special saint watching over us.

January 17
St. Anthony of Egypt (c. 251-354)
Patron of Gravediggers and Graveyards

"By his example and prayers, may we learn to deny ourselves and to love You above all things." This is the heart of the Prayer of the Mass for St. Anthony. The patriarch of all monks, Anthony (also Antony) is remembered as the first abbot who formed a permanent rule for his family of monks, dedicated to divine service. He died at the remarkable age of 105.

What do we have in common with this monk of the fourth century? Perhaps there exists a closer relationship than we might suppose. Anthony took advice to flee the materialism of his time. The same advice applies to you and me: to learn to deny ourselves in material things and to seek God above all. "Things" will either bring us to or take us away from God. One day we will leave them all and give an accounting on how we used them.

— Rev. Thomas J. Carpender

12

TODAY: "Lord, direct me to love people and use things. I must give an account of everything."

January 18
St. Margaret of Hungary (1242-1270)
Princess, Dominican Contemplative

A princess is much in vogue in today's society, attested to by the media coverage of the likes of Margaret and Diana of Great Britain and the late Grace of Monaco. Today's saint was also a member of the royal household of Hungary. The House of Arapad, the first royal family (997-1301), contributed to the communion of the saints through Stephen, Imre, Laszlo, Elizabeth and today's saint, Princess Margaret.

Margaret was the daughter of King Bela IV and Queen Maria (Lascaris). When she was only 10, she entered the convent of St. Mary of the Isle. Her father had built the monastery on an island in the Danube River near the city of Budapest. Unlike today's princesses, Margaret refused proposals of royal marriage three times. She was, instead, consecrated a virgin, and dedicated her life to austerity, meditation and prayer. Although of royal blood, she served her convent and Sisters as the lowest of servants. Margaret was also a mystic, and dedicated her sufferings and deprivations to the Blessed Sacrament. She was only 28 years old at the time of her death. Pope Pius XII canonized her in 1943, exactly seven centuries and a year from the date of her birth.

TODAY: Pray that these 24 hours are better than yesterday and a mirror of all tomorrows.

January 19
St. Germanicus (d. 156)
Martyr, Tamer of Wild Animals

A man seldom sets out to be a martyr, but down through the ages the measure of perfect dedication for every holy man has been martyrdom. This ideal of sacrifice is reflected in the life of St. Germanicus contained in the writings of early Christian persecutions in Smyrna (Turkey). "... The right noble Germanicus fought with the wild beasts in a signal way." Rather than waiting for the animals to attack him, he attacked them. He exerted violence and dragged the wild beasts toward him, "in order that he might perish. *"The Roman Martyrology* says of Germanicus: ". . . (he) was ground by the teeth of a beast, merited to be one with the true bread, the Lord Jesus Christ, by dying for His sake."

St. Catherine of Siena (1347-1380) was fascinated by the martyrs of early Rome. "The blood of the martyrs is a constant fountain," she once wrote, "and invites the living to be strong."

> *TODAY: Look beneath the surface of life, delve deeper into profound mystery, into the suffering of the Son of God.*

January 20
St. Fabian (d. 250)
Pope and Martyr
St. Sebastian (d. 288)
Patron of Athletes and Archers

The Church in Rome was watered with the blood of martyrs copiously during the first three centuries of its existence. Saints Fabian and Sebastian were favorites among the people of Rome. Fabian ruled the Church for 14 years before he was put to death by the Emperor Decius in 250. St. Cyprian wrote of Fabian: "It is helpful and encouraging when a Bishop offers himself as a model for his brothers. . . ."

Sebastian, a Roman legionnaire, was cited by Emperor Diocletian for his bravery and heroism in battle. The valiant soldier was called to be a valiant martyr for Christ and was killed by the same emperor he had protected.

Fabian, indeed, was one of a long line of Popes who died the death of a martyr. To be named to succeed St. Peter meant certain death for the better part of three centuries. It is a mark of real Christian charity to pray for our Pope and bishops. God has set these men apart for the service of the Church, to build up the Body of Christ. It has never been an easy task and it is certainly a lonely one.

— Msgr. Charles Dollen

> *TODAY: I will walk my post in a military manner that I might be a better "soldier for Christ."*

14

St. Agnes (d. c. 304)
Virgin and Martyr, Patron of Girls

This shining young girl! From the very dawn of the Church she has been there as an example of holiness and a model of heroism. She was young, perhaps not more than 12 years old; she had promised herself to Christ, and no power on earth was going to separate her from this love. Such Faith we sometimes find too overwhelming for us, but perhaps that is because we have not really understood the greatness of what we believe or the magnificent God that we worship.

How can St. Agnes be the model of the young? She lived hundreds of years ago, in an age vastly different from our own. She lived in the days of Roman emperors and centurions and cohorts and all kinds of names quite different from the names in our world. She was of a noble patrician Roman family, and most of us come from ordinary homes and ordinary families. Well, she was a determined little lady, and everyone can understand that. She had made up her mind about something; she was holily stubborn for a cause, and she was willing to risk everything for it. She had convictions deeply rooted in Faith, and she would let go of these convictions for no one; not family, not friends, not pain, not suffering, not death.

— **Blase Schauer, O.P.**

TODAY: It is well to recall the words of St. Ambrose: "Agnes was too young to be punished, yet old enough to receive a martyr's crown. . . ."

January 22
St. Vincent (d. 304)
Spanish Deacon and Martyr

St. Vincent was popular in medieval times. He symbolized what his name indicated, "victory," triumph over overwhelming odds, a profile of courage, the spirit of man clinging to God.

In that era, man feared death, perhaps more than we do, because death in those days was usually violent. To stand firm in the face of death, as the martyrs did, as St. Vincent did, to remain unshakable in the presence of terror and violence, to face death unflinchingly, to be "unconquered" by all of this, was the supreme victory and the noblest achievement. Moreover, this strength was linked to Faith, not to mere human endurance. The martyr stood firm in his Faith in God and triumphed over all obstacles.

"These are those who drank the chalice of the Lord," the liturgy for martyrs sings, "and became the friends of God." The very business of living makes many demands on most of us, fidelity to God may make even more. The medieval Catholic emblazoned the example of the martyrs in the stones of his churches and in the rocks of his cities. Victory—"*vincens*"— is possible, and to be reminded of it constantly by the example of a martyr gave one the courage to face one's own particular and peculiar brand of martyrdom.

— Rev. Clifford Stevens

TODAY: O Jesus, Lover of mankind, take us all into Your arms, especially the youth of this 20th century.

January 23
St. John the Almsgiver (560-619)
Patron of the Knights of Malta

Today's saint was born of a noble Cyprus family. We know that he was a very wealthy person. He was chosen Patriarch of Alexandria, and his daily exercise in spirituality provided an example of virtuous living and provision of alms for the poor. John often referred to his "masters," who, he explained were the poor and downcast "who had such great power in the court of heaven to help those who had been good to them on earth." As Patriarch he enacted ordinances protecting the poor from unjust taxes. He also issued laws protecting the poor and gullible from exploitation and cheating by fraudulent manipulators. Legend has him giving away 80,000 pieces of gold from the church's treasury to help build hospitals, hospices and monasteries and to feed and clothe the poor. St. John, also called the Almoner, did his best "to render to God the things that were God's." This was his philosophy, as he died a very poor man.

It was St. John Vianney, the Curé of Ars, who wrote: ". . . we are almost happier than the saints in heaven! They live upon

16

their income and can earn no more. We can augment our treasure at every moment. All we need to do is to cooperate with God's grace, for His grace helps us to walk. . . . God, through His grace, is as necessary to us as crutches are to a lame man. . . ."

> TODAY: *Like our patron, John, I will make almsgiving a giving that "hurts," during those penitential days of fasting and prayer.*

January 24
St. Francis de Sales (1567-1622)
Patron of Authors, Journalists and Writers

St. Francis de Sales is the patron and benefactor of the Catholic Press. These are certainly times when that medium of the apostolate needs a saintly protector. Changes that have come fast upon us in our religion have caused conflict. This was bound to happen as the old ways yield to the renewed. Those opposed to change in any form can find an available target in the reporter of that news. Opposition to the press is akin to the ancient practice of "killing the marathon runner who brought news the king did not want to hear."

It does take great charity to write about the momentum of our days in a meaningful way. It also takes charity to read about what is happening. If everything we read makes us upset, annoyed or explosive, it may not be necessary to change what we read. It might be better to change ourselves. We are taking things too seriously if they get to us in that way.

— Rev. William Joyce

> TODAY: *That I may readily see the who, what, why, where, when, and how of all spiritual elements that will lead me to a better understanding of the Word of God.*

January 25
Conversion of Paul (d. 64 or 67)
Apostle to the Gentiles

After the Resurrection and Pentecost, the single most important happening in the early Church was the conversion of St. Paul.

"Saul, Saul, why do you persecute Me?" is not only a summons to conversion of the murderous Saul, but a call for us to see Christ in everyone. What we say, do, or fail to do to others is the proof of how genuine our love for Christ and faithfulness to His commandments really are. Do we honestly believe Christ is the Head of the Body and each of us is a living member? How we treat others is the exact measure of *how* we treat Christ. Christ and my neighbor are one.   — Rev. Thomas J. Carpender

TODAY: This is the day of our conversion from selfishness to other-centeredness.

January 26
St. Timothy (d. c. 97)
Bishop of Ephesus and Disciple of St. Paul
St. Titus (d. c. 96)
Companion of St. Paul

Saints Timothy and Titus were "second-generation" Christians. They do not belong to the original group of Jerusalem Christians, and in consequence they had to help pioneer a totally new type of Christian community, one that did not have the stability and unity of the Jewish religious heritage. They had to plant the Faith in oddly different communities, scattered over the face of the Roman Empire, and they had to make that Faith the bond of unity for Jew and Gentile, slave and freeman, men and women from all walks of life and of many races and nationalities.

They had to re-echo always the message of St. Paul that rings through most of his Epistles: "Our bond of unity and our salvation come from Faith in Christ, not from any human advantage that we may have." The Good News that they brought was the news that God had become man and had called all men to His Kingdom. It was this new vision of God's love that they preached as they planted the new Christian communities at Philippi, Thessalonica, Corinth and Ephesus. Their Faith enabled them to face new situations unflinching and unafraid. Within a few short years, they had changed the face of Europe.

— Rev. Clifford Stevens

TODAY: "Fight the good fight of the faith; and take hold of the eternal life . . ." (1 Timothy 6: 12).

18

January 27
St. Angela Merici (1474-1540)
Italian Nun and Founder, Institute of St. Ursula,
the Church's first teaching order of nuns

The historical significance of St. Angela Merici is that she is the foundress of the first teaching order of women in the Church, the Ursulines. Today when the world is divided into two great warring camps fighting for the future, we had better grasp the crucial meaning to us of this far-sighted woman of 15th-century Italy. Her merit is that, moved by heroic charity, she saw that the child is the future.

Thus she began to gather about her the neglected poor children of her village to overcome their appalling ignorance. Through the power of her charm and personal beauty, with the forces of her leadership and judgment in a happy union of nature and grace, she accomplished wonders. May her spirit of self-sacrifice, her wisdom and her burning sense of urgency, animate our Catholic girls and young women to rally to the cause of Catholic education today.

— G. Joseph Gustafson, S.S.

> TODAY: *"Be sincerely kind to everyone according to Our Lord's words: 'Learn of me for I am meek and humble of heart'"* (St. Angela Merici, The Spiritual Testament).

January 28
St. Thomas Aquinas (1225-1274)
Patron of Catholic Schools and Education

St. Thomas is perhaps best known by the ordinary Catholic for the Benediction hymns and for the Office of the Feast of Corpus Christi. The *Tantum Ergo* and the *O Salutaris Hostia* were the classical Latin hymns for Catholics and contained the full doctrine of the Church on the Mystery of the Holy Eucharist. "Down before so deep a Mystery," he said in the *Tantum Ergo*, "Let our beings lowly bow; ancient rites pass into history, newly-formed our worship now. Faith gains insight to the Mystery which the senses cannot know." He himself bowed down in adoration before this amazing Mystery and dedicated his whole

19

priesthood to making it known throughout all Christendom.

When he was dying and the abbot of the monastery where he was being taken care of brought him the Eucharist, this big man, a giant of a man, got out of bed and fell on his knees in front of the Blessed Sacrament. "O Price of my Salvation," he said, "for You alone have I labored, for You alone have I written, for You alone have I studied." The Eucharist was the center of his priesthood and his theology. When he wrote about it, he wrote with a pen of flame. — Blase Schauer, O.P.

TODAY: Let us dwell on the words of the "Angelic Doctor," that prayer had taught him more than study.

January 29
St. Peter Nolasco (c. 1182-1256)

Since the revision of the Roman calendar in 1969 some former feast days have been either abolished or regulated to observance in particular places according to local option. Today's saint was originally honored on January 31, since 1936 on January 28.

It's hard to believe today that Peter Nolasco could found a whole religious order (Mercedarians) simply to ransom captives. Well, in the 13th century, the enslavement of pilgrims was just about the most heinous misfortune that Christians could think of. What's more, ransom will forever be a central Christian principle. God sent His own Son to ransom all of us. Redemption is the name of the game. Today, half the world must be rescued from hunger. Ransom is also urgently needed for the victims of ignorance, prejudice, war, disease, poverty. Right around us, we need rescuing from soul-strangling mediocrity, environmental abuse, the spirit of anarchy, and the manufacture of fear. It looks as if ransom will continue to be very much a human need.

It is also a discipline. As Peter Nolasco reminds us today, redemption from any of these things requires that we interpose something of ourselves.

— Msgr. John G. Nolan

TODAY: Like St. Peter Nolasco, ask Mary the Mother of God to rescue us from sin with our daily ransom of prayer and sacrifice.

January 30
St. Bathildis (d. 680)
Queen of France

The story of today's saint could well be the plot of a modern "rags to riches" narrative. St. Bathildis served as a slave in a French palace only to become the wife of King Clovis II in 649. She reigned as Queen of France for seven years following the death of her husband, and was succeeded to the throne by her eldest son, Clotaire III, in 665. Her other sons, Childeric II and Thierry, also wore the crown.

Day by day, Bathildis exhibited that chief characteristic of saintliness by her concern and compassion for the poor and unfortunate. "The King gave her the sanction of his royal authority for the protection of the Church, the care of the poor, and the furtherance of all religious undertakings" (*Butler's Lives of the Saints*). After her sons were enthroned, she left palatial trappings for the religious life in the monastery of Chelles. For 15 years she served in extreme humility and obeyed Abbess St. Bertilla as the least and lowest of Sisters. She died on January 30, 680, leaving a legacy of charity, care of the poor, religious fervor and perseverance.

> *TODAY: I will be happy to imitate this holy queen by freeing myself from snares and entanglements of the riches and trappings of the "good life."*

January 31
St. John Bosco (1815-1888)
Patron of Editors; Founded Salesian Order

This was a winsome saint, who cultivated winsomeness almost as his trademark, but who could also be a shrewd businessman and wheeler-dealer, if it was for the good of his boys. As a young man he was a juggler, an acrobat, because he found that this gave him the attention of those he was trying to lead to God. As an old man, he led one of the greatest armies of priests in the Church, the Salesians, to amazing work for Christ, on almost every continent.

What St. John Bosco realized, and what some religious people never learn, is that few people will be attracted to Christ

21

if those who represent Him do not have attractive dispositions themselves. Rigid, rude and grumpy people, who also claim to be religious, are a scandal to the Church and, in some measure, are traitors to Christ.

Someone has defined rudeness as "a small man's imitation of power," and rude people never realize just how much unhappiness they bring. St. John Bosco made a careful scrutiny of his own personality and rooted out of it anything that would offend others. Only then did he try to bring them to God.

— **Blase Schauer, O.P.**

TODAY: Reflect on the words of Don Bosco: "In the tabernacle there is the greatest treasure that can be found either in heaven or on earth. . . ."

FEBRUARY

February 1
St. Brigid (450-525)
"The Mary of the Gael," Patron of Ireland

The life of St. Brigid written in the seventh century presents her as a new type of Irish woman — the Christian saint. Her countrymen hailed her as "the Mary of the Gael." Her popularity accompanied the early missionaries and pilgrims on their travels to the continent of Europe.

She was born in Offaly, Ireland, and came from the *Fotharta Airbrech* people near Croghan Hill. Her mother was a slave girl, but the child was acknowledged by her father, an Irish chieftain, and given to a foster mother to rear. Having been instructed in letters, the art of embroidery and household chores, she was sought in marriage, only to reject her suitor. She had vowed "her virginity to the Lord." When she was 20 years old, Brigid founded in the Liffey plain a church called Cill-Dara (Kildare), meaning "the church of the oak." A house for pious men, ruled by Conleth the bishop and abbot, was near the convent, and both communities could use the same church. Kildare was thus a double monastery, the only one of its kind in Ireland.

TODAY: Pray to St. Brigid and ask her protection of Ireland from the perils of terror and warfare in Northern Eire:

February 2
Presentation of the Lord
Formerly Observed as the Feast of Purification (Candlemas Day)

What virtues shine forth in the Holy Family. Loving response to the will of the Heavenly Father, made known to them through the prescriptions of the law, blossoms forth as a fruit of their humanity and ready obedience. Christ, a light of revelation to the Gentiles, enters His temple. Archbishop Fulton J. Sheen wrote: "It is the first Offertory of the first Mass." Christ is of-

23

fered through the immaculate hands of His Mother to the Eternal Father. St. Joseph is there, often pictured carrying two turtledoves in a cage — for theirs was the offering of the poor.

Our Blessed Mother played no small part in this mystery. She stands with other women to be purified, "Our tainted nature's solitary boast"! Her silence adds to the beauty of her *fiat*. We listen to Simeon's words of prophecy, as he speaks to Mary: ". . . a sword will pierce through your own soul . . ."(Luke 2:35).

— **Sister M. Barbara Anne, F.M.S.C.**

TODAY: May the Virgin Mother, your patroness and mine, hold us united in the great apostolate of the family.

February 3
St. Blase (d. c. 316)
Physician, Patron of Throat Ailments

Century after century, and year after year, one of the most sought-after blessings is the blessing of throats given on the feast of St. Blase. Exceedingly rare would be the person who has never suffered from some major or minor affliction of the throat; in fact, rare would be the individual who hasn't had several bouts with a soreness in the throat. A physician, Blase became the Bishop of Sebaste in Armenia. His reputation as a miracle worker in the healing of the sick was enhanced by the saving of the life of a small child who was choking to death after swallowing a fish bone. A humble man with strong faith in God, Blase willingly accepted death rather than deny his Creator.

How beautiful and meaningful are the words of the blessing: "Through the intercession of St. Blase, bishop and martyr, may God deliver you from all disease of the throat and from every other evil!"

— **Msgr. Ralph G. Kutz**

TODAY: I will pray — Jesus, in the midst of my own problems do not let me be blind to the pain and suffering of those around me. Help me reach out to those who need my healing and comfort.

February 4
St. Andrew Corsini (1302-1373)
Italian Bishop, Patron of Peacemakers

The parents of the youthful Andrew Corsini were quite disappointed in their son, who was born on the Feast of Andrew the Apostle, and whom they had early dedicated to God under the patronage of the Blessed Virgin Mary, because of his undisciplined and immoral life. One day his mother told him that before his birth she had dreamed she had given birth to a wolf which ran into a church and was changed into a lamb. This impressed Andrew so deeply that he went to church and prayed most fervently before the altar of Our Lady and there resolved to change his way of life. He persevered in this resolution and became a Carmelite friar. Later he was consecrated the Bishop of Fiesole, Italy. — **Paschal Boland, O.S.B.**

TODAY: Be patient with everyone, especially yourself.

February 5
St. Agatha (d. c. 250)
Virgin and Martyr, Patron of Nurses

The early decades of the history of the Church are filled with acts of heroic young Christian women who gave their lives in defense of virginity and purity. Glorious was their courage in the face of the most cruel torments. One of these young women was St. Agatha. Such courage as theirs is rooted in faith. There are times during our lives when we are faced with difficult decisions, and we may be tempted to compromise our faith and Christian principles. Some situations will be more serious than others. The courage to choose the way of Jesus will be easier if it is a way of life for us.

St. Agatha prayed that God, who knew her heart, would possess all of her. She prayed for worthiness — for courage — to overcome the devil and all temptations. She prayed for the patience to suffer. Though our trials are less severe, we too need courage and patience to suffer. — **Linus Merz, S.C.J.**

TODAY: "I would rather subject myself to bodily suffering for a little season, rather than have my silly soul perish forever" (Thomas More).

25

February 6
SS. Paul Miki and Companions (d. 1597)
26 Martyrs, First Canonized Saints of Far East

The city of Nagasaki, in Japan, is forever unforgettable because of the awful destruction of life there by the atomic bomb on August 9, 1945. Yet, Christians knew its name long before World War II as the site of martyrdom for 26 heroes of Christ, in the 16th century.

Twenty-six Christians — Japanese and European, Jesuits and Franciscans, priests and lay people from every walk of life — were crucified and speared like Christ, because of Christ. They all could say with St. Paul: "I have been crucified with Christ; it is no longer I who live, but Christ who lives in me" (Galatians 2:20). One of the martyrs, Paul Miki, in the spirit of Jesus, prayed, "I hope my blood will fall on my fellow men as fruitful rain." So fruitful was the rain of his blood on the hills of Nagasaki that missionaries 265 years later (1862) discovered thousands of secret Christians there.

— Norman Perry, O.F.M.

TODAY: Pray that atomic fallout will never again rain on mankind.

February 7
St. Richard (d. 722)
West-Saxon King

Today, the people of Lucca, Italy, still honor St. Richard as their patron and their "King of the English." He was taken ill and died there while on a pilgrimage to Rome. Richard had traveled through France and part of Italy with his sons Willibald and Winebald, also honored as saints. His daughter, Walburga, is also a saint whose feast day is observed later this month. Biographical accounts of today's saint reveal that in the earlier part of the eighth century "King Richard, by prayer and sacrifice," saw the recovery of his younger son, Willibald, from near death. "The king had placed his son at the foot of a giant crucifix that had been erected in a public courtyard in England." His was an offering seeking God's miraculous intervention.

St. Richard became a saint for his industry. He was not

26

lazy. He knew that heaven could not be his if he merely sat down and did nothing. This English king was blessed with a family of saints, each one giving to their God the honor and love of serving Him. What an ideal for the family of our time.

TODAY: That I remain faithful in my daily prayers to God, and not become lazy in the daily practice of my Faith.

February 8
St. Jerome Emiliani (1481-1537)
Patron of Orphans and Abandoned Children

O my God, my thoughts today turn to one who is hailed benefactor of the orphaned and the abandoned. Today's saint was a soldier and a mayor prior to his ordination to the priesthood. His daily work is found in these words of St. James: "Religion that is pure and undefiled before God is this: to visit orphans . . . in their affliction"(1 James 1:27).

O God, my Father, what can I do? I can pray for them. . . . There are the orphans who are victims of war. There are those left orphans whose parents were killed on our roads; others are orphans because their parents did not want them. Lord, my thoughts pass from orphans to things that made them orphans, and I want to be in league with Your Spirit in the world that helps prevent children from becoming orphans. I am against war and yet I am guilty of waging my own private battles through greed, self-centeredness and distrust.

— **Donald Crowhurst**

TODAY: I know that spiritually I am Your child and You have promised never to leave me or forsake me. I am secure in Your love.

February 8
St. John Matha (1160-1213)
Order of the Most Holy Trinity

John of Matha, founder of the Trinitarians, was devoted to the redemption of Christians held captive by the Mohammedans. He met the specific needs of Christians in his age through his foundation.

The number of Christians held captive today by chains of sin and habits of vice far exceeds the number of Christians held captive by the Mohammedans of old. But their need of redemption is nonetheless real. The liberation of modern captive Christians will be accomplished by modern imitators of John of Matha through daily prayers and acts of mortification and penance.

Engaging in this sort of prayerful activity will certainly make us conscious of the brotherhood of man under the Fatherhood of God.

— Msgr. Edward W. O'Malley

TODAY: The highest tribute we can pay the saints is to imitate their virtues.

February 9
St. Miguel Febres Cordero (1854-1910)
Brothers of the Christian Schools, Canonized
by Pope John Paul II, October 21, 1984

This saint who was born Francisco Febres Cordero, was the first Latin American Brother to make perpetual vows in the congregation. Francisco was born at Cuenca, Ecuador, on November 7 (1854), a month before the promulgation of the dogma of the Immaculate Conception — a fact that he loved to recall. He was born with a "malfunction of the feet," a painful handicap he experienced throughout his life. Having an intense devotion to the Blessed Virgin Mary, Brother Miguel enjoyed several miraculous visions and sought her on many occasions as the "guiding star" of his life.

Brother Miguel spent over 40 years teaching languages and literature at schools in Quito. He wrote and edited his own textbooks and teaching manuals, and the national government of Ecuador adopted many of his texts for use in all schools in the republic. His Spanish-language texts were used in almost all of the countries in South America. The saintly scholar was elected a member of the prestigious Academy of Ecuador and was also named to the Royal Spanish Academy. He excelled in catechetics, and his favorite teaching task was the "preparation of children for First Communion." His community had ordered him to their schools in Paris and later in Belgium. In 1909 he was assigned to a house of training for young men of various nationalities. While at Barcelona, Spain, he faced the anticlerical revolution there and escaped to the Lasallian college of Bonanova. Brother Miguel brought the sacred hosts from the chapel of Premia in order to save them from profanation. Although he always faced difficulty in walking, he managed to walk nearly eight miles without lagging. He died of double pneumonia in his 56th year.

> TODAY: I will try to help the handicapped, calling to mind St. Miguel: "The child who in his cradle was looked upon as an irreparable misfortune was to become a star for Ecuador and for the whole Church."

February 10
St. Scholastica (d. c. 559)
Patron of Convulsive Children

The twin sister of St. Benedict, Scholastica is remembered chiefly for her close spiritual union with God. This consciousness of God's close personal presence in everyday life is certainly a great gift, one that is quite often given to those who practice mental prayer. A practical consequence of this is the ability to see Christ in one's neighbor.

The Benedictine spirit is one of peace and moderation, of stability and perseverance. Without interior peace of mind and heart there is little chance for happy home life and the flexibility that is necessary to keep a home the joyful and secure haven that it should be. Husbands and wives must first be friends before they can be lovers. When the husband-wife relationship is insecure, the parent-child relationship suffers. Moderation is a key to this. A perfectionist makes life a chore for himself and those around him, while the opposite spirit can be characterized only by the words "lazy" or "sloppy." Moderation takes into account the human condition itself.

— Msgr. Charles Dollen

> TODAY: Like Saints Scholastica and Benedict, "with the Gospel as our guide, let us walk His ways."

29

February 11
Our Lady of Lourdes (February 11-July 16, 1858)
Immaculate Conception Appears to Bernadette Soubirous

"If you take away from the midst of you the yoke, the pointing of the finger and speaking wickedness . . . (God will) make your bones strong . . . and you shall take delight in the Lord" (Isaiah 58: 9-14). Again through Isaiah comes the call to change, to abandon old ways and follow the Lord. With it comes a promise of healing and happiness, but not necessarily happiness now. The call of Levi in the Gospel suggests that with the call of the Lord come pain and suffering, suspicion and ridicule, abuse and criticism.

This day in 1858, God began to teach that lesson anew, through Our Lady of Lourdes to St. Bernadette and through her to us. To and through Bernadette came the call to draw near and follow the Lord. The miraculous waters and physical cures were a promise of spiritual healing for those who answer God's call. Yet, in the suffering and derision of Bernadette is the reminder that accepting the call first entails pain, criticism and rejection.

— Norman Perry, O.F.M.

TODAY: Jesus, I need Your healing in my own life. Help me answer Your call and seek my happiness in You.

February 12
St. Ludan (c. 1202)
Pilgrim, Dedicated to Works of Mercy

An ancient English proverb said: "The saint who works no miracles has few pilgrims." Yet, this pilgrim, one of the lesser known saints, surely had some miraculous powers needed in his approach to sainthood. According to tradition, he was the son of a Scottish prince. Like many saints, he refused a luxurious life and gave his inheritance for charitable uses. He built hospices for the care of travelers, strangers and the infirm. His pilgrimage to Jerusalem and the Holy Land was one of penitential obligation — to do as much as he could for Christ. During his pilgrimage, he stopped to rest in a grove near the village of Northeim along the French-German border. Ludan's dream foretold his approaching death. Upon awaking, Ludan asked God that he might receive the "Body of the Lord" before his death. "An angel brought him last Communion." His death caused a miraculous ringing of bells in the country churches.

A small scroll found in his purse was his I.D. card. "My name is Ludan; I am the son of the noble Scottish Prince Hiltebold. For the honor of God I have become a pilgrim."

> *TODAY: Like St. Ludan, I beseech God to give me those graces to receive Viaticum at the hour of my death.*

February 13
St. Catherine dei Ricci (1522-1590)
Dominican, Mystic, Stigmatic

We marvel at the number of young men and women who dedicate their lives to God in the service to the Church and their fellowmen in the seminaries and religious Orders. Alexandrina was born of a noble family in Florence, and was placed in a convent when she was six years old. At 14 she entered the Dominican Order, and at her profession took the name of Catherine. She was named prioress of the order for life when she was 30 years old. Known for her sanctity and wisdom, she was sought by many Church officials and talked with cardinals who later were known as Pope Marcellus II, Clement VIII and Leo XI. During an illness she offered up her suffering by meditating on the passion of Christ.

In 1542, Catherine was favored with the stigmata — wounds in hands, feet and sides. Her head was pierced with a crown of thorns. On Easter Sunday of that year, Christ is to have appeared to her, and removing a ring from His finger, placed it upon the forefinger of her left hand. Biographers note of the incident: "Christ said, My daughter, receive this ring as a pledge and as proof that you do now, and ever belong to Me." Although she could see the ring, others viewed it as a red circle or a fleshy ridge encircling her index finger. St. Catherine dei Ricci "attended to the duties of her office and Order, tended the sick — which was her favorite work — and cared for the poor." Her biography and the account of the events leading to her stigmata afford readers a detailed study of the "spiritual ecstasies."

TODAY: When we say the name of Jesus — it is at once a cry of love, an exclamation of joy, a petition of hope and a strong weapon to use against the devil.

February 14
SS. Cyril (d. 869) and Methodius (d. 885)
Monk and Bishop, "Apostles of the Slavs"

These two brothers were of a senatorial family, born in Thessalonica, Greece. They are regarded as the Apostles of the Slavs, co-patrons of Europe and also patrons of the unity of the Eastern and Western Churches.

Their real mission in life became evident when they responded to the need of Emperor Michael III. He thought of the two brothers when the Prince of Moravia, Ratislav, requested Christian missionaries to teach his people in 862. Both had the necessary background, but were not bishops. So they journeyed to Rome for their consecration, bringing relics of Pope St. Clement with them. Cyril died in Rome, probably before the ceremony. Methodius was consecrated by Pope Adrian II, who also approved of the use of the Slavonic language in the liturgy. The older brother continued the apostolate with success in Moravia, Bohemia, Poland, and the neighboring countries.

— Sister M. Barbara Anne, F.M.S.C.

TODAY: Ask God's blessings on your work, but do not ask Him to do it for you.

February 14
St. Valentine (d. 269)
Legendary Patron of Lovers

Somewhere, and sometime after his death, St. Valentine's name was given to love notes that boys and girls exchanged. Today there are lacy valentines, heart-shaped boxes of candy, flowers, or small gifts sent on St. Valentine's Day with which a man can reveal his romantic interest in a girl who has won his affections.

For the Christian, every day should be St. Valentine's Day. For a Christian ought to love all, the rich and the poor, the well and the sick, the young and handsome, the aged and wrinkled.

Manifesting concern and love should be the usual manner of treating others. We should try to keep ourselves aware of the needs of others, rather than concentrate always on our own.

— Paschal Boland, O.S.B.

TODAY: ". . . let us not love in word and speech but in deed and truth" (1 John 3:18).

February 15
SS. Faustinus and Jovita (c. 121)
Brothers, Martyrs, Patrons of Brescia, Italy

There are innumerable men and women among the early Christians who were put to death because of their belief in Christ, but whose names are known only in heaven. Also, there are many like St. Faustinus and St. Jovita about whom little is known except their names and that they were martyrs. Today, in countries like Hungary and Poland where the Christian faith is still strong, there are innumerable "dry" martyrs: men, women and children who suffer for their Faith by living it, not by dying for it.

By contrast, in free countries many practice their faith with lukewarmness and indifference. They really do not live it, nor would there be much hope that they would die for it. God's revenge is, "Have I any pleasure in the death of the wicked, says the Lord God, and not rather that he should turn away from his way and live?" (Ezekiel 18:23).

— Paschal Boland, O.S.B.

TODAY: To be a Christian is to be a lover of people and to be a lover of the Father, as Jesus is.

February 16
St. Onesimus (c. 90)
Martyr, Disciple of St. Paul

The power of good example is repeatedly recorded in *The Lives of the Saints*.

One of the more outstanding examples of conversion through the power of good example took place in the life of Onesimus, the slave of Philemon. Following a theft from

Philemon, he met St. Paul, who held before him the example of Christ, and then challenged him to imitate Christ in his own life.

The challenge was accepted. Onesimus was converted and grew in wisdom and grace. He eventually gained universal recognition for his good works and perfect imitation of the Savior. At times we may be tempted to think that imitation of Christ is too difficult to accomplish, but when we read of others who have accomplished this difficult task, then their good example is an encouragement for us to at least try a little harder for perfection.

— Msgr. Edward W. O'Malley

TODAY: Ask for a generous measure of the fearless spirit of St. Paul to be used as an antidote for the sickly indifference of society.

February 17
Seven Founders of the Servites (13th century)
Servants of Mary

Can you imagine seven men, three not married, two with wives, and two widowed, mutually deciding to give away their money, all their possessions and entering on a life of prayer and penance together?

Yet in 1233, seven young Florentines did just that. The members of the Confraternity of the Blessed Virgin were: Bonfilius Monaldo its leader, Alexis Falconieri, Benedict dell'Antella, Bartolommeo Amidei, Ricovero Uguccione, Gherardino Sostegni, and Giovanni Buonagiunta. At the insistence of the Bishop of Florence, they wrote a rule of life and agreed to accept other members. They called themselves the Servants of Mary, or Servites.

Each year a great number of young people dedicate their lives to God and to the service of the Church and their fellowmen in seminaries and religious orders. Pray that they be filled with the spirit and humility of these Seven Holy Founders.

— Paschal Boland, O.S.B.

TODAY: Pray that more accept the grace of vocations to the priesthood and religious life. "O Lord, send workers into Your harvest."

February 18
St. Colman (c. 676)
Bishop of Lindisfarne, Ireland

St. Colman is only one of a multitude of Irish saints who are accepted in *The Roman Martyrology*. These include St. Finan, St. Columba, St. Fintan, St. Aidan, St. Kieran and St. Mel. The list could go on for pages.

These men had many things in common besides their Irish birth. They had a burning love of Christ, a deep devotion to the Holy Father as the successor of St. Peter, and a deep respect for learning and scholarship. As the Dark Ages enveloped Europe, these Irish saints preserved the Faith and brought it back to the continent. The Church in the English-speaking world owes its very existence to modern Irish priests and nuns who have covered the globe in England, Australia, Africa, America and the Pacific Isles. St. Colman, a seventh-century bishop and abbot, would recognize modern Irish apostles and approve their worldwide witness to Christ.

— **Msgr. Charles Dollen**

TODAY: That our prayers may join those of Erin's litany of saints in Ireland's plea for justice and unity.

February 19
St. Mesrop (c. 345-439)
"The Teacher"; Translated the Bible into Armenian

When God displays His generosity by granting special gifts and talents to certain of His children, He does not give these gifts as personal possessions, but as talents to be used for the good of religion and the glory of God. Each of us has been given some special talent or ability by Almighty God which, if developed, could lead us closer to God. Others would also be attracted to love Him more.

The early Armenian Bishop Mesrop devoted his entire life to developing a native alphabet and then translated the Syriac Bible into the Armenian language for the instruction and edification of his people.

We should strive to discover what special talent Almighty God has given us for the furtherance of His work on earth, and then develop and perfect that ability for love of God and love of neighbor.

— Msgr. Edward W. O'Malley

TODAY: O God, help me to be as aware of my blessings as I am of my problems.

February 20
St. Wulfric (d. 1154)
English Priest, Hermit; Also Known as Ulrick

Day by day, as we reflect on the stories about the saints, we learn much about their philosophy in holiness, service and dedication to God. The historical setting of today's saint is Haselbury-Plucknett, in Somerset near Dorset, England. St. Wulfric's tomb was a popular pilgrimage site during the Middle Ages. We know that he was ordained a priest and his daily activities of charity and prayer guided him onward to a "fellowship of saints." By scourging and fasting, Wulfric reduced himself to mere skin and bones. In addition to these austerities, he also wore a chain-mail suit next to his skin. The miraculous cutting of the iron links in the suit with an ordinary scissors, "as if it were so much linen," is another legend attributed to our saint of the day. Wulfric was not without idiosyncracies, as biographers mention that he would bathe in cold water daily, even in winter, and loudly sing psalms of praise to God.

TODAY: O heavenly Father, give me the courage to face these physical and mental tribulations, in order that I might suffer a little for You!

February 21
St. Peter Damian (1007-1072)
Cardinal, Doctor of the Church

St. Peter Damian has been described as "one of the most glorious lights of the Church in the 11th century." Certainly he shone outside, but his main honor is that he shone inside the Church and worked zealously for internal reforms.

The word "fellowship" is one of the key words of the New Testament. While the word occurs only 18 times, it is a word with weight. It carries the idea of sharing in the spirit of friendship, practical sharing, partnership in the work of Christ. We help one another by being together and sharing joys, sorrows, burdens, tasks, worship, Faith, and love. We may not shine with the brightness of St. Peter Damian, but we can be light and warmth for each other. This is one reason why attendance at the Mass is important. God meets His people as they meet together, and the fellowship generated is warm and bright. A coal on the hearth goes out. In the grate with other coals, it remains warm and helps the overall heat.

— Donald Crowhurst

TODAY: "Let your light shine before men, that they may see your good works and give glory to your Father who is in heaven" (Matthew 5:16).

February 22
Chair of St. Peter the Apostle (1st century)
Head of the Church on Earth

St. Leo tells us that we ought to celebrate the feast of the Chair of Peter with no less joy than that of his martyrdom. By his martyrdom he was "exalted to a throne of glory in heaven," but in honoring the Chair of Peter with a feast, we rejoice over the fact that "he was installed head of the Church on earth."

Let us recall these words of Christ when He established the primacy of Peter and his successors: ". . . You are Peter, and upon this rock I will build my Church and the powers of death shall not prevail against it" (Matthew 16:18). Peter was named the chief shepherd over His flock with the words of Christ: "Feed my lambs . . . Feed my sheep" (John 21:16-17). The holy martyrs preferred to die rather than separate themselves or deny their allegiance to the Pope of Rome, the visible Head of Christ's Church. In our prayers, we should tell our Lord that we would do the same.

— **Sister M. Barbara Anne, F.M.S.C.**

TODAY: Reflect on these words of the Gospel: "I will give to you the keys of the kingdom of heaven . . ." (Matthew 16:19).

February 23
St. Polycarp (d. 155)
Bishop, Martyr; Knew "John and others
who had seen the Lord"

Just as we treasure the memories of old priests and bishops, especially the missionaries, the early Christians loved to hear of Christ from the lips of the Apostles. When these were gone, the faithful listened to those who had known them well. Such a one was the valiant Polycarp, who had been a pupil of St. John the Evangelist. He was a living link, until his death in 155, with those who had lived with our Lord.

He was finally arrested for his Faith, and burned to death in Smyrna. He had greeted his captors genially, and had dinner served to them. While they ate, his prayers and his words could serve us all as a "going-away" prayer, a sort of last will and testament: "I remember all, both high and low, who at any time have come my way, and the Catholic Church throughout the world." All those who crossed his path in 86 long years — and God's Church everywhere! — St. Polycarp remembered well.

— **Most Rev. Paul J. Hallinan**

TODAY: Heed the words of St. Polycarp to "Stand fast
. . . in the Lord, firm and unchangeable in faith."

February 24
SS. Montanus, Lucius and Companions (d. 259)
Martyrs of Carthage

During the Christian persecution by Emperor Valerian, a revolt broke out in the city of Carthage. Christians were blamed for the outbreak, which cost the lives of many. Seeking revenge, the Roman official, Solon by name, arrested eight disciples and followers of St. Cyprian. The saintly bishop was martyred in 258. *The Lives of the Saints* names today's saints — Victor, Renus, Flavian, Quartillosia, Montanus, Julian, Lucius and Victorinus. When these Christians were told that they would be condemned to death by fire, "they prayed fervently to God to be delivered from that punishment." God granted their prayers, and instead the eight were imprisoned where they underwent cruel physical punishment. The martyrs were all subsequently beheaded. Montanus, who is described as having great strength of mind and body, cried out often during the execution: "He that gives sacrifices to any but the true God shall be utterly destroyed." He also denounced the pride and obstinacy of the heretics, and told them they could know the true Church of God by the number of her martyrs.

> *TODAY: Reflect on the words of St. Cyprian. "The body feels no pain when the soul gives itself entirely to God."*

February 25
St. Walburga or Walpurgis (d. 779)
English Virgin, Abbess; Patron of Thunderstorms, Rabies

This noble lady belongs to a "family of saints." Her father, St. Richard, was King of the West Saxons. Her brothers, Willibald and Winebald, are also venerated as saints.

She was born in Devonshire and educated in Dorset. Walburga was one of the Religious who answered the missionary call of St. Boniface by setting up a convent and abbey in Germany. Later she became Abbess of the convent-monastery at Heidenheim. She is also said to have studied medicine. Historians write that Walburga is interred in the Church of the Cross in Eichstatt, near the tomb of her brother Winebald. With many saints, fame comes to the individual long after death. Walburga is noted for her "miraculous oil — an aromatic watery fluid — of natural medicinal properties, which flows from the crevices of the rocks, the site of her relics." She is still venerated throughout Germany, France and Belgium. Our saint for the day is also known as Walburg, Falbourg and Walpurgia.

> *TODAY: St. Walburga, we pray that you and your saintly kin help us in our role as parents that our Christian family life will be more united and strengthened.*

February 26
St. Victor (c. 610)
Hermit, Patron of Millers

Day by day we learn that God is using people to invite others to conversion and salvation. God uses the saints to bring sinners to a conversion of faith. God also urges good men to better lives.

Victor was a holy priest and hermit who lived in Troyes, France, and later spent his life in prayer at the hermitage of Arcis-sur-Aube in Champagne. "He was a saint from his cradle, and even in his youth sought a life of prayer, fasting and almsgiving." Victor's continual union with God through a life of prayer and spiritual contemplation seemed to "raise him above the ordinary conditions of his mortal life." He was glorified by grace and performed many miracles. His greatest act was the conversion of many sinners through his exemplary life and heavenly intercession.

> TODAY: Like Victor, every one of us should be a spokesman for God, calling people to a conversion of faith and a life of greater holiness.

February 27
St. Gabriel Possenti (1838-1862)
Italian Passionist, Patron of Youth; Also Known as Brother Gabriel of Our Lady of Sorrows

Youth of today move the heart of the Church perhaps more than ever before since the days of Christ. St. Gabriel was one such "mover." His life was cut short at the age of 24, shortly before he would fulfill his lifelong dream of priestly ordination. He was born in Assisi, the town that sheltered the humble Francis (Giovanni di Bernardone). During his formative years, Gabriel Possenti enjoyed the schools of the Christian Brothers and later the Jesuits. In 1856 he received the garb of the Passionist congregation and took the name Brother Gabriel of Our Lady of Sorrows. He was a prayerful person but not an overly demonstrative one. He was said to stand aside, in the shadows of his more devout companions. Writers mention that his great sanctity was covered by the Brother's own humility. In 1862 he was stricken with tuberculosis and died at Isola di Gran Susso, where he is interred at the Passionist retreat.

When Gabriel was beatified on May 31, 1908, by the saintly Pope Pius X, he had been dead less than 50 years. This early beatification was a special privilege, calling the world's attention to the heroics of youth. Twelve years later, in 1920, he was canonized by Pope Benedict XV.

TODAY: Pray that our youth learn the Christian art of sanctifying every thought, word and deed of the day with their prayers and morning offering to God.

February 28
St. Oswald (d. 992)
English Benedictine, Bishop of Worcester

St. Oswald was educated by an uncle, St. Odo, who was the Archbishop of Canterbury. He was ordained to the priesthood and later named dean of Winchester, England. Oswald then went to Fleury, France, where he became a Benedictine monk. Upon the death of his uncle Odo, Oswald returned to England and joined another uncle (Oskitell), the Archbishop of York. "Oswald's piety and grand qualities attracted the attention of St. Dunstan." It was Dunstan who recommended Oswald to King Edgar, who then named Oswald Bishop of Worcester.

Bishop Oswald is credited with building the monastery at Westbury. In 972 he helped Aylwin (cousin of King Edgar) to build the Abbey of Ramsey in Huntingdonshire. Oswald was responsible for many clergy reforms and an overall revival of religion in England. As a bishop, he spent much time visiting throughout his diocese and preaching in its churches. He encouraged the Benedictine monastic philosophy in his diocese and promoted the further education of all his priests. Oswald could be found regularly in worship with the monks in the monastery Church of Our Lady, which he founded. This church was later to become the Cathedral of Worcester, and is the site of the bishop's interment.

TODAY: Reflect on this thought: The power of God is made known, not only through His direct intervention in the affairs of men, but indirectly, through the activity of His saints.

February 29
Leap Year

Every four years we have an extra day in the calendar. Today is a time for us to dwell on those unknown saints and patrons. The lives of the saints are an essential part of the divine plan. They show us what God has done for mankind and how mankind has responded. On this leap year day, it is a great help to realize that there is a vast multitude of men and women who were once on earth, who went through the same trials as our own, who were faced by the same temptations, and who today are watching our struggle with interest and sympathy.

The Church keeps a saint's day almost every day. It is all part of her wise system of keeping supernatural truth before our minds and in our hearts. All of these saints are interested in us. They feel for us more now than when they were on earth, because they see our danger better.

— Albert A. Murray, C.S.P.

TODAY: Heed the words of St. Jerome, who tells us: "A person is always entitled to be called a saint provided he or she repents and gets up after each fall."

MARCH

March 1
St. David (5th-6th century)
Bishop, Patron of Wales; Founded 12 Monasteries

Although David is respected as one of the most celebrated of British saints, much of his biography is legendary. We do know that he was the son of King Sant of Cardigan and of Nonna, daughter of a Welsh chieftain. Dedicated to a religious life, David was eventually ordained to the priesthood. He studied with St. Paulinus, a disciple of St. Germanus, Bishop of Auxerre. Biographers record that David "founded 12 monasteries all for the glory of God. First, upon arriving at Glastonbury, he built a church there; then he came to Bath, and there, causing deadly water to become salutary by a blessing, he endowed it with perpetual heat, rendering it fit for people to bathe in; afterward he came to Croyland and to Repton; then to Colva and Glascwn . . . after that he founded the monastery of Leominster. Afterward, in the region of Gent, in a place that is called Raglan, he built a church; then he founded a monastery in a place which is called Llan Gyvelach in the region of Gower." Finally, "by the direction of an angel," he settled in the extreme southwest corner of Wales, at Mynyw, where he founded the principal abbey. Giraldus, a historian, tells us that Bishop David was "the great ornament and example of his age." The bishop ruled his diocese until he was a very old man.

> *TODAY: Remember that those acts of praise to God are returned to us with His grace in keeping with God's liberality and greatness.*

March 2
St. Chad (d. 672)
English Benedictine, Bishop of Lichfield

We belong to the communion of saints, in which we share spiritual goods — ours and theirs — for mutual benefit and for building up the kingdom of God. We are members of a community of faith, prayers, good works and fraternity which tran-

scends all boundaries of space and time. The saints we honor —
not just the "name" saints but all who are in glory with God —
give us inspiration and offer intercession with God. They have
attained full union with Him.

St. Chad is not a "name" saint, but he was one of four
brothers who were priests in Northumberland. Chad and his
older brother Cedd, also a saint, studied at the "Holy Island" of
Lindisfarne under St. Aidan, who founded that center of spiritual learning. Chad went to Ireland following the death of St.
Aidan. Cedd remained in England and became the Bishop of
London. Later, Chad returned to England and ruled the Abbey
of Lastingham near Whitby. King Oswy named him Bishop of
York. St. Chad devoted himself to "ecclesiastical truth and to
chastity." His priorities were humility, continence and study.
He did not travel by horseback, but on foot, "after the manner
of the apostles." The bishop preached the Gospel in towns,
countryside, in cottages, villages and castles — for he was a disciple of St. Aidan and sought to instruct his hearers by acting or
behaving after the example of his master and of his brother St.
Cedd. Bishop Chad died at an old age, leaving 31 churches dedicated to his name as his saintly legacy.

> TODAY: Offer mutual help and support to one anoth-
> er through prayer; in witnessing to faith in daily life,
> and in carrying out our share of the mission entrusted
> to us by Jesus.

March 3
St. Cunegund (d. 1039)
*Empress of Bavaria, Patron of Bamberg, West Germany
and of Luxembourg; Also Known as Cunegundes*

What surprises most people today is the very humanness of
the saints. We expect them to be somewhat other-worldly, tow-
ering in virtue and aglow with faith and charity. It is surprising
then to learn just how human they were; how down to earth,
how close they are to us.

Cunegund is another one of the "regal" saints. She was a
person of noble civil status, yet humble and charitable despite a
crown or jewels. She was the daughter of Siegfried, the first Earl
of Luxembourg, and the pious Hedwig. Today's patron married

St. Henry, Duke of Bavaria. He succeeded King Otto III to the throne, and in 1013 the king and his wife journeyed to Rome to receive the imperial crown from Pope Benedict VIII. Artists have pictured her walking barefoot without harm over red-hot plowshares. She did this to prove her innocence in slanderous accusations. Cunegund showed that she was chaste and loyal to the emperor. From that moment, we learn, "they lived in the closest union of hearts, striving in every way to promote the glory of God and the advancement of religion." Following the death of her husband, Cunegund became a nun at the Benedictine Convent at Kaufungen, the same convent that she vowed she would build when cured of a lingering illness.

The "humanness" and "down-to-earth" quality of today's saint is recorded thus: "Once she had been consecrated to God in religion, she seemed entirely to forget that she had been an empress and behaved as the lowest servant in the house, being convinced that she was so before God." Mortification and physical penances weakened her body, and after 15 years' service in the convent she died. She is buried near the tomb of her husband, St. Henry, at the Cathedral of Bamberg.

> *TODAY: Dwell on these words by Thomas Merton, a Trappist monk: "The simplest and most effective way to sanctity is to disappear into the background of ordinary everyday routine."*

March 4
St. Casimir (1458-1484)
Polish Prince, Grand Duke of Lithuania,
Patron of Poland and Lithuania

Early biographers refer to Prince Casimir as the "peacemaker" among the Polish people. Another "regal saint," Casimir was a son of King Casimir IV of Poland and Elizabeth of Austria, daughter of Emperor Albert II. Casimir was educated in the royal court, but abhorred luxurious living and secretly underwent penances and mortifications to atone for such luxuries. For the love of God he cared for the poor, giving them all his possessions. He also used all his influence with his father and with his brother Wladislas, King of Bohemia, to improve living conditions for the poor.

Prince Casimir was not quite 15 years old when he was asked by noblemen of Hungary to be their king. The plot involved warfare and leading an army of 20,000 soldiers. The "peacemaker" then returned to Poland where "he could never be persuaded to take up arms. . . ." From 1481 to 1483 Casimir governed the Polish kingdom during the absence of his father, the king, also the officer of the state in Lithuania. Upholding his rule of chastity, Casimir refused marriage. In 1484, while visiting in Lithuania, Prince Casimir died of tuberculosis and was buried at St. Stanislaus Church in the city of Vilna. The saintly prince and peacemaker was canonized by Pope Adrian VI in 1522.

> TODAY: Let us pray! Almighty God, to serve You is to reign in peace. By the intercessory prayers of St. Casimir, help us to serve You in sanctity and justice, that right will replace might in the lives of the suffering people of Poland. Amen.

March 5
St. Kieran (c. 530)
Irish Bishop of Ossory

One of many celebrated Irish bishops, Kieran is designated the first-born of Irish saints. He was one of the Celtic saints who introduced Christianity in southern Ireland, before the arrival of Patrick. When Kieran was 30 years old, he traveled to Rome to study "in order to be fully instructed in the faith." Years later he returned to Ireland accompanied by four missionaries — Lugacius, Columban, Lugard and Cassan — all of whom were raised to the episcopate. (Biographers say St. Kieran was one of the 12 bishops consecrated by St. Patrick upon his arrival to Ireland.) A hermit, Kieran lived in a hut near a stream. This site gave rise to the little village of Sier-Kieran, also known as Saighir, named in the saint's honor. As the first Bishop of Ossory, he converted his own clan of the Osrargs and a great number of the people of the region (area of Kilkenny and Offaly Counties). His mother, Liadan, received the religious veil from her bishop-son, and she joined other pious women in the convent of Killiadhuin. As with many of the Celtic saints, Kieran's biography is a mixture of poetry, love of nature and mostly legend handed down by *shanachies,* the Irish storytellers.

> *TODAY: We learn of one who has done great things for God. Kieran was sanctified by the Holy Spirit, making him an instrument in the sanctification of others.*

March 6
St. Colette (1381-1447)
French Franciscan Tertiary; Reformed the Religious Rules Of the Order of Poor Clares

Religious artists used the lamb and birds as symbolic to the life of St. Colette. The virtues of purity and simplicity governed her life. *The Lives of the Saints* records: "Like her spiritual father, St. Francis, Colette was a lover of animals, especially the weak and gentle. Lambs and doves would gather round her and even the shyest of birds would eat out of her hand." She also had a great affection for children and would play and pray with them and then bless them in the name of God. She was born of devout peasant parentage in Picardy. Unlike other children her age, Colette devoted many hours of the day in prayer and spiritual meditation. She was orphaned at an early age and turned to the convent at Corbie where she later received the habit of the Third Order of St. Francis.

During one of her visions, "the Seraphic Father, St. Francis, appeared and charged her to restore the first rule of St. Clare in all of its severity." She claimed to be unworthy of the task, but when Colette became blind for three days and then unable to speak for another three days, she recognized it as a sign from heaven to proceed with the reformation of the Order of St. Clare. St. Colette also helped correct the schism — three claimants to the Papacy — in the Church. She died in her 67th year at a convent in Flanders.

> *TODAY: St. Colette, like many saints, was inspired and motivated by daily meditation on the passion and death of our Lord. Each Friday from six o'clock in the morning until six o'clock in the evening she meditated on Christ's passion and did not eat or drink during that time. Pray that Christ will motivate us in our daily life.*

March 7
St. Perpetua and St. Felicity (d. 203)
Early Christian Martyrs

T he Church calendar is filled with ancient names and ancient memories of men and women who staked all, gambled all on the promise of Christ. Possessions and wealth meant nothing, and even life itself was cast aside on the strength of His Word. A powerful Faith, we say, but how powerful was the Word! They could not waver for a moment. What strength, we say, what courage, what marvelous devotion. It was more than that. It was the Word of God they clung to that was the marvel. It is that we must examine, if we would understand what manner of men and women they were.

St. Perpetua and St. Felicity were among these martyrs; martyrs in the ancient sense: one who bears witness. Bears witness to what? To God's Word, to the Word of Christ. They clung to it, held fast to it, kept their eyes on it, fastened it to their souls and hopes of steel.

— **Rev. Clifford Stevens**

TODAY: Recall Perpetua's words: "Stand ye all fast in the faith and love one another; and do not let our sufferings be a stumbling-block to you."

March 8
St. John of God (1495-1550)
Founder of the Order of Brothers Hospitallers, Patron of Booksellers, Heart Ailments, Hospitals, Nurses, Printers, The Sick

W hat made saints out of saints was their realization of the love God had for them. Love is a powerful, motivating force. History records stories of people doing fantastic things when motivated by love. It is no wonder, then, when people think about the love God has for them, the love which caused Jesus to sacrifice His life for us, that they find the strength to live and die as saints.

John Ciudad, today's saint, found this love and realized his strength while listening to a sermon by the famous John of Avila, also a saint. He asked mercy on himself as he ran amock in the streets. His conduct seemed that of the mentally dis-turbed, and he was retained in a mental ward. St. John of God spent 13 years in the armies of Count Oroprusa in Castile. He fought in wars between the Spaniards and French, and later fought against the Turks in Hungary. When he was 40 years old he returned to civilian life, remorseful and bitter about his past. He was counseled by St. John of Avila and devoted the re-mainder of his life to the care of the sick and poor. In order to help the abandoned sick, he built a hospital in Granada. His apostolate grew into the Hospitallers, an order of charity and service. It was the Bishop of Tuy who named him John of God, because of his spiritual intellect. The bishop also devised the rules and habit for the Hospitallers, who are still engaged in nursing skills and hospital medicine.

> *TODAY: We learn that one single sermon converted St. John of God from a sinful life and made him a saint. How is it that so many sermons, homilies and pious books produce so little effect in our lives? Could it be because of sloth and a hardening of our hearts to God?*

March 9
St. Frances of Rome (1384-1440)
Organized the Oblates of Mary; Patron of Motorists

Popes, particularly Clement X (1670-1676), have approved of devotion to the angels. Note the word is "devotion" and not "adoration." When we think of Guardian Angels, our mind generally pictures a young boy, shadowed by a winged figure. This motif dates to the 17th century, when there was much de-votion to the angels. However, sometimes in recorded appear-ances, like that of today's saint, they are not "shadowy."

St. Frances of Rome, a wealthy widow and mystic, had the special privilege of seeing her Guardian Angel at all times. His appearance was that of a young boy of about 12 years. His pres-ence gave off such light that she could read at night without any other means of illumination. It was said that if she did some-thing displeasing to God, her angel rapped her on the hand; the strength of the blow depended upon the severity of the inci-dent!

— Jeanne Dageforde

TODAY: Remember that those who follow You, Lord, will have the light of life.

March 10
Forty Martyrs (16th and 17th centuries)
English and Welsh Catholics Martyred for the Faith

Somebody once said, "Taking the easiest way makes men and rivers crooked." Edmund Campion (c. 1540-1581) could have taken the easy way, easily. As a student at Oxford, his sharp mind and brilliant oratory won him the commendation of no less than Queen Elizabeth. For him a golden career was dawning. He had only to grasp at the new age and its new religion. But he chose to obey his conscience, to take the hard way, and in religion to prefer the true to the new.

Ordained in Rome, he returned to England, disguised as a debonair gentleman. Captured by the Queen's agents, he refused to betray his colleagues. "To the revealing whereof I cannot nor will not be brought, come rack, come rope!" He was racked three times. At the hanging, a fellow martyr nodded toward the noonday sun. "Ah, Campion, I shall shortly be above yonder fellow!" Shortly, they both were.

— **Joseph E. Manton. C.SS.R.**

TODAY: Remember those daily martyrs to loneliness, sickness and death.

March 11
St. Constantine (d. c. 598)
Celtic King, First Martyr of Scotland

King Constantine, a rough-riding Celtic warrior, was converted to Christianity by St. Petroc and repented his earlier crimes of plunder and killing. Unlike Saul of Tarsus, Constantine was not hurled from a horse or blinded by a light from heaven (Acts 9:3). However, his new-found faith led him to be a humble lay Brother in the monastery of St. Mochuda in Ireland. "He performed the most menial offices and carried sacks of corn which he ground for his brethren and the poor." According to legend, his regal identity was discovered by a monk who heard the saint laughing over his chores and saying to himself: "Is this indeed

Constantine of Cornwall, who formerly wore a helmet and carried a shield and who now drudges at a handmill?"

In time he was ordained as a priest and later was an abbot of the monastery. He later became a missionary to Scotland and was named abbot of a monastery at Glasgow. While on a mission to the village of Kintyre, Constantine was attacked by a gang of pirates who cut off his right arm. Calling to "his followers, he blessed them as he slowly bled to death." He is buried at the Govan monastery in Scotland.

> *TODAY: The shaping of the heart of a saint is a sublime work, the masterpiece of divine grace.*

March 12
St. Theophanes (c. 752-818)
Abbot, Called "The Chronicler"

Formerly it was the custom for members of religious orders to adopt, or be given, a new name upon taking their formal religious vows. Thus, the only man I ever knew personally by the name of Theophane(s) was a Jesuit Brother who spent decades recruiting candidates for the Society of Jesus. He too, like today's saint, was a bit of a "chronicler" but more of an archivist.

St. Theophanes was born of wealthy parents in Constantinople and from an early age was raised in the court of Emperor Constantine V. Although Theophanes married in his youth, his bride proclaimed her vow of perpetual chastity. She later became a nun and gave away all personal belongings to the poor. Meanwhile, Theophanes built two religious monasteries in what is now northern Turkey, and later became Abbot of Mount Sigriana. He also took part in the Second Council of Nicaea in 787, and supported the decrees on the "uses and veneration of sacred images." In 814, when Leo the Armenian became emperor, the Council decrees were abolished and Abbot Theophanes's faith was cause for his imprisonment, torture and banishment. St. Theophanes "chronicled" a short history of the world — *Byzantine History: A.D. 284-812.* This is the source of his nickname.

> *TODAY: Personal mortification, prayer, hard physical labor, plus historic research and writing, were the keys to this saint's best-seller.*

51

March 13
St. Euphrasia (c. 390-420)
Virgin, Mystic

Archbishop Fulton J. Sheen was once asked, "How long does it take to become a saint?" He replied, "It doesn't take much time. It only takes much love."

Time was of the essence for St. Euphrasia, who died when she was only 30 years old. Yet that was time enough to love and serve God through a life of consecration, asceticism, chastity and obedience. Euphrasia was the beautiful daughter of Antigonus, a nobleman and relative of Emperor Theodosius the Elder. She and her mother, a wealthy and pious woman, left the king's household and settled in Egypt. At the age of seven Euphrasia entered a religious house, where she "matured and became a beautiful girl in the seclusion of the convent." The abbess, in order to discipline her and stifle any vain or worldly imagination, commanded Euphrasia to carry a pile of stones from one place to another. When she finished, Euphrasia then had to carry the stones back and forth another 30 times. Her meekness and humility were extraordinary, and she served God with an abundance of love.

> *TODAY: The greatest gift that God has given us, after life itself, is our capacity to love.*

March 14
St. Matilda (c. 895-968)
Queen of Germany, Symbolized in Art by Purse and Dove; Also called Mechtildis or Maud

Matilda is another of our "regal saints." She was the daughter of Count Dietrich of Westphalia and Reinhild of the royal house of Denmark. Matilda married Duke Henry of Saxony, who became King of Germany in 919. He was a military victor over the Danes, Bohemians, Hungarians and added Bavaria to his kingdom. King Henry himself attributed much of his success to the pious practices and prayers by his wife, Matilda. Biographers infer that "she retained the humility which had distinguished her as a girl, and in the royal palace she lived almost like a religious." She seemed more like a loving mother than a queen to the household servants and members of the court. King Henry and Queen Matilda went out of their way to assist their people. We learn "they planned good and just laws and strove by every means in their power to advance the Kingdom of God." Upon the death of her husband, the oldest son, Otto, was named emperor. Political machination between Otto and young Henry divided the family. Henry was later forgiven and named Duke of Bavaria. Matilda resigned her power and inheritance and moved to the countryside after accusations by her sons that she "emptied the treasury." She later returned to the castle as the queen mother, and deeded to her people everything in sight as gifts. She died during the singing of Psalms and recitation of the Gospels.

> TODAY: We are not able to build convents and monasteries, or rule and govern earthly kingdoms. We are, however, expected to assist in the upkeep of churches and schools and be the holy rulers of our earthly families.

March 15
St. Clement Mary Hofbauer (1751-1820)
Redemptorist, Called "Apostle of Vienna"

One of the popular Redemptorist saints, Clement Mary Hofbauer is called the second founder of the Congregation of the Most Holy Redeemer. Through his efforts the congregation spread throughout Switzerland and southern Germany. He was the vicar-general of the C.SS.R. for the region north of the Alps. From the two Redemptorist houses in Italy came the Religious who would expand the order's missionary role in Europe and later in the Americas. St. Clement was a noted preacher and scholar, a friend of both the rich and the poor. He was popular with learned persons, artists and writers and a teacher-friend of the students.

St. Clement served in Poland (1787-1808), setting up the great Redemptorist center in Warsaw. He was later banished from that city by Napoleon I and returned to Austria. Father Clement "became beloved of the people and also of Emperor

Franz Joseph." This saint, a man named Mary, was the cause for the "spiritual rejuvenation" of Vienna and was named patron saint of that city by Pope Pius X in 1914, five years after his canonization.

TODAY: Grant me the grace, Lord, to accept Your Word and to place my trust in You like Mary, our Blessed Mother.

March 16
St. Abraham Kidunaia (c. 366)
Hermit, Priest, Convert-Maker

Today's saint spent most of his life in or near Edessa in Mesopotamia, now the country of Iraq. Like other desert saints, Abraham sought a life of spiritual solitude. Perhaps that is why he fled from his week-long prenuptial celebrations and hid out for 17 days in the nearby desert. His only view of the outside world was through a small window in an otherwise sealed abode. St. Ephrem, whose feast is noted on June 9, writes of his friend Abraham the hermit: "For 10 years he spent his whole time in praising God and imploring His mercy with many tears." The hermit gave away his inheritance and distributed all his goods to the poor. Ephrem, a Doctor of the Church, also wrote that "Abraham was never seen to smile . . . and he regarded each day as his last."

At the request of the Bishop of Edessa, Abraham left his desert cell and was ordained a priest. He went to the town of Beth-Kiduna, where he converted and baptized 1,000 persons during his three years there. While Abraham knocked down altars and destroyed idols in the village, the citizens retaliated by beating him with sticks, stoning him, and then dragging the saint from the town, leaving him for dead. Abraham revived the physical beating and returned to the people, who realized that he was indeed a holy man.

TODAY: We cannot live a solitary life isolated from a busy world. But we can spend a few minutes in our life, each day, to pray and reflect on the things of God.

March 17
St. Patrick (389-461)
Missionary, Patron of Ireland

On Easter Sunday, Patrick, the once captive swineherd, appeared in full episcopal attire at Tara, where chieftains and pagan priests were gathered for a pagan ceremony. After he had successfully defeated the pagan priests, Patrick began to preach on the true Faith. He plucked a shamrock from the grass and used it to explain the Trinity. That is why the shamrock is held in reverence by the Irish.

The truth of the three persons in one God is the most sublime and most mysterious truth in our Faith. It is a mystery that our limited minds cannot grasp. If it had not been revealed to us, we would never know it. Each time we make the Sign of the Cross, we pay homage to this great mystery. We should also remind ourselves of the debt we have to the Trinity — to the Father because He created us, to the Son who redeemed us, and to the Holy Spirit who makes us holy.

— **Albert J. Nevins, M.M.**

TODAY: Let my Sign of the Cross be a petition for peace in Ireland.

March 18
St. Cyril of Jerusalem (c. 315-387)
Archbishop of Jerusalem, Doctor of the Church

St. Cyril was the first to popularize the catechism as the ordinary way of learning and teaching Christian doctrine. Question and answer, well thought out, clear, concise, easily commited to memory. How many generations of youngsters have squirmed their way through this ancient method, and how many of the same youngsters, grown to man's estate, have blessed God for the knowledge thus pounded into their heads.

St. Cyril would thrill to be alive today. The catechetical program, followed by rote for so many centuries, is benefiting from the best of modern teaching methods. Religious and laity alike are dedicating themselves to the catechetical apostolate with renewed energy and zeal. Truly, a new golden age of the catechism has come. — **Most Rev. Robert J. Dwyer**

TODAY: I will pray for catechists and those being catechized. We may be sure that St. Cyril does not forget his work.

March 19
St. Joseph (1st century)
Spouse of Mary, Foster Father of Jesus,
Patron of the Universal Church

Scripture records not a single word spoken by St. Joseph. The little we know of him portrays him as a man of great faith, prudence and obedience, "a just man."

As protector of Mary's honor in becoming legal father of Jesus, he was entrusted with the duty of providing for the Mother of God and God's Son. What a privileged position! Yet Joseph went about his daily labors as a carpenter in a quiet, unassuming manner, eager to be of service to his family and neighbors. Because he was the divinely appointed head of the Holy Family, Pope Pius IX solemnly proclaimed him Patron of the Universal Church (1870). As such he is the guardian and protector of the family of the Church and all Christian families.

Let us pray to him with confidence for all our needs, to be faithful to the duties of our call in life, and finally for the grace of a holy and peaceful death.

— **Sister Lorraine Dennehy, C.S.J.**

TODAY: Remember, there is no higher praise of a man than saying he is just.

March 20
St. Cuthbert (d. 687)
Bishop of Lindisfarne (England),
"Wonder Worker of Britain"

The Irish, Scots and Britons all claim a piece of St. Cuthbert's ancestry. His name is of Saxon and not Celtic origin, however. As a shepherd lad, Cuthbert enjoyed the peaceful "communing with God" while tending sheep in the folklands of Northumbria. His life outdoors and his love of animals, plants and things of God's natural kingdom remind us of Francis, the peaceful saint from Assisi.

Cuthbert was only 15 years old when he set off to Melrose Abbey to consecrate his life to God. Biographers write: "The saint's hardy constitution enabled him to bear all the austerities demanded by the Columban Rule . . . and even add to them." He assisted Abbot (St.) Eata with the new Abbey of Ripon, but a year later returned to Melrose.

This was an interesting time in Church history, as King Alcfrid, influenced by St. Wilfrid, was a zealous champion of using the Roman calendar and the Easter dates in opposition to the ancient Celtic liturgies still practiced by the followers of St. Columba. The Council of Whitby (664), ruled in favor of the Roman liturgical practices, and St. Colman and some of his monks returned to Ireland. Abbots Eata and Cuthbert remained to enforce the council decisions. Cuthbert was consecrated Bishop of Lindisfarne on Easter Sunday, March 26, 685. He continued to preach, give alms and perform miracles of healing during the "yellow plague," earning his nickname "The Wonder Worker of Britain." His last instructions to his brethren were: "Be of one mind in your councils, live in concord with the other servants of God. . . . Study diligently, observe the canons of the Fathers, and practice with zeal that monastic rule which God has deigned to give you by my hands. . . ."

> TODAY: We, who live in a restless age and so easily lose patience, pray to St. Cuthbert to intercede with God so that we may cultivate more perfectly his spirit of charity and resignation.

March 21
St. Serapion (c. 370)
Bishop of Thumis (Egypt); Called "The Scholastic"

Serapion's nickname "Scholastic" indicates that this great bishop was especially noted for his learning. He was also head of the catechetical school in Alexandria. We may not possess the brilliant intelligence of a Serapion, but we surely can strive to imitate his zeal for truth.

Today's saint was a friend of St. Athanasius (see May 2), a Father and Doctor of the Church, and St. Anthony of Egypt (see January 17). Serapion left the life of academe and went into the desert for the prayer life of a monk. He was later recalled from his solitude to be named Bishop of Thumis, a famous city in lower Egypt. He supported St. Athanasius in defense of the Catholic faith and also took part in the Council of Sardica in 347. Historians write that St. Serapion was banished by the Emperor Constantine for refuting Arianism and the Manichean heresy. St. Serapion's formula of Christian perfection was summarized with these words: "The mind is purified by spiritual knowledge (or by holy meditation and prayer), the spiritual passions of the soul by charity, and the irregular appetites by abstinence and penance."

> TODAY: We "can't find time to study"? What we read — and how we go about it — may be a gateway to the coming of Christ into our lives.

March 22
St. Deogratias (c. 457)
Bishop of Carthage

Today's saint is an unusual priest having a most unusual name. *Deo gratias* is a Latin expression meaning "Thanks be to God." He was named Bishop of Carthage, which see had been vacated for 14 years. Historians noted that Deogratias "was a holy priest, who, by his example and teaching, strengthened the faith of his people and succeeded in winning the respect of pagans and Arians alike." In 455, Genseric, King of the Vandals, invaded Rome and returned with captives from Italy, Sicily, Sardinia and Corsica. Bishop Deogratias sold the gold and silver vessels and the jeweled ornaments of the altar to ransom these captives and help unite their broken families. The bishop also provided two large churches to shelter the captives. Attempts were made on the bishop's life, but were unsuccessful. In the words of historian and chronicler Alban Butler, Bishop Deogratias "was worn out through his efforts in serving the Church. He died after an episcopate of a little over three years, and was deeply mourned by his own flock and by the exiles who had found in him their great protector."

> TODAY: Pray to our heavenly Father to help us be more like the saintly bishop so that we too are our brothers' keepers.

58

March 23
St. Turibius de Mongrovejo (1538-1605)
Lawyer, Professor, Archbishop of Lima

Although St. Joseph is the patron saint of Peru, the memory of St. Turibius is likewise venerated in the South American Republic. One biographer writes that St. Rose of Lima was befriended by St. Turibius, who also confirmed her. He was the first to die but was not canonized for some 55 years after her, in 1726.

Today's saint is also known as Toribio Alphonsus and he was born in Mayorga, Spain. He became a distinguished lawyer and also professor of law at the University of Salamanca. In 1575, King Philip II appointed him chief judge of the Court of Inquisition in Granada. Even though he was a layman, Turibius was appointed Archbishop of Lima. Peru was under Spanish rule at that time. He championed the rights and interests of the Indians, and also built churches, schools and hospitals. In 1591 Archbishop Turibius built what was to be the first seminary in the Americas. He traveled about the vast diocese and lived among the Indians as he taught them about God, their loving Father. When cautioned about the dangers he would face in the Andes Mountains, Turibius replied: "Christ came from heaven to save men, and that we ought not fear any danger for His glory."

> *TODAY: At Mass, we pray: "Lord, through the apostolic works of St. Turibius and his unwavering love of truth, you helped your Church to grow. May your chosen people continue to grow in faith and holiness. . . ."*

March 24
St. Catherine of Sweden (c. 1331-1381)
Daughter of St. Bridget, First Superior of the Bridgettine Order

A guidebook for Sweden provides the following information for the prospective traveler: "The Middle Ages produced Sweden's great religious genius, St. Bridget of Vadstena. Founder of the Bridgettine Order and a mystic whose revelations exercised a lasting influence, she was also eminently practical, admonisher of popes and monarchs and a builder who put her stamp on the town of Vadstena. The Blue Church she designed ranks high among Swedish architecture." St. Catherine also eloquently followed the path of her mother to continue in the formation of a religious order of nuns, and later to join Mother Bridget in the Communion of Saints. She visited her mother in Rome and, upon the death of Catherine's husband, Eggard, remained there as a constant companion to Bridget.

St. Catherine's charitable qualities endeared her to many. But the natural beauty of the saint was only a mirror of the innermost graces of her soul. Upon the death of St. Bridget (see July 23), Catherine accompanied the corpse back to Sweden and the convent church at Vadstena. It was St. Catherine who secured the final approval for the religious order from Pope Urban VI.

> TODAY: Do I mirror the religious fervor of my parents? Could I spend four hours of prayer and meditation on the suffering of Our Lord? St. Bridget and her daughter St. Catherine did.

March 25
Annunciation of the Lord (Observed since 430)
Archangel Gabriel announced to Mary that she was to become the Mother of Christ

This feast deserves the thundering dignity of its long name, because it differed so much from all other mere "announcements." There have been announcements of the birth of princes, and of the assassinations of kings; announcements of new Presidents and new Popes; announcements of wars declared and peace treaties signed — thousands of announcements.

But in the headlines of history there never has been an announcement like this: "God Comes On Earth!" For the Feast of the Annunciation celebrates the day when the Archangel Gabriel announced to the Virgin Mary that she was to become the Mother of Christ. And when she consented, the Word was made Flesh — to be born nine months later on the twenty-fifth of December. It all began today. Everything that went before, patriarchs and prophets, were preparation. Everything after-

ward, a natural effect. This *the* event of salvation history.
— Joseph E. Manton, C.SS.R.

TODAY: Reflect on these words of St. Irenaeus: "The Father's purpose in revealing the Son was to make himself known to us all."

March 25
St. Dismas (1st century)
The "Good Thief," A Patron of Prisoners

When the penitent thief offered his prayer, "Jesus, remember me when you come in your kingly power" (Luke 23:42), it was Jesus' darkest hour. One of His Apostles had betrayed Him. Another had denied Him. All had fled except the one standing near the cross. They had all heard the Master's lessons and doctrine. They had seen His miracles. Yet their faith was not proof against His sufferings and humiliations!

Dismas had probably never heard a word from the lips of Christ until His prayer of forgiveness for His murderers. He knew nothing of the Savior's doctrine or miracles. That day on Calvary, though, he surpassed the Apostles in constancy and courage. This saint of the 11th hour made a public declaration of his faith under circumstances that were more likely to shake the strongest faith. With grace, the weakest of men become strong. The strongest become weak without it. And grace comes through prayer. After Dismas, who can doubt the power of prayer?

— Thomas M. Brew, S.J.

TODAY: Let this patron of prisoners be a guide to us as we treat those criminals now in jail.

March 26
St. Ludger (c. 744-809)
Missionary, First Bishop of Munster (Germany)

Day by day we learn that the saints were fearless in their work for God because they relied entirely upon prayer for their physical assistance and support. St. Ludger allowed nothing to interfere with his daily prayers and devotions. Legend has it that Charlemagne requested Ludger's presence before the royal court. A servant summoned Ludger for his royal appearance, only to find the saint kneeling during morning prayers. Ludger said that he would follow the servant when he finished his devotion. The emperor had called for him three times and was now growing angry and impatient. When asked why Ludger did not obey Charlemagne's summons immediately, the saint replied: "Because I believed the service to God was to be preferred to yours or to that of any man. . . . Such indeed was your will when you invested me with the office of bishop, and therefore I deemed it unseemly to interrupt the service of God, even at the command of Your Majesty."

St. Ludger was born and educated in The Netherlands and later studied with Blessed Alcuin at York, England. Upon his return to his homeland in 771, Ludger was ordained to the priesthood. Following the Saxon invasion of 804 he was named first Bishop of Munster.

> *TODAY: Do we begin and end each day with prayer to our heavenly Father? We should put first things first in our daily priorities. After all, God is the alpha and omega in our life.*

March 27
St. John of Egypt (c. 304-394)
Carpenter, Famous Desert Hermit

Obedience to a religious superior, regardless of how foolish be the task, is a common quality found among the saints. St. John of Egypt was no exception. In fact, we learn that he spent a whole year watering a dry (dead) stick as if it had been a living plant, in blind obedience to his spiritual mentor. Common sense leads one to believe that this activity is futile. Yet, how many miracles have sprung from one's obedience to any act when performed for the love of God!

The Lives of the Saints mentions this about today's saint: "Excepting St. Anthony (see January 17), no desert hermit acquired such widespread fame as St. John of Egypt, who was consulted by emperors and whose praises were sung by St. Jerome, St. Augustine . . . and others." John was a carpenter by trade, and when he was 25 years old he entered a monastery and spent his remaining years as a hermit living in a cave near today's city of Asyut, along the Nile River. He was noted for his prophecies to the Emperor Theodosius, numerous miracles and reading one's thoughts.

TODAY: Saintly hermit of God, help me find your spiritual solitude in the frenzied pace of a busy world.

March 28
St. Gontran (524-592)
King of Burgundy and Orleans (France)

Biographers write that although Gontran found his way into *The Roman Martyrology*, "his claims to sanctity would scarcely qualify him for canonization today." His court life involved kidnapping, murder, quarreling with his brothers and their widows. On the other hand, King Gontran was considered a popular ruler, and would visit his people in their homes, where he ate at their tables.

St. Gregory of Tours (538-594), a historian and writer, describes Gontran's regal heritage. "He was one of four sons of King Clotaire and a grandson of King Clovis I and St. Clotilda." At age 36 he inherited a fourth of the French kingdom and became the King of Burgundy and Orleans. He is also identified with the name Guntramnus. Benziger's *Little Lives of the Saints* says this about today's saint, "The prosperity of his reign, both in peace and in war, condemns those who think that human policy cannot be modeled on the maxims of the Gospel, whereas nothing can render a government more flourishing."

TODAY: Let us dwell on the words of Christ to His disciples: "Blessed are you when men revile you and persecute you and utter all kinds of evil against you falsely on my account ... your reward is great in heaven ..." (Matthew 5:10-11).

March 29
St. Jonas and St. Barachisius (d. 327)
Persian Brothers, Monks, Martyrs

The Persians were at constant war with the Romans. When Christianity was adopted by Rome, King Sapor of Persia began his persecution of the followers of Christ and destroyed all churches and monasteries in that country. The war was seen as a religious struggle between Christianity and Zoroasterism. This philosophy hailed the emperor as "king of kings," and sought the worship of deities represented through natural elements of sun, moon, fire and water.

This was the setting for the story of today's saints, brothers and monks at the monastery of Beth-Asa in Hubaham in Persia. The two monks encouraged Christians to "persevere in their faith" even as they faced torture and certain death. These saints refused homage to the emperor, "king of kings," and were sentenced to die. Their homage belonged to God, and their fidelity belonged to the Christian Church. Jonas and Barachisius were subject to barbarous tortures, acts of savagery unequalled in the Church's epic of saints.

> TODAY: Fashions, fads, gimmicks and gadgets lend themselves to help us "do our own thing," many times to the detriment of a holy life. They tend to break our spirit and stifle our dependence on those Christian virtues.

March 30
St. John Climacus (c. 569-605)
Hermit, Abbot, Writer, Also Known As
"John the Scholastic"

The dates surrounding the life of today's saint vary, according to numerous references. We do know for certain, though, that he was a monk and ascetic in a monastery on Mount Sinai. John spent considerable time in a hermitage where he developed his spiritual treatises and wrote the instructions of faith for all catechumens. Prayer was his chief occupation, and "he acquired such a gift of beholding God in everything that it became a second nature" to him. Historians refer to him as one of the most learned of the "desert saints."

The name Climacus originated with the title of his writings, "Climax of Perfection." This is often referred to as his "Heavenly Ladder." John formulated 30 steps necessary in the spiritual preparation for Religious. These steps relate to the 30 hidden years in Christ's life. The final step is that crown of glory merited by a life of faith, hope and charity. This shepherd of souls was also a miracle worker and a popular pilgrimage figure. Pope (St.) Gregory the Great (see September 3) sought the holy abbot's prayers and sent him money and beds for the welfare of all the pilgrims to Mount Sinai.

> TODAY: *The ways to sanctity differ from one person to another. Remember, Jesus Christ is the epitome, the norm, the Divine Model for all.*

March 31
St. Benjamin (d. 424)
Persian Deacon, Martyr

Recalling our entry of March 29, relating to Jonas and Barachisius, we find that, even after 94 years, the Persians "carried on the persecution with greater inhumanity." We also learn the very "recital of the cruelties exercised on Christians strikes us with horror."

Benjamin, a deacon of the Church, had spent a year in prison when the emperor in Constantinople promised him freedom on condition that he would not mention his religion or preach to the people. As a "minister of the Gospel," Benjamin proclaimed his fidelity to God and again preached about Christianity. This action enraged the emperor, who again imprisoned the deacon and subjected him to "barbarous" physical torture resulting in Benjamin's death by impalement with a "knotty stake."

> TODAY: *Not everyone is called to be a martyr, but every person in Christ will pray for the spirit, the determination and the courage required of the martyr.*

APRIL

April 1
St. Gilbert (d. 1245)
Scottish Patriot, Bishop of Caithness

Fellow countrymen regarded St. Gilbert as a great patriot for defending the freedom of the Scottish Church against England. After he had received Holy Orders, Gilbert became archdeacon of Moray. He was an eloquent speaker and a favorite of Scotland's rulers, William and Alexander. He was a high steward (office similar to modern business manager), appointed by the king and vested with great temporal as well as spiritual power in keeping with the traditions of that civil office.

In 1225, King Alexander nominated Gilbert as Bishop of Caithness, and he cared for the diocese for 20 years. St. Gilbert supplied provisions and hospices for the poor. He also supervised the building of the grand Cathedral of Dormoch. His personal philosophy is summed up in his dying words: first, "Never (to) hurt anyone, and, if injured, never to seek revenge"; second, "to bear patiently whatever suffering God may inflict"; third, "obey those in authority so as not to be a stumbling block to others."

> TODAY: *How many times have I been the stumbling block to those seeking my help or advice? St. Gilbert, please help me pick up those loose "blocks" or barriers along my neighbor's pathway.*

April 2
St. Francis of Paola (1416-1507)
Italian Hermit, Founded the Order of Minim Friars;
Patron of Seafarers

Francis of Paola, a fearless Italian hermit, won his saintly crown through the literal acceptance of Christ's words: "Blessed are those who hunger and thirst for righteousness . . ." (Matthew 5:6). He was a defender of the poor and oppressed and was fearless in pleading their cause before the kings of

France. Although he was born at Paola in Calabria, Italy, Francis spent a quarter of his lifetime teaching at the courts of King Louis XI and King Charles VIII in France.

As a young adult, Francis joined his companions to form an eremitical community, later known as the Minim Friars. Penance, charity and humility were its prerequisites, while a law of fast and abstinence was added to bolster the community. Francis of Paola is credited with many miracles and prophecies. He was the subject of paintings by numerous Italian masters, and one concept describes the miracle of walking on the open sea. This image and others dealing with boats and water led Pope Pius XII, in 1943, to declare Francis patron of sailors.

> TODAY: Reflect on the words of Christ to His disciples on the mount: "Let your life so shine before men . . . and give glory to your Father who is in heaven" (Matthew 5:16).

April 3
St. Richard of Wyche (1197-1253)
Chancellor of Oxford University, Bishop of Chichester, England

St. Richard was the Bishop of Chichester in England during the troubled reign of King Henry III. He was renowned for his pastoral ministry and his great generosity.

This prayer which he composed has been set to music and is a great favorite with many folk Mass singers.

> Thanks be to You, my Lord Jesus Christ, for all the blessings and benefits which You have given me, for all the pains and insults You have borne for me.
>
> O most merciful Friend, my Brother and my Redeemer, may I know You more clearly, love You more dearly, and follow You more nearly, day by day, day by day. Amen.
>
> — Msgr. Charles Dollen

> TODAY: Our love for God and neighbor must grow constantly, day by day.

April 4
St. Isidore of Seville (c. 560-636)
Spanish, Bishop of Seville, Doctor of the Church

I sidore was one of a saintly quartet born of a noble Hispanic-Roman family in Carthagena, Spain. The fact that his two brothers Leander and Fulgentius, and his sister Florentina, are also saints has much to say about the family's spiritual legacy. We do know that sanctity develops from within the person. It does not consist merely in copying the actions of another but rather it is motivated through an undying love of God. Our Savior teaches us this lesson very clearly: "Learn from me, for I am meek and humble of heart."

St. Isidore, even as a youth, was considered to be a great scholar and one of the learned men of the times. He is credited with founding diocesan schools (similar to our seminaries), and of fostering the study of liberal arts, medicine and law. Early biographers refer to him as "The Schoolmaster of the Middle Ages," and for centuries his *Etymologies* (encyclopedia) remained a favorite textbook in schools. St. Isidore of Seville is considered to be "the last of the Latin Doctors," and was named a Doctor of the Church by Pope Benedict XIV in 1722.

> *TODAY: It was the Curé of Ars who said: "Virtue passes from the heart of the mother into the hearts of her children, because they willingly do what they see done."*

April 5
St. Vincent Ferrer (1350-1418)
Spanish Dominican, Famed Preacher; Patron of Brick and Tile Manufacturers, Pavement Workers, Plumbers

"W hatever you do," said St. Vincent, "think not of yourself, but of God." Imbued with this spirit of dedication, he preached and God spoke through him. If we also meditate in this spirit and listen in this manner, we shall hear the voice of God. Our Lord himself told Vincent to go forth into the world and convert sinners. And this he did. Vincent spent 21 years preaching throughout Spain, Switzerland, France, Italy, England, Ireland and Scotland. As many as 10,000 penitents followed him. By his preaching he effected the banishment of gambling, blasphemy, and vice from the lives of thousands who were former enemies of the Church. Through him, they were reconciled with the Church.

Vincent's influence with Ferdinand of Castile, and the demise of the antipopes in 1416, saw the end of the Church's Great Schism.

> TODAY: Like St. Vincent Ferrer, help me endure everything with patience; help me meditate on Christ's passion, and give me deprivations, that I may grow humble on my way to saintly perfection.

April 6
St. Marcellinus (d. 413)
Martyr, Secretary of State to Emperor Honorius

One chronicler of saints mentions seven individuals by the name of Marcellinus, one of whose feast days is linked to that of St. Cletus and is celebrated later this month. Today's saint, however, was particularly singled out by St. Augustine in his book *The City of God*, dedicated to "my dear friend Marcellinus."

St. Marcellinus represented Emperor Honorius at Carthage in the year 413, when he presided over a special meeting of Catholic and Donatist (heretical) bishops. After three days' deliberation, Marcellinus as judge and assessor ordered the Donatists to desist and return to the "communion of their Catholic brethren." With his brother Apringius, he enforced the ruling with much severity. In retaliation, the Donatists implicated the brothers in the uprising. General Marinus, who was the officer in charge of putting down the insurrection, arrested Marcellinus and Apringius and put them in prison. Shortly after, they were executed. The emperor reprimanded the general and vindicated Marcellinus as "a man of glorious memory."

> TODAY: The cry "give us peace" echoes around the world. Peace is a special gift from God, but we can help bring it to others by example in the way we live and talk and pray.

69

April 7
St. John Baptist de la Salle (1651-1719)
*French Priest, Patron of Teachers, Founder
of the Brothers of the Christian Schools*

John Baptist de la Salle was born in Reims, France, in 1651 and was ordained a priest in 1678. He is the founder of the Brothers of the Christian Schools.

La Salle's educational system was characterized by his insistence on the use of the vernacular instead of Latin, his practice of "simultaneous" or class teaching as opposed to individual instruction and his preference for the Socratic to the lecture method. His published writings are concerned with both educational and ascetical subjects. He was gentle and kind in his dealings with others, even when they were not honest or persecuted him. In teaching any Christian virtue, he was first in practicing it. He was canonized by Pope Leo XIII in 1900. Pope Pius XII declared him patron of all schoolteachers. Here is a great Christian leader who preached and taught people by making out of himself an accurate (true) image of Christ.

— **Ricardo Colin, M.G.H.**

TODAY: The banishment of God from our modern educative process is disastrous. If even greater sacrifices are required for the preservation of our Catholic schools, we should be prepared to make them.

April 8
St. Dionysius (c. 180)
Bishop of Corinth

Dionysius has the reputation as being one of the foremost leaders of the Church in the second century. He was a prolific writer and wrote numerous letters to various Christian communities. The *Ecclesiastical History* written by Eusebius contains a few epistles in which Dionysius championed the orthodox teachings of the early Church. He fought against heresies and instructed his people on ways to be better Christians. A special letter to the Church in Rome thanked the reigning Pontiff for the alms and generosity of the Roman people in supplying food and money for the Christians in Corinth.

The letters written by Dionysius were read aloud to the congregations as they worshiped. Following the reading of Scripture and the celebration of the "divine mysteries," the celebrant would read the instructions from the bishop. Could this be the origin of today's homily or sermon? Although Dionysius appeared to have died in peace, the Greeks venerate him as a martyr because of his immense suffering for the Faith.

> TODAY: Remember all those unhappy souls who resist the heavenly call, and also those still unhappier souls who have fallen from grace and lapsed into heresy.

April 9
St. Mary of Cleophas (1st century)
Holy Woman of Galilee, Witness of Christ's
Crucifixion and Resurrection

A study of the Gospels will provide a most accurate biography of today's saint. We know that she was one of the holy women who followed Jesus from Galilee and "ministered to Him"; that she stood with Mary Magdalene beside the cross; that she was careful to observe where His body was laid; that, with Mary Magdalene and Salome, she brought spices that they might anoint Jesus.

We know the women found the sepulchre empty; were told by angels that Jesus was risen; were told to carry the message to the disciples and to Peter. On their way back they met Christ himself, who said to them: "All hail."

Legend has Mary going to Spain, where she died at Ciudad Rodrigo. She is also said to have accompanied Lazarus, Mary Magdalene and Martha to Provence in France. St. Mary Cleophas is also known as Mary Clopas.

> TODAY: Read those passages of the New Testament relating to Mary Cleophas's role as witness to Christ. See: Matthew 27: 56; Mark 15:40 and 16:1; Luke 24:10; John 19:25.

April 10
St. Macarius (d. 1012)
Also Known as Macharius of Ghent, Patron of Flanders,
Patron Against Epidemic Diseases

Today's saint was a popular figure throughout Flanders; however, many of the feats attributed to him are legendary. As Alban Butler wrote: "In the case of uncanonized saints honored locally, fiction steps in where history is lacking."

According to legend, Macarius was an Archbishop of Antioch in Pisidia who gave everything to the poor and went on a pilgrimage to Jerusalem. During his journey, he was captured by the Saracens, imprisoned and tortured. In a miraculous way, Macarius managed to escape his captors and continued on a journey through Europe. He is credited with many miracles occurring in the cities of Mainz, Cologne, Malines, Combria and Tournai. When he arrived at Ghent in Flanders, "he was hospitably received as a poor pilgrim" at the monastery of the monks of St. Bavo. Macarius himself was a victim of the deadly plague. He had prophesied that the pestilence would cease at the time of his death. Many of his relics remain in the Cathedral of Ghent.

> TODAY: Let us proclaim the mystery of faith with this acclamation: "Dying you destroyed our death, / rising you restored our life, / Lord Jesus, come in glory."

April 11
St. Stanislaus (1030-1079)
Polish Bishop, Martyr, Patron of Poland;
Principal Patron of the City of Krakow

To be born to wealth is not ordinarily considered conducive to holiness. St. Stanislaus's parents were of the nobility, but very virtuous. When they died, he gave away everything that he had inherited, became a priest, then bishop, and crowned an austere life with martyrdom. He was put to death because of heroic opposition to the evil King Boleslaus the Bold. St. Stanislaus was canonized by Pope Innocent IV in 1253.

At times we make ourselves believe that under different circumstances we would serve God more faithfully. We must, of course, avoid the occasions of sin which accompany our mode of life. Other than that, the barriers to a good Christian life are within ourselves, and would have to be overcome no matter what our situation. It is self-deception to think otherwise.

— Most Rev. Joseph M. Marling, C.PP.S.

TODAY: We are where God wishes us to be. Fidelity to Him is fidelity to the duties which currently we are called upon to perform.

April 12
St. Zeno (d. 371)
Bishop of Verona, Italy; Patron
Against Floods and Drowning

In the Basilica of St. Zeno Major, in the city of Verona, a 13th-century polychrome statue depicts Bishop Zeno as "the saint who smiles." At least the sculptor has delivered us from one of the "sad-faced saints."

Zeno was born in Africa, and according to St. Ambrose (397), our saint for today was named Bishop of Verona in the year 362. He lived during the time of the great Christian persecutions and underwent much suffering and anguish. Historic accounts of St. Zeno show him to be a pastoral-minded bishop who sought a sound liturgical and sacramental life for his people. He purged the Church in Verona from heresy and pagan superstitions. He also taught that hospitality, charity and care of the poor were top priorities for Christians. Bishop Zeno once told his followers that "you have opened your homes to travelers. . . . For a long time (in Verona) no one alive or dead has gone naked. The poor no longer need to beg for food."

Two centuries later a miracle occurred through the intercession of St. Zeno. In the year 598, the Adige River flooded, submerging the city of Verona. Although the water level was at window-height, the people who had found protection in the Basilica of St. Zeno were kept dry and safe.

TODAY: Lord, renew in me the praises of springtime. Keep me safe from nature's torrential outbursts.

April 13
St. Martin (d. 655)
Tuscan Pope, Last of Popes to Die a Martyr

This Martin, who was Pope in the seventh century, died a broken man in exile because he would not hedge on the question of "Who is Christ?" When the Emperor Constans demanded that Martin go along with the current eastern heresy, holding that Christ actually was human but had a divine will, the Pope held firm. Truth is truth, and the Faith handed down from Christ and the apostles could not be thinned out. "No," said Martin, "Christ has two natures. He is true God as He is true man." Because he would not compromise, he died.

It is the same underlying heresy today. The worldlings don't want a Christ who is truly alive, unchanging. They want a modern, congenial sort of Christ — a blend of Santa Claus and Albert Schweitzer, ministering to the sick and poor, and pouring out his soul in sonorous organ solos. But Christ is alpha and omega, the same yesterday, today and forever. To lift our lives to the supernatural by His blood and cross, He came. Again, He comes to judge us.

— **Rev. Robert L. Wilken**

TODAY: "... The Son of man also came not to be served but to serve, and to give his life as a ransom for many" (Mark 10:45).

April 14
St. Bénézet (d. 1184)
"Little Benedict the Bridge Builder";
Patron of Avignon, France

Unlike today's generation who dream of building castles, Bénézet — the shepherd — was destined to build bridges. Responding to three requests occurring during a vision, the shepherd hastily approached the Bishop of Avignon with the proposal to build a bridge over the Rhône River, to safeguard the many travelers lost there each year. Miraculously, the bishop allowed Bénézet to proceed with his gigantic task. Bridge construction began in 1177, and Bénézet was still working on the stone spans at the time of his death in 1184. At that time, the bulk of the engineering problems had been resolved. It is fitting that Bénézet was interred upon the bridge itself. According to *The Lives of the Saints*, "the wonders which attended the construction from the laying of the foundations, and the miracles performed at Bénézet's tomb induced the city to build a chapel on the bridge in which the body lay for nearly 500 years."

TODAY: God . . . teaches us all that we need to know, as we are ready. As we work and play, think and pray, stumble and fall. God is touching us — day by day!

April 15
St. Ruadan of Lothra (d. c. 584)
Founding Abbot of Lothra Monastery, Ireland

The power of God is made known, not only through His direct intervention in the affairs of men, but indirectly through the actions of His saints. This special power is given to the saints because of their exceptional love of God and a daily life of prayer and self-denial.

Although little factual material is available on today's saint, we do know that he is honored as one of the 12 Apostles of Ireland. He lived in the western part of Leinster and was a disciple of St. Finian at the Monastery of Clonard. Ruadan founded and was made abbot of the Monastery of Lothra in County Tipperary. He was the spiritual father of 150 who spent their monastic life in work and in prayer. St. Ruadan was often called the "Lamp of Lothra," because of his scholastic influence in the Church at that time.

TODAY: With today's saint, may our mortal lives be crowned with the ultimate joy of rising with Him who is love for evermore.

April 16
St. Bernadette Soubirous (1844-1879)
Visionary of Lourdes, Canonized in 1933

"I do not promise you happiness in this world, but in the next." — Our Lady to St. Bernadette.

As Pope Pius XII said, "The Queen of Heaven came to Bernadette, made her her confidante, helper, the instrument of her maternal tenderness and of the all-powerful mercy of her Son in the restoring of the world to Christ, by a new and incomparable outpouring of the Redemption."

Our Lady chose Bernadette, an illiterate child and shepherdess, such as were Lucy, Jacinta and Francis of Fatima, as were also Melanie and Maximin at La Salette, to proclaim her message to the world: "Do penance. Build a chapel. Have processions. Pray for sinners."

— Paschal Boland, O.S.B.

TODAY: Our Lady of Lourdes, pray for us.

April 16
St. Benedict Joseph Labre (1748-1783)
"Beggar of Rome" and "Saint of the Forty Hours"

St. Benedict Joseph Labre was a wanderer, a seeker. In his early years he went from one religious house to another, looking for the place in which God wanted him to spend his life. He stayed in none of them because he fitted into none. Thereafter he became a pilgrim, tramping the roads of Europe from shrine to shrine. In 1770, however, after a fifth visit to Einsiedeln, his pilgrimages ceased and he stayed in Rome.

He was a curious figure to look upon: ragged, unkempt, hardly clean. The people who saw him casually at one or another shrine may easily have thought him a sort of freak. He certainly was without roots, either of place or of conformity. Actually, though, he was firmly rooted — in God. Actually he was a strict conformist — to God. His vocation seems to have been to set vividly before men the truth that in this world we are not at home but on pilgrimage and that we must hold the world, its ways and its good opinion as nothing and seek to please God alone.

— Msgr. John S. Kennedy

TODAY: O holy patron, pray for me and teach me to be like thee!

76

St. Stephen Harding (d. 1134)
English Cistercian, Abbot of Citeaux (France)

Stephen Harding was one of a threesome who founded the Monastery of Citeaux. Although St. Robert of Molesme founded the Order of Citeaux, it was Stephen who formulated the "Charter of Charity" which became the constitution and rule of the Cistercian Order.

As a student he traveled to Scotland, Paris and Rome. On the journey to Rome, Stephen and his companions would recite the entire psalter together. It was at the Monastery of Molesme that Stephen found "holy fellowship in prayer, mortification and poverty," as exemplified in the Rule of St. Benedict. As the community grew, however, it also grew more worldly, and many restrictions and rules were not enforced. St. Stephen said: "The spirit of the place seems to have departed." He sought a reform in the community to return to a strict observance of the Rule, but only 18 monks were in accord with his plans. Early in 1098, Abbot Robert, Prior Alberic and Subprior Stephen and others received permission from the papal legate at Lyons to form a new community, the Order of Citeaux. Later St. Robert returned to Molesme and Alberic became Abbot. St. Stephen Harding was named Abbot of Citeaux at the death of Alberic. Historians write: "It took time to convert the virgin forest (at Citeaux) into arable land, and the brethren were often reduced to great straits. Nevertheless they continued to serve God according to the strict rule of St. Benedict. . . ." The appearance of St. Bernard (see August 20) and his troop of 30 men at Citeaux marked the continued growth of the community and the beginnings of a new saintly personality.

TODAY: Like St. Stephen, help me observe the rules of life without any laxity.

April 18
St. Apollonius the Apologist (c. 190)
Roman Senator, Martyr

Apollonius was a prominent senator who became a Christian following the persecuting reign of the Emperor Marcus

Aurelius in the year 180. The senator, a well-educated statesman, was also versed in philosophy and the Holy Scriptures. He enjoyed a prominent social position in Roman society.

A household servant reported Apollonius's conversion to the Church and his Christian activities to the local *praetorium*. As was the law, the servant-informer was executed. However, authorities set out to have the senator denounce his newly won religion. Perennis, the prefect of the council of soldiers, delivered Apollonius to his fellow senators so that they might pass judgment on him. In the debates with other Roman senators, Apollonius refused to renounce his faith, and instead preached about Christ and the formation of the Christian Church. His masterful display of logic and his command of philosophy earned for him the title of apologist. Despite all his heroics and the friendship of fellow statesmen, Apollonius was condemned to death by those with whom he had served.

> *TODAY: St. Apollonius leaves us with these words of reflection. "Love of life does not make me afraid to die." Rather, "there is nothing better than the life eternal, which gives immortality to the soul that has lived well. . . ."*

April 19
St. Leo IX (1002-1054)
Pope (February 12, 1049, to April 19, 1054), Bruno of Alsace

Pope Leo IX is probably best remembered for his part in preparing the way for the election of popes by vote of all the cardinals of the Church. The current practice dates back to 1059. Another fascinating biographical item was the mention of Bruno's early military skill as a deacon. Also, as Pope Leo IX he commanded an army against the Norman invaders at Civitella. However, he was captured and then imprisoned at Benevento. St. Peter Damian (see February 21) is said to have reprimanded Leo for this avocation — "a Pope acting as a military commander and leading an army."

Bruno was born of noble parents in Alsace, at that time a part of the Holy Roman Empire. He studied at Toul and later was tutored by Bishop Adalbert of Metz. While he was a deacon at St. Stephen's in Toul, he was named "counselor" to Emperor

Conrad the Salic. Later, upon the death of Pope Damascus II, Bishop Bruno of Toul was chosen as the new Pontiff under the name of Pope Leo IX. Music was a hobby of the Pope; he enjoyed religious music and promoted the study of sacred chant. He also stressed a collegiate atmosphere in seminaries and traveled throughout Christendom enforcing Church reforms and regulations, stemming much heresy in the land. Pope Leo IX died in Rome shortly after his release by Norman captors.

TODAY: We praise the Lord by a forgiving love of others. "You shall not take vengeance or bear any grudge against the sons of your people, but you shall love your neighbor as yourself . . ." (Leviticus 19:18).

April 20
St. Agnes of Montepulciano (c. 1268-1312)
Dominican Nun, Abbess of Procena Convent

Saints are exemplars of the fruit of a prayerful life. We realize that this one, now a companion of God, was once, as is each of us, a traveler along the pathways of this world. Saints were tempted and saints were sinners. But saints were persons of prayer — persistent prayer, confident prayer — who were in constant communication with God in order to receive guidance to those heavenly things. They also received protection against the darkness of the devil. Saints learned well the lesson of Christ's teachings so that they would be strong, constant and victorious in their combat with the devil.

Today the Church has such a saint. Agnes of Montepulciano knew the problems pitting good against evil and the fires of temptation. Greater than these, however, she knew the purpose and value of prayer. Her prayer life led her to become one of the great saints of the Dominican Order. Agnes received a special dispensation from the Pope in order to be named abbess of the convent of Procena when she was only 15 years old. She was gifted with prophecy and the working of miracles. She also founded a church in honor of Our Lady in the city of Montepulciano, and placed the convent under Dominican patronage.

TODAY: "Let your light so shine before men, that they may see your good works and give glory to your Father who is in heaven" (Matthew 5:16).

April 21
St. Anselm (c. 1033-1109)
Missionary, Bishop, Doctor of the Church

The saints show us how to imitate Jesus. St. Anselm was an Italian monk who was a missionary to England and became Archbishop of Canterbury. He fought valiantly for the faith, which is another way of saying that he always remained loyal to Jesus. He was a courageous pastor of souls "in season and out of season." He defended Christianity against the ambitious tyranny of the English King William Rufus. Jesus had purchased with His blood freedom for His followers, and Anselm would not let the king subject them to slavery again.

St. Anselm knew that Christ was everything and that only with Christ is man truly free. Leonardo da Vinci understood this when he said, "Only through the God-man can man become truly human." People living without God are filled with fear. St. Anselm was fearless. St. Anselm was strong in faith and an opponent to all who tried to subject man to slavery. He knew that "religion gives the answers to the mysteries of life." Anselm stood with Christ in refuting confusion.

— Rev. Rawley Myers

> TODAY: "Keep the commandments of the Lord your God, by walking in his ways and by fearing him" (Deuteronomy 8:6).

April 22
St. Opportuna (c. 770)
Benedictine Nun, Abbess

The Latin adjective *opportuna* means: suitable, fit, convenient, advantageous and useful. How fitting a name to describe today's saint. Opportuna was born in Normandy of royal blood. As a young girl she entered the Benedictine convent of Montreuil, and received the religious veil from her brother, Bishop Chrodegang of Séez. Like lives of other members of the community, her life was spent in mortification, humility, obedience and prayer.

Those of us distressed with weight and dietary problems would do well to look to St. Opportuna for help in meeting our problems. On Sunday she ate a little fish; Wednesday and Friday she abstained from all food, and the remaining four days of the week she subsisted only on a piece of barley bread. The nuns and novices were edified by her saintly austerity and piety as abbess of the convent. The tragic death of her brother proved a great shock to St. Opportuna, and she died shortly afterward.

> TODAY: As Americans, we shy away from saintly roles; yet, it is advantageous for us to be close friends of God and grow in a life of grace within us.

April 23
St. George (d. c. 300)
Martyr, Patron of England

Internationally, St. George is the most popular saint in philately. He is honored on more stamps, by more countries, than any other saint. In most of these stamp designs, St. George is shown on horseback in battle with the dragon.

One of the best known legends about St. George symbolizes the conquest of paganism by Christianity. According to it, the country around Salena, in Libya, had been terrorized by a terrible dragon demanding a daily toll of human life. One day, St. George was riding across the country. He met a procession being led by the king's daughter whose lot it had fallen to be devoured by the dragon on that day. Learning of it, St. George charged the dragon, wounded and captured him. Then he bound the princess's sash about the dragon's neck. Thereupon, she was able to lead him as she wished. Returning to the city, St. George told the populace it was God's grace which had enabled him to overpower the demon. He exhorted them to accept Christianity.   — Marie Layne

> TODAY: We will learn to conquer the little things in life, and let the dragons fall where they may.

April 24
St. Fidelis of Sigmaringen (1577-1622)
Mark Rey, Martyr, Known as the "Poor Man's Lawyer"

This German martyr was "the advocate of the poor." He was a Franciscan who preached mightily the Word of God. And because of his love for the truth, he was martyred. He defended the Church with his life.

The Church was vital to the martyrs. They knew that man needs a guide, and that is why Jesus graciously gave us the Church. Man almost always gets off balance in his thinking about religion when he tries to go it alone without the Church. As Monsignor Knox reminds us, "Our memories are too short, our loyalties too weak, and our instincts too rebellious" to be able to travel the right path without guidance. The Church then is our lighthouse in the darkness all about us.

How foolish many moderns are who think they do not need the Church. They find out too late that whereas they thought they were going in the right direction, they have been wandering around in circles, totally lost, ending in disaster and despair.   — Rev. Rawley Myers

TODAY: Like all martyrs we must strive to be guardians of the Faith and zealots for Christ.

April 25
St. Mark (c. 74)
Evangelist, Author of 2nd Gospel, Patron
of Venice and of Notaries

In *The Roman Martyrology* for this date is this summation: "At Alexandria, the birthday of blessed Mark, evangelist, disciple and interpreter of the Apostle St. Peter. He wrote his Gospel at the request of the faithful of Rome, and taking it with him, proceeded to Egypt and founded a church at Alexandria, where he was the first to announce Christ." St. Mark faced many tribulations for his beliefs, we learn: ". . . arrested for his faith, he was bound, dragged over stones and endured great afflictions. Finally he was confined to prison, where, being comforted by the visit of an angel, and even by an apparition of Our Lord himself, he was called to the heavenly kingdom in the eighth year of the reign of Nero. . . ."

This soldier of Christ is interred at St. Mark's Cathedral in Venice. Day by day, with Mark and the other saints, we learn that physical suffering is or will be the lot of many of us. By offering up our suffering in reparation for our own and others' sins, we can make it eternally profitable.

TODAY: Like St. Mark the Evangelist, give me the strength of the lion when facing life's dangers.

April 26
St. Cletus (d. 91) and St. Marcellinus (d. 304)
Popes and Martyrs

St. Cletus and St. Marcellinus, commemorated today, were both Popes, both martyrs. But there were some 200 years between their pontificates. St. Cletus was the third Pope, a convert of St. Peter's and his successor after St. Linus. He was martyred in 91. St. Marcellinus ruled the Church from 293 to 304, and in the latter years he gave his life in witness to Christ during the savage persecution of the Emperor Diocletian.

These men are links in that living, unbroken, and illustrious chain which runs through the tumultuous centuries from Christ's commissioning of St. Peter to the reign of the present Holy Father. Everything else in the world has changed many times over, but the divinely established Church, built on the rock of the divinely established papacy, has stood fast. Men have done their utmost, their worst, to strike down Peter, but he remains proof, like the Church, against the gates of hell. Are we sufficiently grateful for the totally undeserved privilege of being members of his flock?

— **Msgr. John S. Kennedy**

TODAY: Dear Lord, do I have the faith and courage of the early martyrs to stand up for You?

April 27
St. Zita (1218-1278)
Patron of Housekeepers and Servants

Zita is known as Italy's "little maid." When she was 12 years old she became a servant in the Fantinelli household in the village of Lucca. Zita's parents and family were very poor but equally pious. They provided her with "spiritual equipment" that would last her a lifetime. At times she was disliked by fellow servants. Some even despised her austere way of living in order to feed the poor and help the handicapped. She is credited with numerous miracles through her charitable acts of giving and sharing with people she met who were even less fortunate.

Biographers write that Zita's "work indeed was part of her religion." Her philosophy is summed up in her words: "A servant is not pious if she is not industrious. Work-shy piety in people of her position is sham piety." St. Zita served the same family for 48 years. She was dear to the Fantinelli children, and she also became a friend and confidante of the entire household. She was later freed from domestic chores and was able to live her life in prayer and works of mercy.

> TODAY: "Hear us, O God, our Savior, so that, as we rejoice in the feast of Thy virgin, blessed Zita, we may also be taught the spirit of pious devotion, through Christ, our Lord. Amen" (Roman Missal).

April 28
St. Peter Chanel (1803-1841)
Missionary to Oceania, First Martyr in the South Seas

Here is another martyr, someone who loved Christ so much that he gave his life for Him. He was a missionary to Polynesia and was murdered in the last century for his faith, the first martyr of Oceania.

To love Christ, to be loyal to Him, that is the first characteristic of the martyr. And it should be the mark of every Christ-follower, great or small. We cannot be heroic missionaries, most of us; we will never baptize thousands or go halfway around the world to bring the Word of Christ to pagan people. We will never work great miracles, and we will never be known throughout Christianity for our wondrous deeds. We are little people and we can only do little things. But Christ expects each one of us to do something. When that beautiful soul Mother Teresa of Calcutta started out helping the poor, she was only one person alone. But she thought of the saying of Confucius: "Better to light one candle than to curse the darkness." Christ wants every Christian to do what he can.

— Rev. Rawley Myers

> TODAY: Reflect on the fact that this proto-martyr's death brought about the conversion of the Fortuna islanders to Catholicism.

84

April 29
St. Catherine of Siena (1347-1380)
Doctor of the Church, Patron Saint of Italy

One of the loveliest modern monuments in Rome is dedicated to St. Catherine. It stands alongside the Castle of San Angelo, and honors her as the greatest woman of Italian history. This 14th-century Dominican tertiary was a woman without fear. If the Lord had a mission for her to accomplish, she would carry it out though hell would bar the way.

When our Lord gave her the stigmata, the five wounds, she recognized a problem for a busy woman like herself. If she had to go around with hands and feet bleeding and bandaged, she might be a seven-day wonder, but she would also be a good deal of a nuisance. So she asked that they be invisible. The compromise reached was that they would be, as they were later described, luminous, but to make up for it, doubly, nay, triply painful. Bargaining with God is a ticklish business, even with the best intentions. It is just as well not to advertise our virtues. If they are real, they will be found out. If they are a fraud, we will be found out. And a good test of whether they are real or not is whether they hurt.

— **Most Rev. Robert J. Dwyer**

TODAY: Remember all the holy virgins and widows; ask all holy saints of God to intercede for us.

April 29
St. Peter the Martyr (1205-1252)
Dominican Martyr, Preacher, Inquisitor

In most of the frescoes of the great Dominican artist Fra Angelico, you will see, in a corner, or somewhere off in the background, a friar with a gaping wound in his head. That is St. Peter Martyr, the painter's celestial patron, and it is likely that no patron saint ever received greater honor from a client than he. Actually, he lived in 13th-century Italy, found his way into the Dominicans soon after their foundation and, because of the vigor of his preaching against the revived heresy of the Manicheans, was assaulted by a hired assassin and murdered in cold blood. He died reciting the Apostles' Creed.

Fra Angelico put his saint everywhere, at the Annunciation, at Bethlehem, at the foot of the cross, at the Resurrection. Perhaps his point is that if these things are real enough to us, if we believe tham with all our heart, then in truth we are there. Faith is presence. — Most Rev. Robert J. Dwyer

TODAY: Prepare to meet those saintly persons in your life and begin to follow their virtues.

April 30
St. Pius V (1504-1572)
Dominican Pope and Reformer, Also Known as Cardinal Alessandrino

Antonio Ghislieri of Alessandria, Italy, was destined to be the Church's 225th Pope. He became a Dominican friar and later taught philosophy and theology. As Cardinal Alessandrino he became the Church's grand inquisitor, serving Pope Pius IV. Upon the death of that Pontiff in 1565, Cardinal Alessandrino was elected to succeed him as Pope Pius V. He continued to enforce the decrees enacted at the Council of Trent, and he witnessed numerous reforms in the pastoral and liturgical life of the Church. A high point during his reign was the publishing of the *Roman Breviary* and *Missal* to replace older editions. Pope Pius V was involved in international politics with the excommunication of Queen Elizabeth I of England in 1570, and later with his support of Mary Stuart.

During his pontificate he sought a league of Christian nations to stem the advance of the Ottoman Turks who threatened Europe. The naval victory at Lepanto (October 7, 1571) saw his efforts crowned with success. It was Pope Pius V who announced the Feast of Our Lady of Victory (now the Holy Rosary) in honor of Mary's intercession in the victory of Don Juan and others over the Turkish navy. This popular Pontiff died less than six months later. Succeeding him was Pope Gregory XII (1572-1585).

TODAY: Our present Pontiff is the most international of traveling Popes. Pray that he may be safe from any further attempts on his life during his travels in warring and terror-stricken nations.

MAY

May 1
St. Joseph the Worker (Feast established in 1955)
Protector of Workers, Patron of Social Justice

Many people wonder why they are discontented, why they feel frustrated, why they find life dull, why they are always running a fever of vague unhappiness. It is because they do not give themselves to their work. Work is one of the greatest blessings given to man. But it is a hidden blessing. It can be discovered only by working — and by giving one's best to one's work. Too many of us have lost pride in our work and substituted a half-hearted attitude that is alarming. You will find this resentment and indifference in factories, offices, shops, restaurants, almost everywhere.

To remain great, the people of a nation must take pride in their work and make every effort to give a decent day's work for a decent day's pay. St. Joseph the humble carpenter, spouse of Our Lady and guardian of the Holy Child, is offered to us today as a great model of work. Pray to him.

— **Albert A. Murray, C.S.P.**

TODAY: Look to Joseph for consolation in relieving the humdrum in today's workaday world.

May 2
St. Athanasius (c. 297-373)
Father and Doctor of the Church

"Athanasius against the world," is an old proverb. It not only sums up today's saint but also the times in which he lived. Athanasius was an Egyptian bishop. His time was the fourth-century world which St. Jerome described when he wrote: "The whole world groaned . . . to find itself Arian." For 45 years Athanasius was Primate of Alexandria. For most of that half-century, the Christian world was troubled and confused by a single unorthodox sentence, the teaching of a priest named Arius: "Once the Son of God did not exist." For half a century

Athanasius fought that heresy. For half a century he proclaimed to the Roman Empire that the Son of God is eternal, as God the Father is eternal. For that Faith Athanasius lived, for it he suffered, was exiled from his see five times, for it he was ready to die, if need be. — Thomas M. Brew, S.J.

> TODAY: "Graciously hear our prayers, we beseech Thee, O Lord, while we offer in solemn commemoration of blessed Athanasius, Thy confessor and bishop; and by the merits of him who worthily served Thee, absolve us from all our sins."

May 3
St. Philip (1st century)
Apostle, Martyr
St. James (d. 62)
Apostle, Martyr, Patron of Pilgrims

Philip of Bethsaida, a disciple of John the Baptizer, referred to Jesus of Nazareth, the son of Joseph, who had told him, "Follow me." With childlike enthusiasm, Philip told Nathanael he had found the one of whom the prophets had written. His friend asked. "Can anything good come out of Nazareth?" Philip simply answered, "Come and see" (John 1:43-46).

Jesus, always the teacher, explained that the way to the Father was through Him, for once the disciples really knew the Son, they would know the Father. How frustrated Jesus must have become when moments later Philip said, "Lord, show us the Father, and we shall be satisfied." Philip still had not understood Jesus' words, "I am in the Father and the Father (is) in me" (John 14:6-10).

James the younger, Apostle and cousin of the Lord Jesus, became Bishop of Jerusalem and author of the Epistle (James). Cephas and James cordially welcomed Paul to Jerusalem after Paul's conversion. James, martyred by the same people who had so much esteem for his great sense of justice, was and still is called "James, the Just." — Dorothy Travers Zisa

> TODAY: To think of the Apostles is to recall their zeal and sacrifices as they followed the footsteps of Our Lord for the spreading of Christ's kingdom.

May 4
St. Florian (d. 304)
Roman Martyr, Patron of Poland and Upper Austria

Like St. Sebastian (January 20), who was martyred only 16 years earlier, Florian too was an officer of the Roman army. He was also a Christian martyred for his Faith during the persecution of Diocletian. St. Florian was attached to an army garrison in Austria. He freely gave himself up to fellow soldiers who were rounding up Christians for arrest. Bravely he confessed his belief in God, for which he was scourged and half-skinned alive. He was then thrown into the Erns River with a rock around his neck. This soldier for Christ was entombed at the Augustinian abbey near Linz. The body was later removed to Rome in 1138, when Pope Lucien III gave some relics, of the saint to King Casimir of Poland. Many miracles of healing are attributed to St. Florian's intercession. He is also a patron of those in danger from fire or water.

> *TODAY: Remember in prayer all the soldiers and servicemen who gave their life for God and country. For them — Day is Done.*

May 5
St. Angelo (d. 1220)
Carmelite Monk, Martyr

According to tradition, our Lord appeared to Angelo on Mount Carmel and told him he was needed in Sicily. The fact that he converted sinners through his teaching and example speaks well of his popularity. In Palermo, more than 200 Jews were baptized as a result of his evangelism.

During May — Mary's month — the beautiful story is told of the conversion of his Jewish parents to Christianity. Angelo's mother and father were gifted with a vision of our Lady, who told them that the "Messiah had already appeared and had redeemed His people." Mary also predicted a holy life and martyrdom for their son Angelo.

St. Angelo was preaching in the town of Leocata in Sicily when he was beaten by a band of terrorists and then stabbed many times. Angelo's dying prayer was one of forgiveness for those who attacked him, but especially for a man called Berengarius who fatally wounded him.

> TODAY: Pray to Him whom the Jews called "Anointed of God."

May 6
St. Evodius (c. 64)
Bishop of Antioch

It is believed that this saint was the first person to describe the followers of Christ as Christians. According to the Acts of the Apostles, the word Christian was first used in Antioch and it describes one who believes in the divinity and teaching of Jesus Christ.

Tradition has it that Evodius was one of the 70 disciples who had been ordained by the Apostles themselves. Also, he was probably consecrated Bishop of the Church at Antioch by St. Peter. At the death of Bishop Evodius, St. Peter named Ignatius (October 17) to succeed him to the See of Antioch. St. Evodius teaches us that without perseverance there can be no sure way to holiness.

> TODAY: Lord, help me be faithful to Your teaching, and do not let me tire of doing Your will.

May 7
St. John of Beverly (d. 721)
English Benedictine, Bishop of York

Today's St. John is only one of 69 saintly Johns mentioned in a popular catalogue of saints. St. John of Beverly also had the distinction of teaching Venerable Bede, one of England's first and greatest men of letters. As Bishop of the See of Hexham, St. John also ordained his pupil and scholar, Bede. The shrine of St. John at Beverly Abbey was one of the most popular pilgrimage sites in England prior to the Reformation.

As a young man, John studied under a holy abbot, St. Theodore of Tarsus, at Kent. He then became a monk at Whitby Abbey. John was named Bishop of Hexham in 687, and 18 years later he was named Bishop of York, succeeding St. Bosa. Today's saint was noted for his holiness, devotion to contemplative life and also performed many miracles. Venerable Bede's *Ecclesiastical History* contains a historical account of St. John of Beverly.

> *TODAY: Like St. John of Beverly, let us plant the seeds of Jesus' love in the garden of our hearts.*

May 8
St. Boniface IV (d. 615)
Benedictine, 67th Pope (August 25, 608 - May 8, 615)

St. Boniface was a Pontiff who governed the Church for six years. He is reported to have been a student of St. Gregory the Great in Rome. He succeeded Pope Boniface III to the Chair of Peter. Today's saint was also responsible for converting the Roman Pantheon (temple of all gods) into a Christian church, dedicated to our Lady and all martyrs. The church is now called Santa Maria Rotunda, for its circular architectural shape.

At a synod of Italian bishops, the Pope called for a restoration of discipline in the Church. He also met with St. Mellitus, Bishop of London, to discuss the affairs of the Church in England. Boniface also received a letter from St. Columban, who chided the Pope for some of his theological stances, yet proclaimed his devotion and loyalty to the Holy See. Pope Boniface IV is buried in the Basilica of St. Peter in Rome. It was St. Deusdedit, otherwise known as Pope Adeodatus I of Rome, who succeeded him as Supreme Pontiff.

> *TODAY: Lord, help me strengthen my faith in the Church, and firm up my allegiance and loyalty to the Holy Father.*

May 9
St. Pachomius (c. 292-348)
Egyptian Abbot, Founder of Cenobitic Monasticism

Today is also the feast day of St. Beatus and St. Gerontius. Beatus, a second-century saint, is often called the "Apostle of Switzerland." Gerontius, an Italian bishop, was murdered on his way home from Rome in 501. Like those of other early saints, their lives are greatly intertwined with legendary prose and fictitious biographies.

As a youth, Pachomius was drafted for service in the Egyptian army. During his travels the troops were befriended by numerous groups of Christians. The soldier never forgot their kindness, and when he was discharged from service, he returned to his home (Kasr as-Syad), where he became a catechumen in the Christian Church. He was attracted to the prayer life of the desert hermit, and a life of austerity, fast and abstinence, mixed with daily work and prayer. Pachomius built a monastery at Tabennisi, situated along the Nile River, and his followers soon numbered in the hundreds. Later, he built six more monasteries in Egypt, and lived to see 3,000 monks and nine monasteries under his care. His rules of monasticism were the guidelines for the Rule of St. Benedict written in the sixth century. Pachomius was 56 years old when he died during an epidemic.

TODAY: "Let us love one another." May our life be an example to those around us.

May 10
St. John of Avila (1499-1569)
*Spanish Priest, Preacher, Missionary;
Patron of Southern Spain*

It is only fitting that the teacher — the master — would some day follow in the paths of those he served and guided as their spiritual advisor. So it was with St. John of Avila, a friend of St. Ignatius Loyola (founder of the Society of Jesus), and spiritual advisor to St. Teresa, St. John of God, St. Francis Borgia, St. Peter of Alcantara and the mystic Louis of Granada (the saint's biographer).

St. John of Avila is recognized as one of the great religious leaders of 16th-century Spain. Although he was of a wealthy family, he gave his entire inheritance to help the poor. His oratorical eloquence is described in this passage from *The Lives of the Saints*: "When he preached, he spoke like one inspired. . . . The only preparation he ever made for his sermons was his daily meditation of four hours." When asked how to become a good preacher, St. John told a young priest that the only way he knew how was to love God very much. His charge that "the rich could not get to heaven," and his accusations of sin and vice among those of high society led to his imprisonment during the Spanish Inquisition. After his release from prison he continued preaching throughout the country. He is buried at the Jesuit church in Montilla. St. John of Avila was canonized in 1970 by Pope Paul VI.

> TODAY: *It has been said that God does not count our prayers; He weighs them. What really matters is quality not quantity!*

May 11
St. Ignatius of Laconi (1701-1781)
Capuchin, Peacemaker and Beggar of Alms

At first it was procrastination — delay, delay, delay — as a youth. Then as a Capuchin lay brother it was prompt obedience — punctual, punctual, punctual. Today's saint was canonized in 1950 and is also known as Ignatius Vincent (Peis). His main duties were gathering and begging alms for the Capuchins' support. He did what he was supposed to do when he was supposed to do it.

A once popular song, "Slowpoke," told about the aggravation of people kept waiting. A most needed modern virtue in this speedily paced world is promptness. Lateness is often a large wound in the heart of charity. For many people the dawdling latecomer is a frustrating, upsetting, disturbing human being. At times, detaining someone is actually cruel. On the other hand, being on time brings gladness, smiles, cooperation and friendliness. It gets a meeting, dinner, class or Mass off to a bright start. Pronto appointments oil the machinery of our daily dealings with others, initiating achievements that hum along happily.

— Donald Costello

> TODAY: *St. Ignatius of Laconi, ever on time, as up the pathway to heaven you'd climb, with your help we hope never to be late, so that no one, for us, will have to wait.*

May 12
SS. Nereus and Achilles (1st century), St. Pancras (c. 304)
Roman Martyrs

Nereus and Achilles were soldiers of early Rome who became
Christians and then refused to bear arms under Emperor Trajan.
They were beheaded and buried in the cemetery of Domitello.
St. Gregory the Great (540-604), in his homily for the day, said:
"These saints, before whom we are assembled, despised the
world and trampled it under their feet when peace, riches and
health gave it charms."

Almost 250 years after the martyrdom of Nereus and
Achilles, a 14-year-old youth by the name of Pancras was also
beheaded for proclaiming his Christian beliefs. Pancras was
born in Syria and moved to Rome, where he was converted to
the Church with his uncle. St. Pancras was called "the avenger
of perjuries" by St. Gregory of Tours. He asserted that God
would punish those who lied or made a false oath in the presence of the saint's relics.

> *TODAY: " They threw away their shields, armor and
> blood-stained javelins ... to confess their faith in
> Christ" (Pope Damasus).*

May 13
St. Servatius (d. 384)
Bishop of Tongres in Belgium

Today's entry in *The Roman Martyrology*, reads: "At
Maestricht, St. Servatius, Bishop of Tongres, whose grave, as a
public sign of his merit, was free from snow during winter
(though everything around was covered with snow), until the
inhabitants built a church over it." Servatius was an Armenian
by birth and is also known by the name Servais. He befriended
St. Athanasius and also provided refuge for him during his banishment. He fought against Arianism (a denial of Christ's
divinity), despite the Arian majority at the Council of Rimini in
359. Servatius died from a fever during his return from a pilgrimage to Rome. Bishop Servatius was popular for the miracles
that he performed benefiting the sick and wounded. His prophecies also included the invasion of the continent by Attila.

TODAY: We must all strive to stand for something and be zealous for it; but first we must be sure that it is the cause of Christ, and not someone leading us away from Him.

May 14
St. Matthias (1st century)
Apostle, Martyr

T oday we celebrate the feast of St. Matthias. He was the Apostle elected to take the place of Judas. He has one thing in common with most of us: history knows little about him. Yet he was a close personal friend of the Apostles, and closeness to Christ's friends is an honor which was denied to many of the greatest figures in human history. How fortunate we are, therefore, that we may count so many of our friends among the saints of God.

Just think what it must have been for St. Matthias to hear St. Peter and the rest describing our Lord's teachings and works; His love and His death. We too can learn of Christ from those He has appointed to give us His message and His Sacraments, and today would be an ideal day to thank Him for His Apostles and His Church.

— **John C. Selner, S.S.**

TODAY: Reflect on the words of the first chapter in the Acts of the Apostles. "They put forward two, Joseph called Barsabbas, who was surnamed Justus, and Matthias . . . and the lot fell on Matthias; and he was enrolled with the eleven apostles" (1:23, 26).

May 15
St. Isidore (1070-1130)
Patron of Farmers and Laborers

T oday's saint was a Spanish farm servant. Physically and spiritually he demonstrated to all that "a farmer's work is never done." Farm people depend upon the weather, and they learn a great deal of patience, a virtue that many of us lack. Today we seem to want instant results and we become frustrated if God doesn't do everything precisely when we want it. Someone has called this the "slot machine" complex. We put in our quarter's worth of prayers and we expect the jackpot every time. Well, slot machines don't work that way, and neither does God. Cardinal Newman reminds us that although Jesus said, "Ask, and you will receive," He did not say "right away." Sometimes God tests us in prayer, to see if we will persevere.

Parents don't give a child everything he wants. Some things the child begs for would be bad for him. Nor does God give us everything we pray for. At times we can look back and truly say, "Thank You, God, for not answering my prayer." The late Archbishop Fulton J. Sheen told us that God doesn't give us everything we want, but He always gives us everything we need.   — Rev. Rawley Myers

TODAY: Pray to St. Isidore for a huge harvest of souls.

May 16
St. Simon Stock (d. 1265)
English Carmelite; Fostered Scapular Devotion to Mary

This is the feast of the apparition of Mary to St. Simon Stock in 1251. Born at Aylesford, Kent, England, Simon joined the Carmelites in Jerusalem and became the Prior General of the Order of Mount Carmel in 1247. The Carmelites are said to have been founded by the Prophet Elijah on Mount Carmel in Israel. Mount Carmel was the first place dedicated to the Blessed Virgin, even before her Assumption. The revised rule of the Order was approved by Pope Innocent VI in 1237. Simon died at Bordeaux on May 16, 1265.

The Carmelite Scapular, which signifies shouldering the "yoke" of Jesus Christ, has been most popular in the Church. The Carmelite Orders of men and women are devoted to contemplation. St. Teresa of Avila and St. John of the Cross are the champions of their spirit.   — Julian Woods

TODAY: "Shoulder my yoke and learn from me."

May 17
St. Paschal Baylon (1540-1592)
Patron of Eucharistic Congresses and Societies

The great international Eucharistic congresses, held at intervals in various parts of the world, attract millions and present a spectacle of unparalleled majesty and grandeur. It is in keeping with the ways of God, even though paradoxical, that they have as their heavenly patron a humble and simple lay brother who lived in Spain in the 16th century — St. Paschal Baylon.

St. Paschal's devotion to the Blessed Eucharist was most extraordinary. Attracted to it as if by a magnet, he led his life, as it were, in that holy presence. In contrast are our coldness, unconcern and plain neglect. Just as we expect our children to appear other than those in India, for example, who are entirely deprived of good food, so should our lives differ from those of individuals about us who never partake of the Bread of Life. But is this the case? How shall we explain this matter to ourselves?

— **Most Rev. Joseph M. Marling, C.PP.S.**

TODAY: Christ is present always in the Blessed Sacrament to counsel and love us. In Holy Communion He comes to make us a part of Him and himself a part of us.

May 18
St. John I (d. 526)
Martyr, 53rd Pope (August 13, 523, to May 18, 526)

Although King Theodoric, who had ruled Italy for over 30 years, was responsible for Pope John I's role as an ambassador to Constantinople, the Goth king was also responsible for the martyrdom of the Pontiff. On the other hand, Emperor Justin I of Constantinople greeted Pope John I warmly, and on Easter Sunday he pontificated in the cathedral of that city.

Theodoric's fear of the growing friendship between the Latin and Greek Churches was the cause of a change in attitude, and persecution began in Rome once more. During the Pontiff's absence Theodoric executed St. Severinus Boethius, a philosopher, and his father-in-law, Symmachus, on charges of treason. Theodoric regarded the friendly relationship between the Pontiff and the Emperor as part of a conspiracy against him. Pope John I was seized by Theodoric's guards upon his return to Ravenna, where he died in prison.

TODAY: "Let your desire be to see God; your fear, that you may lose Him; your sorrow, that you are not having fruition of Him; your joy, that He can bring you to himself. Thus you will live in great peace" (St. Teresa of Avila).

May 18
St. Venantius (d. 257)
Seventeen-year-old Martyr of Camerino

According to a tradition of long standing, St. Venantius was a teenaged youth when dragged before a pagan judge in the middle of the third century, savagely tortured, and finally beheaded for the Faith.

The Church has many youthful saints whom she holds up to the young men of today. Without exception they are superb models of manliness and spirit. We confess, however, that our youth are often falsely accused of being flighty and rebellious. How often they amaze us by their maturity when put to a test. Many times they are listless because they are not challenged to seek goals which lie beyond the ordinary. Uppermost in the minds of those who are older must be the example which they place before those who are just developing. Failure in this respect is the key to much of the waywardness and heedlessness associated with our contemporary youth.

— Most Rev. Joseph M. Marling, C.PP.S.

TODAY: Let us heed the words of Matthew (18:7): "Woe to the world for temptations to sin! ... woe to the man by whom the temptation comes!"

May 19
St. Celestine V (c. 1214-1296)
Pope (Peter of Morrone the Hermit)

St. Celestine V is the only Pope in history to resign. Chosen in 1294, at 84, with a reputation for holiness after years spent chiefly as a hermit, he soon saw and immediately admitted that he was poorly equipped for the papacy. With unfeigned humility he inquired if he could abdicate, and upon receiving an affirmative reply, stepped down from the papal throne, after five months, to the bare cell that was his delight.

Lack of humility leads us to overlook our shortcomings,

and to strive for positions beyond our capabilities. Humility is commonly considered the foundation for a good life. To cultivate it is to draw many blessings upon ourselves, and to be spared pitfalls and blunders without number. Let us never make the mistake of deeming humility a mark of weakness. Only the strong are humble. It is the badge of solid character.

— Most Rev. Joseph M. Marling, C.PP.S.

TODAY: To know God is to love Him; to love God is to live within the realm of God's Word.

May 20
St. Bernardine of Siena (1380-1444)
Italian Franciscan, Preacher, Missioner;
Patron of Italy, also of Advertisers

Biographical accounts of today's saint lead one to believe that Bernardine was truly one of those "take charge" personalities. The son of a Sienese governor, Bernardine was only 17 years old when he joined a confraternity dedicated to our Blessed Mother. He was only 20 when he took charge of the La Scala Hospital in Siena during a virulent plague. Several years later Bernardine joined the Franciscan Order. He was to become one of the Church's most popular preachers, after suffering a chronic hoarseness of his throat which left his voice weak and inaudible. It was through faith and prayer that his voice was restored. He spoke to open-air audiences throughout Italy because no church or forum could accommodate the multitude of followers. Bernardine was especially devoted to the Holy Name of Jesus, and everywhere he spoke he displayed a special placard with the letters IHS.

In 1430, Bernardine completed his missionary labors to take charge of the Strict Observance movement in the Franciscan Order, as its organizer and second founder. His followers in the strict rule grew from 300 to 4,000 members. Several years before his death, Bernardine again returned to the mission field, preaching throughout Italy. This "People's Preacher" was indeed God's take-charge saint of the 15th century.

TODAY: We begin our waking hours by dedicating our day to God. Please, God, be the "take charge" Savior of my soul!

May 21
St. Crispin of Viterbo (1668-1750)
Franciscan Capuchin Brother

Although this was the first saint canonized by Pope John Paul II (June 20, 1982), it is likely that you could find St. Crispin of Viterbo on a Franciscan calendar before that declaration. Here was a humble Capuchin brother, a gardener, a cook, a beggar for the Order, a "picker-upper" of unwanted babies left at the door. Maybe a better title for him would be "St. Jack of all Trades."

That is what every practicing Catholic must be, a joy-filled, holy "Jack of all Trades." Around the home, office, or factory, it is our profession. On the street or highway, in our daily dealings with others — the mailman, the barber, the bank teller, the grocery clerk, the teacher, the newsboy — we must be prepared. As "Jack," our vocation is to perform that act of kindness, to say that uplifting word, to find a "Gospel solution" to a difficulty. The "trades" are easily spelled out by Matthew, Mark, Luke and John, in beatitudes, in parables, in miracles and in the Passion of Our Lord and Savior Jesus Christ!

— Donald Costello

TODAY: St. Crispin, gardener, beggar, cook, guide me in my daily Christian trades and tasks.

May 22
St. Rita of Cascia (1381-1457)
Widow, Cloistered Augustinian Religious;Patron of the Impossible and Desperate Cases

Contained in *The Roman Martyrology* are these thoughts for the day. St. Rita, "after being disengaged from her earthly marriage (of 18 years), loved only Christ, her eternal Spouse." She is also likened to St. Jude (October 28) with the title "patron of the impossible and the advocate of desperate cases." Modern advertising patter would say: "We do the impossible — all other things may take a little extra time."

Today's saint is like numerous religious women. As a girl, she desired to enter the Augustinian convent in her hometown of Cascia; however, she was promised in marriage by her parents. Her husband was murdered, a possible "victim of a vendetta," and the two sons swore vengeance for the crime. Their mother, St. Rita, prayed that her sons would die rather than commit murder. They were felled by a fatal illness. Rita was denied entry into the convent because she was a widow and not a virgin. She was 32 years old when she finally was accepted by the religious order. All that she said or did was prompted by a fervent love of God. Because of her special devotion to the passion of Jesus Christ, she miraculously was marked with a bleeding stigmata on the forehead, as if a thorn from Christ's crown were imbedded in her flesh. St. Rita is symbolized with a rose.

> *TODAY: May I be more like St. Rita in my love for enemies or those who would do bodily harm. Grant me the love and grace to combat all physical pain and torture.*

May 23
St. Julia (5th century)
Patroness of Corsica, Virgin and Martyr

In 438, Genseric took Carthage. A noble maiden, Julia, was sold as a slave to a pagan merchant of Syria. She bore her fate with fortitude, performing each assigned duty, devoting her spare time to prayer and reading. Her gentle cheerfulness and fidelity endeared her to her master. He esteemed her as his most valuable possession.

On a trip to Gaul, he took her with him. At Corsica, he landed to join an idolatrous festival. Julia remained apart. Her absence, an implied censure, was deeply resented by Felix, the governor. Fiercely, he demanded she be brought before him. He caused her to be struck on the face and then crucified. This saint is generally shown with a wreath and veil of a virgin, standing by the cross, through which she found both death and eternal life. In one hand, she holds the palm of martyrdom; in the other, the open Scriptures, over which she bends in an absorbed mood, evidence of her great love for God and His teachings.

— Marie Layne

> *TODAY: Like St. Julia may I too be a slave for God and His Church.*

May 24
St. David I (c. 1080-1153)
King of Scotland, Son of St. Margaret

Prince David was the youngest of six sons of King Malcolm III and his Queen, St. Margaret. As king, David was one of Scotland's more popular rulers, noted for his beneficence to the Church. He established bishoprics (dioceses) throughout the island and founded many convents and monasteries.

On his deathbed, when requested to rest, David prayed: "Let me rather think about the things of God, so that my spirit may set out strengthened on its journey from exile to home." David continued to pray: "When I stand before God's tremendous judgment-seat, you will not be able to answer for me or defend me; no one will be able to deliver me from His hand." St. David is enshrined at Dunfermline Abbey, which was founded by his mother and father.

> *TODAY: "He who does justice will live in the presence of the Lord."*

May 25
St. Bede the Venerable (c. 673-735)
Benedictine, Doctor of the Church;
Father of English History

One of the most beautiful prayers in the Bible is Mary's *Magnificat*. It really isn't a very original prayer, since Mary, the Jewish maiden, so filled with the hymns, psalms and canticles of the Old Testament, was bound to pray in those terms.

St. Bede the Venerable, in his commentary on St. Luke's Gospel, takes each phrase and weaves his thoughts around it. It shows us a very pleasing form of mental prayer. For openers, Bede tries to amplify Mary's opening phrase: "The Lord has exalted me by a gift so great, so unheard of, that language is useless to describe it and the depths of love in my heart can scarcely grasp it. I offer them all the powers of my soul in praise and thanksgiving."

— Msgr. Charles Dollen

TODAY: Let St. Bede be your mentor in your pursuit of knowledge in history and literature.

May 25
St. Mary Magdalene de Pazzi (1566-1607)
Italian Carmelite, Contemplative

Our age boasts that it has given women position and opportunities previously denied them. But a host of great women of the past rise to acknowledge that the Church did not restrict their talents, and actually did much to give them status. Among them would be St. Mary Magdalene de Pazzi, who died at Florence in 1607 at the age of 41.

The effect of the saint's holy life upon her era is all the more remarkable since she led a hidden existence as a cloistered Carmelite. From this we learn that those who live as contemplatives are not as removed from the world as it first appears. They supplement the intense activity that God asks of most individuals in the fulfillment of His holy Will. This is another reminder that we sanctify our daily life, and move toward heaven, by being faithful to the duties which our state of life imposes.

— **Most Rev. Joseph M. Marling, C.PP.S.**

TODAY: Heavenly patron, grant that I may be not too "far out" of this world that I should neglect my duties to family and Church.

May 26
St. Philip Neri (1515-1596)
Founded the Congregation of the Oratory

St. Philip Neri was born in Florence, Italy, in 1515, son of a notary of noble family. Sacrificing the favor of a wealthy uncle, he became a private tutor. After his studies, he sold his books for the benefit of the poor and ministered to pilgrims and convalescents in Rome. He was ordained a priest in 1551. Large numbers of people came to his confessional. He founded the Congregation of the Oratory. Neri was the most popular saint in Europe since St. Francis of Assisi.

Jesus makes clear to us *nowadays* that any renunciation for the Gospel's sake will be blessed with a spiritual fruitfulness far more recompensing, both on earth and in heaven, than the possession of all other things. — **Ricardo Colin, M.G.**

TODAY: St. Philip is noted for his humor and wit. His cheerful manners and outgoing personality could well be the daily pattern for us to follow.

May 26
St. Mariana Paredes y Flores (1618-1645)
"Lily of Quito," Canonized in 1950

Little known in North America, St. Mariana of Jesus is Ecuador's patron saint. Her town of Quito is a tourist's paradise of natural beauty. She lived the secular Franciscan (third order) way, in the environment of her hacienda, her home. It is a superb lesson.

Certainly she could be a special patron of the home. For the "Lily" it was a place of education, of prayer and fasting; meditation and mortification; charitable words and charitable works.

You can do the very same! Give your home "atmosphere" with a crucifix, holy water font, saints' images and religious reading. Fill that "atmosphere" with your very own personal brand of Christ-like-ness! Too many forfeit the peace of home for the casinos of Atlantic City and Las Vegas; the theaters of New York and Los Angeles; the strident streets and the maddening malls. The hallowed function of the homestead must not be engulfed by worldly desires and media attractions. Home is a fortress of faith. — **Donald Costello**

TODAY: Lord, with Your power and strength, give my folks a big boost; make Christian life flourish in our little roost.

May 27
St. Augustine of Canterbury (d. 604)
Missionary, Patron Saint of England

The 11th chapter in the Gospel of Mark, reveals Christ's triumphal entry into Jerusalem. We read that He entered the temple precincts and dispersed those who were engaged in marketing — buying and selling. He cautioned all with these words: "Is it not written, 'My house shall be called a house of prayer for all the nations'? But you have made it a den of robbers . . ." (Mark 11:17). The chief priests and scribes were angered with Christ, because "all the multitude was astonished at His teaching." As humans, we are also domiciles of prayer, but many times we steal from our spiritual life, like the "den of thieves" who carried their wares through the temple. Today there is time to put our prayer life in order.

A missionary, St. Augustine, converted England's King Ethelbert and his kingdom to Christianity. Canterbury is known as the birthplace of Christ's teachings on the island. As today's missionaries, let St. Augustine be our guide as we "Go in God's Name." — **Dorothy Travers Zisa**

> *TODAY: Reflect on these words of St. Gregory directed to St. Augustine: "All the elect do not work miracles, and yet the names of all are written in heaven."*

May 28
St. Germain (378-448)
Bishop of Auxerre in France; Also Known as Germanus

While still a young man, Germain was a member of the imperial civil service, and later he was assigned to Gaul as a military governor. In 418, upon the death of St. Amator, Germain was named Bishop of Auxerre.

A beautiful Marian reflection is credited to St. Germain in his message on the Feast of the Presentation. He spoke these words: "Hail, Mary, full of grace, holier than the saints, higher than the heavens, more glorious than the Cherubim, more honorable than the Seraphim, to be reverenced by every creature. Hail, holy and immaculate building, most pure palace of God, adorned with the magnificence of the Divine King. Hail, holy throne of God, divine treasury, house of glory, chosen and sacred mercy-seat for the whole world. O virgin most pure who brought forth a Son, and Mother who knew no man, hidden treasure of innocence and holiness. By your prayers to your Son, direct all those who govern the life of the Church and lead us to the harbor of Peace." — **Msgr. John J. Duggan**

> *TODAY: "Blessed be the Lord! for he has heard the voice of my supplications" (Psalm 28:6).*

May 29
SS. William, Stephen, Raymund and Companions (d. 1242)
Martyrs of Toulouse

Pope Gregory IX commissioned William Arnaud and other Dominicans to combat Albigensianism in the area of Languedoc, France. This heresy denied the humanity of Christ and questioned the teaching authority of the Church. Albigensian fanatics attacked Dominicans, driving them out of the cities of Toulouse and Narbonne. Undaunted, the friars continued their journey, chanting the *Salve Regina* and the Apostles' Creed on their way. At Avignonet, the group preached a mission assisted by other priests. They were the guests of Count Raymund VII of Toulouse and stayed at his castle. During the night, a military patrol secretly entered the castle and beheaded the holy men as they slept. The martyrs included William Arnaud and two other Dominicans, Stephen and Raymund, plus two Franciscans, two Benedictines, four secular priests and a layman. Many miracles and cures were reported at the site of their grave.

> *TODAY: "Hail to the Queen who reigns above, Mother of clemency and love. . . ." Pray for us, O holy Mother of God, that we may be made worthy of the promises of Christ.*

May 30
St. Joan of Arc (1412-1431)
"Maid of Orléans," Patron of France and of Soldiers

St. Jeanne d'Arc of Domrémy — "La Pucelle" (the maid of Orléans) to fellow soldiers, but more more popularly known as Joan of Arc — was the maiden-warrior who led the French army against English invaders at the city of Orléans.

St. Joan was only 13 years old when she began having visions of supernatural origin. These visions would "lead her through the path of patriotism and also to death at the stake." The manifestations included the voices of St. Michael, St. Catherine and St. Margaret who revealed to Joan that she, a simple peasant girl, was destined to save France. During a battle in 1429 she received several wounds but returned to her troops.

The next year, however, she was captured at Compiègne and remained a prisoner of the Duke of Burgundy. She was ransomed by the English, who condemned her to death as a heretic and sorceress. She was not yet 20 years old when she was burned at the stake in Rouen. Joan called to Jesus and Mary as the flames consumed her. In death, as in life, she carried the banner of Christ and Mary and proclaimed her fidelity to Christ and His Church. John Tressart, a secretary of King Henry, was noted as saying, "We are lost, we have burned a saint!" St. Joan's innocence was declared by the Church in 1456. She was canonized by Pope Benedict XV on May 16, 1920.

— **Albert A. Murray, C.S.P.**

TODAY: As we are nearing the end of May, let us again pray: Mary, Queen of the Holy Rosary, pray for us and all soldiers of Christ.

May 31
Visitation of Blessed Mary the Virgin
Commemorates Mary's visit to her cousin Elizabeth after the Annunciation and before the birth of John the Baptist

Every "Hail Mary" commemorates this unique event. Two cousins, the Blessed Virgin Mary and St. Elizabeth, are expecting babies; one, the Lord Jesus Christ, true God and true man; the other, His herald, St. John the Baptist. Both women with child expressed prayerful and loving joy in their waiting.

Yes, waiting, anticipation, even suspense is part of the fabric of life. It ought to be Christianized. *Holy* expectancy, *prayerful* anticipation and *sacred* suspense typified the manner in which our Lady awaited her Son. Just as with the nine months of life in the womb, God sets time schedules for many occurrences — apples to grow, bruises to heal, paint to dry, pies to bake. The Gospel's "watch and pray" might well be "wait and pray." If we bide our time prayerfully, God gives us amazing results and sometimes adds a pleasant surprise.

— **Donald Costello**

TODAY: You expectant Mothers rejoiced, without ever a complaint. Lend light and joy to the times we must wait, to spend each moment in prayerful state.

JUNE

June 1
St. Justin (100-165)
Martyr, Philosopher, Apologist, Teacher, Writer

A characteristic of almost all the saints is single-mindedness. Whatever else they did — and most of them did a great deal in the time they had on earth — they put the search for God first.

St. Justin is an outstanding example of this. He was born less than a hundred years after the death of Christ in a pagan Roman town in Galilee — where our Lord had spent a great deal of His life. But Justin was born ignorant of Christ, and, thirsting for God, he set out across the world in search of the truth. He tried one philosophy after another, and finally encountered Christ. He described it this way: "A fire blazed up suddenly in my soul. I was seized with love for the prophets and for these men who had loved Christ; I reflected on all these words and decided that this philosophy alone was true and profitable." He gave his life as a martyr for Christ, illustrating what he had written so beautifully of others: "Nobody believed in Socrates deeply enough to die for his teaching. . . . But for Christ, not only philosophers and men of letters, but even artisans and uneducated men have made light of fame, fear and death."

— Msgr. Peter Coughlan

TODAY: Each one of us has the obligation to defend and proclaim the Faith. St. Justin proved his love of Faith by dying for it.

June 2
SS. Marcellinus and Peter (d.c. 304)
Roman Martyrs

Our Lord planned to leave us a pattern of life. The Prince of the Apostles noted this from the start: "Christ . . . suffered for you, leaving you an example, that you should follow in his steps" (1 Peter 2:21). The saints marked the Lord's footprints, and we follow in theirs. Theirs are often closer to our pattern.

St. Marcellinus and St. Peter, whose feast we celebrate today, appreciated and followed the teaching of Christ and the
Apostles on the sacraments as sources of the Spirit. Marcellinus
and his server risked and gave their lives to administer the sacraments to converts. Their devotion won them a place in our
Mass daily in the second list of martyrs. We pray at Mass "that
we may be inspired by the example of those in whose merits we
rejoice" to treasure the sources of the Spirit, the fountains of
grace, the virtues and sanctity.   — Conrad Louis, O.S.B.

*TODAY: Like the saints, seeking to know God better
leads to loving Him more which, in turn, leads to a
closer union with Him.*

June 3
SS. Charles Lwanga and Companions (d. 1886-1887)
Martyrs of Uganda, Canonized by Pope Paul VI in 1964

In Paul's second letter to Timothy, he writes: "If we endure, we
shall also reign with Him" (2:12). Few individuals have under-
gone the trials and tribulations which befell the Apostle Paul.
Despite these agonies, he was able to counsel Timothy to endure
all things for the sake of Christ. His advice to Timothy was not
limited to the latter and has been accepted by saintly persons of
every succeeding age as persecution continues even to our very
day.

Persecutors vary, but their tactics follow patterns from the
past. The persecution methods of the early Roman emperors
were adopted in 1886 when the first martyrs of black Africa —
Charles Lwanga and 22 companions — met their deaths. Recent
converts to the Church, they were willing to suffer and die a
fiery death for Christ so as to live with Him forever. Charles
Lwanga and the other martyrs were pages in the court of King
Mwanga of Uganda in East Africa.

— Msgr. Ralph G. Kutz

*TODAY: Persecution may never face us, but our fideli-
ty to God is subject to many tests. We can disown God
in our daily living . . . we can be faithless to Him . . . we
can display the lack of the all-important virtues of
which martyrs are made.*

June 4
St. Vincentia Gerosa (1784-1847)
Co-founder of the Sisters of Charity of Lovere

One reason for honoring the saints is that they always give us ordinary Christians an extraordinary example of Christian life. A sample of that life is found in these words of St. Vincentia: "He who has not learned what the crucifix means knows nothing, and he who knows his crucifix has nothing more to learn."

Born Catherine Gerosa, Vincentia was in her forties when she helped organize a holy institute to help the sick and the poor and to educate poor children. Her partner in the foundation of the Sisters of Charity of Lovere was St. Bartholomea Capitanio, also of Lovere. The spiritual rule was patterned after that of the Sisters of Charity of St. Vincent de Paul. St. Vincentia continued to direct the community after the death of St. Bartholomea in 1833. She was a humble and spiritual lady and was known for her organizational and leadership qualities. Pope Pius XII canonized Sister Vincentia on July 14, 1950.

TODAY: When self is the motive, the results cannot be greater than self. When the love of God is the motive, there are no such limits.

June 5
St. Boniface (Winfrid) (680-754)
Benedictine, Bishop, Martyr, "Apostle of Germany"

The Holy Bible was the focal point of the spiritual life of the English hero St. Boniface, apostle to Germany, evangelizer and civilizer of the great central region, organizer and creator of its hierarchy. The lively, colorful details of his apostolate tend to hold our attention at the expense of an understanding of the motives which lay behind them.

One reads with fascination how Boniface hacked down the sacred oak of Doner which the natives superstitiously venerated; how he crowned an emperor; founded the famous Abbey of Fulda (735), and at the end accepted martyrdom from the hands of savages, at Dukkum in Holland. He was a great missioner, indeed; but first of all he was a great lover of the Word of God.   — G. Joseph Gustafson, S.S.

TODAY: Let us look at the name Boniface or Winfrid. The words mean a doer of good. This is not the same as a "do-gooder."

June 6
St. Norbert (1080-1134)
Founded Order of Norbertines (Premonstratensians)

The saint of today was not only the Archbishop of Magdeburg, Germany, but the founder of a monastic order. I remember him best as the author of a very concise but quite comprehensive definition of a priest which has been on my desk and, I hope, in my head and heart, for many years. Our saint for today was also a champion in devotion to the Blessed Sacrament. A famous sermon on the priesthood by the eloquent Father Lacordaire is more often quoted. He said that the priest is "a member of every family but belongs to none." That is true, happily true.

I grew up in a small parish, which made it possible for our pastor to come for occasional visits and share a meal with us. It was never regarded as a purely social event. It had a special character, a deeper meaning. I cherish those memories. They made me wonder why any priest would not wish to be called Father.

— **Most Rev. Leo A. Pursley**

TODAY: Ponder awhile these beautiful hymns to the Blessed Sacrament: "O saving Victim, opening wide the gate of heaven to man below." And the response: "You have given them bread from heaven, containing in itself sweetness of every kind."

June 7
St. Antony Gianelli (1789-1846)
Bishop of Bobbio (Italy), Founder of the Missioners of St. Alphonsus Liguori, and Sisters of St. Mary dell' Orto

The month of June is, for many, the most beautiful month of the year. It is noted for its summer weather, anniversaries of weddings, graduations and — for many in religious life — fond memories of ordinations and ceremonies of vows. Today's saint

111

is representative of the month; in fact, the religious order he founded is known as the Sisters of St. Mary "of the Garden."

Antony was of a middle-class family who lived in Genoa. An outstanding scholar, he was ordained a priest before the regular age for ordination. The priest-educator also gave missions, preached regularly and functioned as an ordinary pastor of a parish. He was not yet 40 when he started two religious congregations, one for men and one for women. Both were teaching and nursing orders that spread throughout Europe and the United States. Antony was consecrated Bishop of the See of Bobbio in 1838. He was canonized by Pope Pius XII on June 6, 1951.

> TODAY: Our goal is to follow Christ. Our life's commitment is to follow in His path.

June 8
St. Cloud (c. 605-696)
Bishop of Metz (France)

The first geographic evidence of such a name occurred to me as a young editor working on the *St. Cloud Visitor* newspaper. St. Cloud is for real, as it is a key city in central Minnesota as well as being the name of a diocese of the Church.

Today's saint is also listed as Clodulf, or Clou. He was a son of St. Arnoul, also a Bishop of Metz. The country at that time was part of the Holy Roman Empire. Cloud was a devout layman and later a model pastor. He succeeded St. Godo as Bishop of Metz in 656. Like his father, Bishop Cloud gave of his inheritance to aid the poor. He ruled the See of Metz for 40 years and was in his 90s when he died.

> TODAY: Lord, give us the trust, the faith, and the wisdom to come to You, that we may experience Your healing power in our lives.

June 9
St. Ephrem (c. 306-373)
Doctor of the Church, "Harp of the Holy Spirit"

One of the changes inaugurated by the Second Vatican Council was the restoration of the Permanent Diaconate, a Major

Holy Order which goes back to the Apostles. That they might devote more time to prayer and preaching, they appointed and ordained worthy laymen to assist them chiefly in the ministry of charity.

In recent years a growing number of men have prepared themselves to serve as permanent deacons. They have such patrons as St. Stephen, the first martyr, and they can add to the list the saint we honor today. St. Ephrem is described as a "great teacher, orator, poet, commentator and defender of the Faith." He is called "the Harp of the Holy Spirit" because he enriched the liturgy with his homilies and hymns. Such men are rare, but we need them to keep the standards high and to keep us humble and prayerful as we reach for them.

— Most Rev. Leo A. Pursley

TODAY: This saint was a poet, writer and musician who virtually lived for Christ with his songs in his heart.

June 10
St. Bogumilus (d. 1182)
Archbishop of Gniezno (Poland)

Bogumilus and his twin brother, Boguphalus, were born of noble Polish parents in the city of Dobrow. They studied in Paris, where they were ordained to the priesthood. Bogumilus returned to Poland and built a church dedicated to the Holy Trinity in his native city. An uncle, Archbishop John of Gniezno, appointed Bogumilus chancellor of the archdiocese. In 1167, he succeeded his uncle as Archbishop of Gniezno. This city was the first capital of Poland, and is often referred to as the "legendary cradle" of the Polish nation.

Archbishop Bogumilus was the benefactor of a Cistercian monastery of Coronowa, and endowed it with funds and property from the family estate. Five years after the archbishop's consecration, diocesan clergy rebelled over the strict discipline demanded of them. At that time Bogumilus resigned his office and joined the Camaldolese Order. He died at the monastery at Uniedow, and later his remains were transferred to Holy Trinity Church in Dobrow.

*TODAY: Help me always pray, not "My will be done,"
but rather, "Thy will be done!"*

June 11
St. Barnabas (1st century)
Apostle, Companion to Paul, Martyr

St. Barnabas is honored as an apostle, although he was not one
of the Twelve. St. Luke writes of him: "He was a good man, full
of the Holy Spirit and of faith" (Acts 11:24). In Jerusalem
Barnabas stood sponsor for Paul when all the disciples "were
afraid of him, not believing that he was a disciple."

When Barnabas needed help in Antioch, he "went to
Tarsus to look for Saul; and when he had found him, he
brought him to Antioch" (Acts 11:25-26). On the first missionary journey, Barnabas was the companion of the great
Apostle. St. Barnabas showed his dedication to the Gospel when
he "sold a field which belonged to him, and brought the money
and laid it at the apostles' feet" (Acts 4:37). He made that dedication complete when he yielded his position as leader to one
greater than himself. In the first instance he gave his possessions; in the second he gave himself — a worthy proof of his
apostolic heart.   **— Most Rev. Henry A. Pinger, O.F.M.**

*TODAY: Scripture relates of Barnabas: "He was a
good man, full of the Holy Spirit and of faith." Can the
same be said about me?*

June 12
St. Leo III (d. 816)
96th Pope (795-816)
St. John of Sahagun (San Facundo) (d. 1479)
Spanish Monk, Preacher, Martyr

Cardinal Leo of the Church of Santa Susanna was unanimous-
ly elected Pope, succeeding Pope Adrian I, December 27, 795.
He was to be known as Pope Leo III. Several years later the Pontiff was a victim of a plot by followers of Adrian who sought to
oust him from the papal throne. Pope Leo miraculously withstood a physical beating by enemies who attempted to blind him
and cut out his tongue. He escaped to Paderborn and sought the

protection of Charlemagne, who escorted the Pope back to Rome. At the Synod of 800, Pope Leo was exonerated of all charges made by his persecutors.

It was Pope Leo III who crowned Charlemagne "Emperor of the Romans," at St. Peter's Basilica, Rome. This marked the actual beginnings of the Holy Roman Empire in the West. Pope Leo III governed the Church successfully until the death of Charlemagne in 814. The Saracens then began to land on the coasts of Italy, and Pope Leo was again a victim of subterfuge and murder plot. After a reign of 20 years in the Chair of Peter, he was succeeded by Pope Stephen IV (816-817).

A popular preacher, John of Sahagun gave up his rich benefices to become an Augustinian and eventually prior of the monastery in Salamanca. Keeping discipline by example rather than severity, he healed local divisions in sermons without respect to social class. He is said to have been poisoned by a woman whose married lover he had converted from sin.

> TODAY: *Without God, our personality would be without a center, and the parts would remain dispersed like the pieces of a broken doll.*

June 13
St. Anthony of Padua (1195-1231)
Evangelical Doctor, "Wonder Worker"

St. Anthony is one of the bright stars in the constellation of popular saints. He was an Augustinian monk before joining the Franciscans about 1220. St. Francis of Assisi named him the first theologian of the Friars Minor, whose intellectual tradition he influenced with the thought and spirit of St. Augustine. He was an outstanding preacher, with a reputation for holiness that resulted in his canonization in 1232, a year after his death. His expertise in Sacred Scripture earned him the title "Evangelical Doctor," conferred by Pope Pius XII in 1947. He is remembered principally because of his care for the poor, a concern shared by those who receive "St. Anthony's Bread" and give some of their own to those who are less fortunate.

Legends connected with the life of St. Anthony include those of an apparition of the Child Jesus, and of himself as an

intercessor for the recovery of lost articles, through bilocation.
— Felician A. Foy, O.F.M.

TODAY: "To believe without bothering to perform good works, amounts to laughing in the face of God." St. Anthony, performer of miracles, pray for me!

June 14
St. Methodius I (d. 847)
Patriarch of Constantinople

Another great saint by the name of Methodius. Today's saint was born and educated in Syracuse, Sicily, and went to Constantinople hoping to work at the imperial court. When he arrived at Constantinople, he changed his plans, became a monk and built a monastery on the island of Chios.

The Eastern Church regards Methodius with great veneration because of his part in the overthrow of iconoclasm and his heroic stance during the persecution by Leo the Armenian in the year 815. Greeks called Methodius "The Confessor," and "The Great." He was later exiled and imprisoned. When he was called before Emperor Theophilus, Methodius said: "If an image is so worthless in your eyes, how is it that when you condemn the images of Christ you do not also condemn the veneration paid to representations of yourself? Far from doing so, you are continuously causing them to be multiplied!" The Patriarch convoked a synod at Constantinople that endorsed the Council of Nicaea's decrees on the veneration of sacred images.

TODAY: "Arm thyself with the sign of the cross as with a shield . . . sign thyself not only with the hand, but with the mind" (St. Ephrem).

June 15
St. Vitus (c. 300)
Youthful Martyr, Patron of Actors, Dancers, Epileptics

Among the saints, other than our patronal namesake, the stories about St. Vitus were the favorite of the editor as an eight-year-old pupil in Sister Michael's classroom. This School Sister of Notre Dame developed solid reading habits in her classes that would see her students advance through educational and professional careers. Her source book for reading was Benziger's *Little Pictorial Lives of the Saints*. In our free time we were treated with the stories of the daily heroes for Christ.

St. Vitus was the son of Senator Hylos of Sicily. Unbeknown to his pagan parents, Vitus was baptized a Christian when he was 12 years old. When his miraculous cures of chorea (nervous palsy often called "St. Vitus's dance") and his Christian messages became more popular in the community, he was summoned by Valerian, the mayor, and asked to denounce his newfound religion. Neither threats nor torture could "shake the boy's faith" in God. At Rome, St. Vitus is said to have cured the Emperor Diocletian's son of "evil spirits." Instead of being thankful, the emperor was angered by Vitus's refusal to worship idols and accused him of sorcery because of the many miracles he had performed. Many hideous tortures attempted on St. Vitus proved futile, but he and his companions later died of their sufferings after being freed by an angel, according to legend.

> *TODAY: Let St. Vitus be our guide in loving and treating those souls shaken with epilepsy and other defects of the nervous system.*

June 16
St. John Francis Regis (1597-1640)
French Jesuit, Preacher, Confessor

It was the year 1806, some 166 years after the death of St. John Francis Regis, when a student for the priesthood made a pilgrimage to the tomb and shrine of the saint at La Louvesc. This same student later became known as the Curé of Ars, or St. John Vianney. The Curé of Ars credited today's saint as the source of his priestly vocation. In many ways the two saints lived identical lives.

St. John Francis Regis spent his mornings in the confessional, at the altar and in the pulpit; in the afternoon he would be found in prisons and hospitals. He brought thousands of fallen-aways back to the Church and converted many others in that mountainous region in southeastern France. It is interesting to note that this Jesuit had applied for overseas missionary work among the North American Indians, but was turned down because of his mission success in France. He was 43 years old when taken by death. His last words being: "Brother! I see our Lord and His Mother opening heaven for me!"

> *TODAY: Lord, help us treasure each moment or person that comes our way as the source of holiness and a path to God.*

June 17
St. Rayner (d. 1160)
Also Known as Rainerius of Pisa

Manners make the man, to some extent. To be *mannerly*, polite, cheerful, pleasant is to be Christian. These represent a Christian ideal. St. Paul wrote: "Conduct yourself wisely toward outsiders, making the most of the time. Let your speech always be gracious, seasoned with salt, so that you may know how you ought to answer every one" (Colossians 4:5-6).

St. Rayner was a troubadour and played and sang to the enjoyment of all. When his attention was called to the fact that he might have scandalized some of his listeners, he threw his violin into the fire and cried till he was almost blind. As a saint, he regaled his hearers with his wit and converted many to a better life. To look and sound cheerful is a perfection of Christian charity.

— Conrad Louis, O.S.B.

> *TODAY: There's nothing more attractive than a smile. Perhaps this is the saints' secret for success with people.*

June 18
St. Gregory Barbarigo (1625-1697)
*Cardinal, Bishop of Padua, Canonized
by Pope John XXIII, June 17, 1960*

A popular biographer refers to St. Gregory as a "second St. Charles Borromeo," because of his exemplary conduct and the zeal with which he conducted his priestly life.

Gregory was born and educated in Venice. His was a historic time in the Church, and in 1648 he accompanied the Italian Ambassador Contarini to the Congress of Muenster for the signing of the Treaty of Westphalia with France, Germany and Sweden. This act ended the 30-Years' War. At the congress, Gregory impressed the Apostolic Nuncio Fabio Chigi. When Chigi became Pope Alexander VI, he appointed Gregory Bishop of Bergamo. In 1660 Gregory became a cardinal, and four years later was named Bishop of Padua. The popular cardinal sponsored a college and seminary, endowing them with a library, and also presented a printing press to the seminary. Could this saint also be a patron of printers and pressmen?

> TODAY: It is fitting that the illustrious Pope John XXIII, a native of Bergamo, canonized one of the city's bishop-sons as St. Gregory of Barbarigo.

June 19
St. Romuald (951-1027)
Founded Camaldolese Benedictines

Shocked by seeing his father kill a man in a duel over some disputed property, the hitherto not-so-religious Romuald left his luxurious and comfortable home to become a Benedictine monk. Three years later he exchanged the austerities of the monastic life for those of a hermit. He later founded several monasteries under the Rule of St. Benedict, but in these houses he integrated some ascetical practices of his own, which are now known as the Camaldolese Observance.

Sometimes we are shocked by some crimes or injustices that cause us to examine a facet of our lives to see if we are guilty of a similar fault or sin. Many are now becoming conscious of injustices that have been taken for granted in regard to minorities; injustices that disregard the basic rights of human beings. "Love one another" — John 13:35.

— **Paschal Boland, O.S.B.**

> TODAY: God works in mysterious ways. His grace will always find a door to the soul, but it opens only from the inside.

June 20
St. Silverius (d. 537)
58th Pope, Martyr

Patience was the glory of Pope St. Silverius. By his patience, he saved his soul and the Church. He was faced with many trials from difficult people. The Empress Theodora tried to intimidate him. When she failed, she accused him falsely; then the Byzantine General Belisarius arrested and deposed him.

The Pope took these indignities as our Lord did, suffered, waited, offered all for the benefit of the faithful and the Church. An inscription in his honor near the tomb of St. Peter bears witness to his reward: "Accept these praises which will be read by all the pilgrims who, led by devotion to St. Peter, will come hither from the ends of the earth. . . . Thou hast healed the wounds of thy people." Thus by patience he became another rock upon which the Church rested.   — **Conrad Louis, O.S.B.**

TODAY: Each Christian must be patient in his turn and time to be a rock for someone in Christ's Church.

June 21
St. Aloysius Gonzaga (1568-1591)
Italian Jesuit, Patron of Youth: "I am a piece of twisted iron. I entered religion to get it twisted straight"

St. Aloysius died at the age of 23. Yet he achieved sanctity during his short life. Death came from caring for the plague-ridden in a Roman hospital. Two Popes have offered him to the Christian world as a patron of youth. Aloysius was unquestionably an idealist, as are so many young people. He had no time for cynicism, the vice of the disappointed idealist. Rather, he saw a need and threw himself into the battle.

All around are people and causes that need the solid strength of dedicated Christian idealism. This comes from individuals willing to commit themselves in the spirit of Christ. Am I willing to throw myself into the fray for Christ? The world belongs to the courageous.   — **Kevin A. Lynch, C.S.P.**

TODAY: This is one saint for the younger set to emulate. He was one of the Church's noblest teenagers.

June 22
St. Paulinus of Nola (d. 451)
French-Born Bishop, Writer
St. John Fisher (1469-1535)
English Cardinal, Martyr
St. Thomas More (1478-1535)
English Chancellor, Martyr, "Man for All Seasons"

The liturgy of today's Mass offers us a choice of three saints to commemorate — Paulinus, John Fisher and Thomas More. Two of them, Paulinus and Thomas, were married men and lawyers. After baptism, by consent of his Spanish wife, Paulinus became a priest, a bishop in Italy and a literary friend of such great contemporaries as Ambrose, Augustine and Jerome.

Of the two English martyrs who literally lost their heads over the Church, thanks to Henry VIII, John Fisher was Bishop of Rochester who stood out as a giant in the hierarchy of his time and place, the only one who refused to be silently subservient to his king. The other, Thomas More, was the first layman to hold the high post of Chancellor of England. He is widely known in our day. His life and death have been ably dramatized for stage and screen. He was, indeed, *A Man for All Seasons*, but mainly a man of, with and for God. These two men had what we desperately need in dealing with the encroachment of civil powers upon the realm of religious faith and moral principle — a conscience that cannot be confused, a conviction that cannot be compromised, a courage that cannot be conquered even by the fear of death.

— Most Rev. Leo A. Pursley

TODAY: Our holiness lies in being faithful to our work and everyday life.

June 23
St. Joseph Cafasso (1811-1860)
Moral Theologian, Spiritual Advisor to Don Bosco;
Canonized by Pope Pius XII in 1947

Father Joseph Cafasso encouraged one of his younger students by the name of Don Bosco to continue working with youth, orphans and the imprisoned. Because of his close relation to the

121

Salesians, many thought Joseph to be a member of that community.

He was born in a country town in the Piedmont region of Italy, and was educated at the seminary in Turin. His family were of peasant farmer stock and noted for their piety and practice of their religion. Joseph's nephew later became Canon Joseph Allamano, founder of the Missionary Priests of the Consolata in Turin. In addition to teaching and lecturing, Joseph also was well known as a preacher. He is said to have instructed St. John Bosco in this manner: "Jesus Christ, the Infinite Wisdom, used the words and idioms that were in use among those whom He addressed. Do you the same!" In Italy, Joseph is noted for his many prison reforms, for the founding of orphanages and schools, and the starting of vocational training for delinquent youth.

> *TODAY: How many of us will be remembered by a saint? St. Joseph Cafasso, who died at the hour of the morning Angelus, had St. John Bosco, one of the best preachers of his time preach his eulogy.*

June 24
Birth of John the Baptist (1st century)
"Among those born of woman none is greater"
(Luke 7:28)

The heavenly "birthday" of St. John the Baptist by beheading is celebrated August 29. Today, however, the Church also honors his earthly birthday. Because of St. John's close association with the earthly life of our Lord, this particular feast became known as the "Summer Christmas," and three solemn Masses were celebrated in imitation of the custom of the "Winter Christmas."

What more poignant moment in the history of the Incarnation is there than that joyful recognition of the prenatal St. John at the visit of the Mother of God, carrying the prenatal Jesus in her womb. St. Luke says the baby John leaped for joy! It is with that same expectancy that we too must welcome the visit of Christ and His Mother into our lives. St. Paul couldn't say it more clearly when, in the Epistle to the Philippians, he wrote:

"Rejoice in the Lord always; again I will say, Rejoice" (4:4).
— Ann Hill

TODAY: The birth of John to an elderly couple shows the almighty power of God and teaches me that nothing is impossible to God. Perseverance in prayer is always a necessity.

June 25
St. William of Vercelli (1085-1142)
Abbot, Founder of Hermits of Monte Vergine

Although he was of noble parentage, William was orphaned in infancy and cared for by a relative. As a youth he began a pilgrimage to Compostella in Spain. He later returned to Italy and spent several years as a hermit at Monte Solicoli. He was only 21 when he restored sight to a blind man. His fame grew as a "wonder worker," and he withdrew from the monastic settlement and joined his friend St. John Matera. His spiritual life and disciplines as a hermit drew many to that penitential lifestyle, and he formed a community in 1124. The Hermits of Monte Vergine were an austere foundation, and Abbot William was criticized for the strict rules and lifestyle imposed on clergy and laity. William and John later started communities of hermits at Monte Laceno in Apulia, Monte Cognato, Conza, Guglietto and Saleras. St. William of Vercelli later became the advisor of King Roger of Naples, who also was a benefactor of the numerous religious establishments in Italy.

TODAY: Am I one of those who criticize the strict observance of our Faith? St. William of Vercelli, please help me with my prayer life.

June 26
SS. John and Paul (d. 362)
Roman Martyrs, Brothers

Today's saints are often confused with the Apostles John and Paul. They were army officers serving under Emperor Constantine, and responsible for the security of the emperor's palace. Later they were commissioned by the emperor to serve in the expeditionary forces of General Gallicanus. The saintly brothers warned their general of a possible defeat by the Scythian forces at Thrace, but promised him victory instead if he would become a Christian. General Gallicanus gave his assurance of the promise, and according to legend "a legion of angels put the enemy to flight."

John and Paul denounced the apostasy of their new Emperor, Julian, and refused to obey his commands. They were then seized by members of the Imperial guard and executed at their home on Rome's Coelian Hill.

> TODAY: *Do we have the courage to face death for our religious beliefs? Lord, make us strong and steadfast like those early martyrs of the Church.*

June 27
St. Cyril of Alexandria (c. 376-444)
Bishop, Doctor of the Church

St. Cyril of Alexandria, declared a Doctor of the Church in 1882, was one of those men to whom the words of Sirach apply: "Peoples will speak of his wisdom, and in assembly sing his praises" (39:10). The praises are due for his ministry as Bishop of Alexandria from 412 to 444 and for his extensive teaching and writing in a period of serious controversies over basic doctrines of faith. The controversies concerned the Trinity, the Incarnation (subverted by Nestorians), and the necessity of supernatural grace for salvation (denied by Pelagians, who contended that man in his natural state is capable of salvation). Cyril presided in 431 over the third ecumenical Council of Ephesus, which defined Mary's title, *Theotokos* (Bearer of God), as revealed truth, meaning that the Son of Mary is the Son of God.

Cyril is one of 30 men and two women honored with the title Doctor of the Church.

— Felician A. Foy, O.F.M.

> TODAY: *Rejoice, O Virgin Mary; you alone have put down all heresies in the whole world.*

June 28
St. Irenaeus (130-202)
Bishop of Lyons, Apologist, Martyr

St. Irenaeus lived at a time when many groups of Christians were breaking away from the Church because they insisted on various ideas about Christ and salvation which the Church would not accept. We know that St. Irenaeus was tireless in combatting the false ideas of these groups, but rather strangely, he also opposed those who wanted to use harsh, repressive measures against them. In this way, he earned the name of "Peacemaker" — Irenaeus in Greek.

St. Irenaeus knew something that many of us forget: that there is no contradiction between holding strong views about something and desiring peace with those who disagree. Whether it is a question of politics, or religion, or just in our daily dealings with one another, we can never let our strongly-held beliefs lessen our goodwill to all men. But we can try to "correct" our righteous anger into an active desire to bring peace among men, wherever there is discord. Both our love of truth and our love for men spring from our love for God. And God "prefers mercy to judgment," and has called peacemakers His sons.

— Msgr. Peter Coughlan

TODAY: "Blessed are the peacemakers, for they shall be called sons of God" (Matthew 5:9.)

June 29
SS. Peter and Paul (1st century)
Apostles, Martyrs

When Pope Paul VI proclaimed 1967 a Year of Faith, he set the opening date on the Feast of Saints Peter and Paul, commemorating the 1900th anniversary of their martyrdom in Rome. This observance was intended to help us renew within ourselves the spirit of the Faith which these two Apostles preached so vigorously and for which they died so joyfully.

It was inevitable that their names would be linked in the history of the Church. Our Lord gave Peter his name, "Rock," symbol of the primacy and permanence of his office as Vicar of Christ and Visible Head of His Church. No other Pope has ever borne that name. Saul of Tarsus became Paul, Apostle of the Gentiles, by an overwhelming intervention of our Lord on the road to Damascus. He was, indeed, a "vessel for noble use" (2 Timothy 2:21). His missionary zeal has inspired many through the centuries. It has been surpassed by none. What a privilege to meet these two men in heaven!

— Most Rev. Leo A. Pursley

> TODAY: Like Peter the fisherman, grant that I may be a fisher of men. Too, I will read the Acts of the Apostles and learn of Paul's steadying influence in the early Church.

June 30
First Martyrs of the Church of Rome (c. 64)
"Unknown Soldiers" for Christ and His Church

We come to the end of the month which prompted the poet Lowell to ask: "What is so rare as a day in June?" Now we can count them. We began liturgically with the Feast of St. Justin, Martyr, and we close with a general commemoration of the First Martyrs of Rome. The Church keeps us aware that the sign of our Faith is not merely a cross but a crucifix. There is blood on it, the lifeline of the Mystical Body of Christ. There is no way to escape it and remain Christian, no hope of heaven without it.

I think it was John Keble, Anglican divine and friend of Cardinal Newman, who wrote this verse which I quote from memory:

"There lies thy cross.
Beneath it meekly bow.
It fits thy stature now.
If you pass it with averted eye,
It will crush you bye and bye."

— Most Rev. Leo A. Pursley

> TODAY: These martyrs, known only to God, are described in The Roman Martyrology as "the first fruits with which Rome, so fruitful in that seed, had peopled heaven."

JULY

St. Oliver Plunket (1629-1681)
Irish Martyr, Archbishop of Armagh

This popular Irish saint was canonized by Pope Paul VI in 1975. He was the last Catholic to die a martyr's death at Tyburn, and the first of the Irish martyrs to be canonized. His namesake was the youth Oliver Plunket, who was killed during the Spanish massacre at County Kerry in 1580. The Plunket family were Catholic noblemen who helped King Charles I in his fight for Ireland's freedom from English rule.

Oliver was educated by the Benedictine Fathers in Dublin. He was 16 years old when he entered the Jesuits' Irish College in Rome, and was ordained in 1654. Because of the political uprisings in Ireland, the priest stayed in Rome and became a theologian and consultor of several sacred congregations of the Church. In 1669, Pope Clement XI selected Dr. Plunket to succeed Edmund O'Reilly, the exiled Archbishop of Armagh and Primate of all Ireland. Irish Catholics again faced persecution in 1673, and the prelates were either banished from the country or went into hiding from the law. During the infamous Titus Oates "plot" furor, all clergy and bishops were expelled from the isles. Archbishop Plunket was falsely accused of conspiracy and was imprisoned at Dublin castle, where he was sentenced to be "drawn, hung, disembowelled and quartered," at Tyburn.

> TODAY: *We begin the month dedicated to the Precious Blood of Jesus. Reflect on the bloody death of St. Oliver and others who were martyred by enemies of the Church.*

July 2
SS. Processus and Martinian (c. 1st century)
Roman Martyrs

Today is also the feast day of St. Monegundis, a holy widow who lived during the sixth century at Chartres, France; and a

12th-century German bishop-statesman, St. Otto of Bamberg.

The Roman Martyrology identifies Processus and Martinian as guards at Rome's Mamertine prison during the imprisonment of Saints Peter and Paul. These wardens, along with 40 others, were to be converted to the Christian Faith by the two Apostles. They were baptized by St. Peter. Using a miraculous spring of water flowing from the floor of the prison cell, St. Peter was able to christen the guards and prisoners. Paulinus, the officer in charge, killed Processus and Martinian with his sword because they would not reject Christ or deny their faith in God. St. Gregory the Great preached over their tomb in a basilica on the Via Aurelia. The martyrs' relics are at St. Peter's in the Vatican, in an altar repository dedicated to them.

> *TODAY: "... Their sufferings only wrung from them the words, 'Blessed be the name of the Lord.' "*

July 3
St. Thomas (1st century)
Apostle, Martyr, "Apostle of India," Patron of Architects

He was a simple fisherman in Galilee, called by Jesus to be one of His 12 Apostles. His surname was Didymus (the twin). I wonder if the other twin was living and, if so, ever converted. Thomas showed enthusiastic love for our Lord when he was ready to accompany Him to the house where Lazarus had just died, though the other Apostles feared being stoned by the Jews. Thomas said: "Let us also go, that we may die with him" (John 11:16).

He has come to be called "Doubting Thomas" from his refusal to believe in our Lord's resurrection when told of it by the other Apostles. A week later, however, when he was present at our Lord's second apparition, Thomas uttered that timeless act of faith: "My Lord and my God!" (John 20:28), repeated by the faithful ever since at the Consecration of the Mass and at Benediction. Then it was that our Lord blessed us for our Faith in Him: "Blessed are they who have not seen and yet believe" (John 20:29).   — Msgr. John J. Duggan

> *TODAY: At times, like St. Thomas, I have also refused to trust others. I have been so hurt by being fooled in*

the past that I am reluctant to believe what people tell me. Like our patron for the day, teach me to say, "My Lord and my God."

July 4
St. Elizabeth of Portugal (1271-1336)
Queen, "The Peacemaker"

A saint on a nation's throne. How improbable today. For Portugal, though, in the early 1300s it was a reality. Elizabeth was a model mother for her family and for her people. Her particular charism was that of peacemaker . . . within her family and realm and among kings and kingdoms.

Whatever your status in life, here's a saint for our times. She strove to educate her children in the fear of God, to please her husband; above all, to please God and show it in compassion for the poor. Today's Mass takes note of her special talent for restoring peace. Each of us must lend his best talent to the building of the kingdom of God among men. What is your talent? Are you investing it in the service of your family, community, church? — **Msgr. David P. Spelgatti**

> *TODAY: In the divine office we read: "Elizabeth, the mother of peace and for her people, now triumphs in heaven. Give us peace!" The woman who fears God deserves to be praised.*

July 5
St. Anthony Mary Zaccaria (1502-1539)
Founded Congregation of St. Paul — the Barnabites

St. Anthony was always mindful of the Lord's presence and of His injunctions. Seeing the need of the poor for medical treatment, he studied medicine at the famous University of Padua. But after starting practice as a doctor, he decided that he must learn to cure souls as well as bodies, for the two are inseparable. So he studied theology, which enabled him not only to comfort the sick but also to teach Christian doctrine to young and old.

After his ordination in Milan in 1530, he encouraged some holy women to found a congregation called the Angelicals to rescue girls fallen into evil ways. Then with four fellow priests he formed the Clerks Regular of St. Paul, or Barnabites, approved by Pope Clement VII to promote public preaching, even on street corners, and faithful ministering of the sacraments in Milan's many churches. By these works St. Anthony blunted the attacks Luther was then making against the Church. He was canonized by Pope Leo XIII in 1897.　　　　　— Paul Kocher

> *TODAY: Love humanity as St. Anthony did. All humans are creatures of God; you and I, those in Africa, Asia, Latin America and all the world. No one is excluded from the love of Christ.*

July 6
St. Maria Goretti (1890-1902)
Italian Virgin-Martyr; Model of Purity, Patron of Children

On June 24, 1950, the whole Christian world praised a modern teenager as Pope Pius XII proclaimed officially and infallibly that Maria Goretti was a saint. Maria became a saint because she had the courage to say "No" to the impure advances of the young man who became the "Killer of a Saint." Maria died violently, being stabbed 14 times, rather than give up her life of grace. How many aren't there today, with no life at stake, who willingly give up the precious gift of grace for a few moments of sinful pleasure?

Ask Maria Goretti to help you avoid the occasions of sin ... ask her to help you in your fight against impurity. Who could better understand the problem you face in this sex-mad world than one who died to save her purity? Only the pure of heart shall see God.　　　　　— Msgr. Harry J. Welp

> *TODAY: The martyrdom of a young girl to preserve her virginity reminds me, in these permissive days, that chastity is still one of the highest Christian virtues.*

July 7
St. Palladius (d. 432)
Bishop, Missionary to Ireland

Biographers say that Palladius was ordained a deacon in Rome during the pontificate of Pope St. Celestius I (422-433). In his chronicles, St. Prosper of Aquitaine writes that in 430 or 431 "Palladius was consecrated by Pope Celestine and sent the Irish (Christians) as their first bishop." Bishop Palladius landed in County Leinster near the town of Wicklow. He founded three churches in Ireland but encountered opposition in converting the people to Christianity. The chronicle further notes that Palladius, "seeing that he could not do much good there — and wishing to return to Rome — departed to the country of the Picts (Scottish borderlands)." He died soon after leaving Ireland and was buried near Aberdeen in Scotland.

> TODAY: *The life of a missionary is painful and laborious, but it is also a course of love and faith. Lord, let those of every nation join in praising You.*

July 8
SS. Aquila and Priscilla (1st century)
Jewish Martyrs

Aquila and his wife Priscilla (or Prisca) left Rome for Corinth when the Emperor Claudius banned the Jewish people from Rome. Chapter 18 of the Acts of the Apostles relates that they were befriended by St. Paul, who converted them to Christianity. They also accompanied Paul in his mission travels.

Pope John Paul II, in his *Exhortation on the Role of the Family in the Modern World* (November 22, 1981), mentions today's saints. He writes: "Just as at the dawn of Christianity Aquila and Priscilla were presented as a missionary couple (Acts 18; Romans 16:3-4), so today the Church shows forth her perennial newness and fruitfulness by the presence of Christian couples and families who dedicate at least a part of their lives to working in missionary territories, proclaiming the Gospel and doing service to their fellow man in the love of Jesus Christ. Christian families offer a special contribution to the missionary cause of the Church by fostering missionary vocations among their sons and daughters, and, more generally, '. . . by training their children from childhood to recognize God's love for all people' (2nd Vatican Council, *Apostolicam Actuositatem*, 30)."

> TODAY: *That I may teach my family reverence for a divine calling to religious vocations, and to sacrifice ev-*

ery natural tie at the call of God. Missionary work first begins in the home.

July 9
Martyrs of Gorkum (d. 1572)
19 Priests and Religious Slain in Gorkum, Holland

Nineteen priests and religious sought martyrdom at the hands of Calvinist forces at the Franciscan monastery during the fight over Spanish control of the town of Gorkum. The martyrology names 12 of those who were hanged because of their Catholic belief in the Eucharist and papal primacy. They are: Nicholas Pieck, Jerome Weerden, Leonard Vechel, Nicholas Janssen, Godfrey van Duynen, John van Oosterwyk, John van Hoornaer, Adrian van Hilvarenbeck, James Lacops, Andrew Wontera, Antony van Willehad (who was 90 years old), and Nicasius van Heeze.

The anti-Spanish (Calvinist) forces were called the "Sea Beggars" or "Ragamuffins," and had seized the Dutch towns of Gorkum, Briel, Flushing and Dordrecht. The martyrs were tortured and imprisoned an entire month prior to their deaths at an old Augustinian monastery in Ruggen. During a truce between Spain and the United Provinces in 1616, the remains of the Gorkum martyrs were transferred to the Franciscan church in Brussels, Belgium.

> TODAY: *Like the martyrs of Japan, England and Wales, of North America, and of Uganda, give me the grace to live a holy life dedicated to the Catholic Faith.*

July 10
The Seven Holy Brothers (d. c. 162)
SS. Januarius, Felix, Philip, Sylvanus, Alexander, Vitalis and Martialis

These brothers suffered martyrdom under Marcus Aurelius in Rome around the year 162. Their mother was St. Felicitas, who had a very high social position in Rome but refused to worship the gods. The pagan priests stirred up the emperor with threats of catastrophes if this woman and her children were not forced to venerate the gods, and Marcus Aurelius gave orders for a trial.

Like the Maccabees of old, the children of Felicitas were steadfast in their loyalty to their God. With their mother standing by, encouraging their faith, they were all tortured and finally martyred. The legend goes on to recount that she told them, "Lift up your eyes to heaven, my children; there Christ waits for you; fight for your souls; stay firm in His love." However accurate the details of this account may have been, we can learn from it that faith in Christ and love for Him have ultimate and transcendent values.

— John C. Selner, S.S.

TODAY: This is the true brotherhood which overcame evil.

July 11
St. Benedict (c. 480-547)
Abbot, Established Benedictine Abbey of Monte Cassino;
Father of Western Monasticism, Patron of Europe

When St. Benedict was born in Italy, manual labor was regarded as the degrading work of slaves. Later, when he founded his monastery at Monte Cassino, Benedict made physical labor part of his rule and gave dignity to work and workingmen. His motto: "To work is to pray." Today men have lost sight of Benedict's teaching. Work is something to be avoided. The goal seems to be to do as little work as possible.

In everything Christ did, He was God. He chose to be born into the family of a laborer. He became a carpenter, thus a laborer himself, in order to demonstrate the dignity of work. He wanted to teach us that man is happiest when his powers and talents are challenged. He wanted to convince us that there is great satisfaction when a man helps to fill the needs of his family and community through his labor. The Church prays today that we follow St. Benedict, whom God made an outstanding guide.

— Albert J. Nevins, M.M.

TODAY: We cannot do better than imitate St. Benedict, "that in all things, God might be glorified."

133

*Inspire me to pray and work for Your glory, to respect
God in all persons and creation.*

July 12
St. John Gualbert (11th century)
Abbot, Founder of the Vallumbrosans

Would-be murderer becomes a saint. This is the story of our
saint for today. He sought the life of the man who had killed his
brother. As he was about to give the fatal blow, he stopped, in
answer to the man's plea for mercy. Nor is this the end of the
story. John went to a monastery and became a monk and began
a branch of the Benedictine Order at Vallumbrosa, Italy. He died
in 1073 and was canonized in 1193.

St. John Gualbert teaches us the value and importance of
forgiveness. "Father, forgive them for they know not what they
do" (Luke 23:34). We must forgive others who have hurt us, in
the spirit of Christ-like love. We promise forgiveness every time
we pray the Our Father: "Forgive us our trespasses as we forgive those who trespass against us." That's a big order — to be
forgiven in the measure that we forgive. Perhaps we are indict-
ing ourselves.

— **Titus Cranny, S.A.**

TODAY: Put aside hatred and love will conquer all.

July 13
St. Henry (972-1024)
Emperor of Bavaria

St. Henry the Emperor is not your usual run-of-the-mill saint,
if there are any such. He was born the son of the Duke of
Bavaria, and his mother was of the Burgundian nobility. From
birth, he was destined to rule.

After succeeding his father to the throne in 995, he was
elected to rule the Holy Roman Empire in 1002. From this pin-
nacle of success he had to govern an unruly empire, engage in
wars and politics, and look after the needs of the people. In the
midst of all this, Emperor Henry II did not neglect his own soul
or the needs of the Church. In the midst of imperial splendor he
did not allow himself to become enmeshed in worldly goods, or

become attached to things. This regal example of poverty of spirit is a splendid lesson for us today.

— Msgr. Charles Dollen

TODAY: I am expected to make the best use of the gifts and time God has entrusted to me.

July 13
St. Eugenius (d. 505)
Bishop of Carthage

Benziger's aging *Pictorial Lives of the Saints* illustrates the saint for the day with a woodcut showing the saintly bishop meditating while standing in a prison courtyard. St. Eugenius became Bishop of Carthage in the year 481. The Arians raised a loud protest against him, and King Huneric, perhaps out of fear, forbade Eugenius to exercise his ministry. After some time in exile, he returned to Carthage under a more benign ruler, but in 486 he was again exiled and remained so until his death in 505.

There are many saints who were made such by the very futility of their lives. According to human standards they seemed to fail, but in fact they were really a magnificent success in God's eyes because of their close union with Him. St. Eugenius was one such saint. Former accounts from *"The Lives"* imply that he was martyred in company with others, but later research indicates that he died while in exile at Albi in southern France. So it was not one stroke of martyrdom which made a saint of him, but the little martyrdoms he endured day by day.

— John C. Selner, S.S.

TODAY: The very vocation of the Christian encourages me to follow Christ to perfection. Let it be a lifetime occupation for me.

July 14
St. Camillus de Lellis (1550-1614)
Founder of the Camillians, Patron of the Sick and Nurses

Chronic illness is hard for anyone to bear. It takes a lot of God's grace to be a cheerful sick person. St. Camillus de Lellis cared for the sick and dying by founding a congregation known as the Ministers of the Sick, even though he himself suffered constantly from an incurable running sore in his leg.

There is not one of us who has never experienced physical pain and illness. All of us can offer up our pains in reparation for our sins and the sins of others. When we are ill for a short time, we can pray for those who are incurably ill and dying. We can pray that God in His mercy and love will grant them repentance and hope for life eternal. Many times we suffer even greater mental ills. Mental anguish is sometimes harder to bear than physical pain. Let us pray also for those who are suffering the cruelest kind of pain — the tortures of mind and soul.

— Margaret Hula Malsam

> TODAY: Try to see in hardships both a challenge and an opportunity to develop and put to good use the talents that God has entrusted to us.

July 15
St. Bonaventure (c. 1217-1274)
Franciscan Cardinal-Bishop, Called "Seraphic Doctor"

At the age of four, John Fidanza (surnamed Bonaventure) was cured of a serious illness by the prayers of St. Francis of Assisi. At the age of 17 he became a Franciscan. He received his Doctorate in Theology on the same day with his close friend St. Thomas Aquinas. He was only 36 when he was elected Minister General of the Franciscan Order, and he held this office for 16 years.

St. Bonaventure ordered that a bell should be rung and the Hail Mary recited at nightfall in each monastery in honor of the Annunciation (for it was popularly believed to have taken place at that hour). From this pious practice the Angelus seems to have taken its origin. Pope Gregory X made him a Cardinal. When the papal legates arrived at the monastery in Florence, they found him washing dishes and were told to hang the Cardinal's hat on a nearby tree until he had finished. He wrote and spoke so beautifully about heavenly matters that Pope Sixtus V named him The Seraphic Doctor.

— Msgr. John J. Duggan

TODAY: St. Bonaventure reminds us — "If you seek Jesus without Mary, you seek Him in vain."

July 16
Our Lady of Mount Carmel (1250)
*Pope Benedict XIII extended the feast
to the Universal Church in 1776*

The motherhouse of the Carmelite Order stood on the top of Mount Carmel in the Holy Land. In 1251 the Blessed Virgin Mary appeared there to St. Simon Stock, a general of the order, and gave him the scapular, with the promise that anyone dying while wearing it would be saved. She asked him also to have the Carmelites dedicate themselves to her service and to wearing the scapular.

Even Mary as Queen of Heaven never speaks for herself only. She speaks for her Son, our Lord. Therefore, in her later appearances at Guadalupe, Lourdes, Fatima and elsewhere, she is acting as God's favored messenger to us. We ask her to intercede for us with Him whom she loves and who loves her. No intercession by the saints is so powerful. We do well to heed what she tells us. She heals at Lourdes. At Fatima in 1917 she asked us to pray fervently to her Son, lest Russia's errors contaminate the whole world. We can see we have not prayed enough.   — **Paul Kocher**

TODAY: That I might be a loyal child of Mary in thought, word and deed!

July 17
St. Alexis (5th century)
Called "The Man of God"; Patron of the Alexian Brothers

The life of St. Alexis, a Roman, is intensely interesting, even dramatic. Here indeed was the rich man who *found* the kingdom of heaven. He is said to have fled from the altar during the ceremony of his marriage. While this gesture was by no means required for sanctity, it indicated how sincerely he wished to devote his whole life to the poor and to the love of God.

He mingled with the mendicants in far-off Syria and, much later, returned to Rome, unknown. He went back to his father's house and asked to lodge under the staircase. "I consent," said his father, not recognizing him, "provided you pray God to send back my son." For 17 years he went out from his hiding place, begged bread for the poor and visited the churches. One day Pope Innocent I went in search of this holy man to beg prayers, and in company with Alexis' father, found him dead — under the stairs — but, to their amazement, holding a parchment which gave his name and history.

— John C. Selner, S.S.

TODAY: Remember your concern for the sick when you first heard this listed as a corporal work of mercy? Have I persevered in that youthful resolution?

July 18
St. Bruno (1049-1123)
Bishop of Segni in Italy, Abbot of Monte Cassino

For the believers, Christ is present always in the Blessed Sacrament to counsel and love us. Christ comes to us in Holy Communion to make us a part of Him and himself a part of us.

Today we return to the 11th century for the story about the Canon of Siena. St. Bruno defended the doctrine of the Blessed Sacrament and Christ's presence at Rome's Council of 1079. Pope Gregory VII appointed Bruno Bishop for the See of Segni a year later. He had accompanied Blessed Urban II in 1095 into France, where the Pontiff launched the first Crusade to the Holy Lands. Bishop Bruno later withdrew to Monte Cassino Abbey and received the monastic habit. He was named abbot of the famed monastery. It was Abbot Bruno who rebuked Pope Paschal II because of his political concessions in Germany. The Pope ordered Bruno to resign from Monte Cassino and return to the diocese of Segni. Our saint for today was noted for his commentaries on Holy Scripture and for fostering liturgical devotions among clergy and faithful.

TODAY: Today we are not treated as often to the continuous exposition of the Blessed Sacrament during 40 Hours devotions — or to the liturgical devotion of Benediction — but we can receive the Eucharistic body and blood, at daily Mass.

July 19
St. John Plessington (d. 1679)
Canonized Among the 40 Martyrs of England
and Wales, by Pope Paul VI in 1970

Father Plessington was neither a traitor nor a criminal of the state. He was condemned to death because of his priesthood in the Church. He was arrested as a victim of the "popish plot" fabricated by Titus Oates to murder King Charles II. Father Plessington was also known as William Pleasington or Scarisbrick upon his return to England from his schooling in Spain. He is especially famous for his last words at the scaffold in Barrowshill.

"Dear countrymen," the priest said, "I am here to be executed, neither for theft, murder, nor anything against the laws of God, nor any fact or doctrine inconsistent with the monarchy or civil government." Despite the perjured charges against him, Father John said, ". . . Nothing was laid to my charge but the *priesthood*; I am sure that you will find this to be neither against the law of God nor monarchy or civil government. You have but to consult either the Old or the New Testament. . . . I profess that I, undoubtedly and firmly, believe all the articles of the Catholic faith . . . by the assistance of God, I would rather die than doubt any point of faith taught by our Holy Mother the Roman Catholic Church."

TODAY: In the words of today's saint, let us pray: "I commend myself to the mercy of my Jesus, by whose mercy I also hope for mercy."

July 20
St. Joseph Barsabas (1st century)
Disciple of Christ, Surnamed "The Just"

St. Eusebius identified today's saint as one of the 72 disciples of Christ. Along with Matthias, Joseph Barsabas was nominated to take Judas Iscariot's place among the 12 Apostles. Both Disciples were nominated for their holiness and as followers of Jesus Christ from the time of His baptism until Christ's resurrection.

Mention of today's saint is found in the Acts of the Apostles (1:23-26), where we read, "And they put forward two:

Joseph called Barsabas, who was surnamed Justus, and Matthias. And they prayed and said, 'Lord, who knowest the hearts of all, show which of these two thou hast chosen to take the place in this ministry and apostleship from which Judas turned aside, to go to his own place.' And they cast lots for them, and the lot fell upon Matthias; and he was enrolled with the eleven apostles."

> TODAY: Grant that we continue to seek God in all that we do. As laymen, let our example be greater than our words, in seeking others for Christ.

July 21
St. Lawrence of Brindisi (1559-1619)
Franciscan Capuchin, Proclaimed Doctor of the Church by Pope John XXIII in 1959

St. Lawrence, at the age of 16, became a Franciscan Capuchin friar. Subsequently, while studying philosophy and theology at the University of Padua, he learned to speak six languages, including Hebrew, besides acquiring an intimate knowledge of Holy Writ.

With this background, he became an impressive preacher. Then in 1596 Pope Clement VIII charged him to use his knowledge of Hebrew to work for the conversion of Jews. Later his Order sent him to Germany to establish the Capuchins there as a bulwark against Lutheranism. He founded friaries in Bohemia, Austria and Syria before being elected general of the Capuchins in 1602. The Emperor Rudolf then sent him to persuade the Christian German princes to form an army to stop the advances of the heathen Turks. He became its chaplain general, and on one occasion led a charge, armed only with a crucifix, against the Turks. He was beatified by Pope Pius VI in 1783, and canonized in 1881.

— Paul Kocher

> TODAY: The saintly Capuchin wrote: "Preaching is a duty that is apostolic, angelic, Christian and divine." Pray that the priests of our time may spread the Word of God effectively.

140

July 22
St. Mary Magdalene (1st century)
Among the Women at the Crucifixion of Jesus Christ

In sports, politics or any human endeavor, Americans love a "comeback." We admire people who pick up the pieces of their lives to construct something wholesome and worthwhile. We love a winner, but we love even more those who make successful comebacks.

Such is the story of Mary Magdalene. A known sinner, rejected by her society, she is touched by the healing grace of Christ. She abandons her old life of sin, and she is among the final four faithful friends who stand at the cross as Christ surrenders His life for us. Her loyalty did not go unrewarded. It was to Mary Magdalene that our Lord appeared on Easter morning, telling her, the former sinner, to announce to His Apostles that He had risen. Her "comeback" was complete. Christ chose her to be the messenger of His greatest accomplishment, His Resurrection. — **Rev. Thomas J. Carpender**

> *TODAY: Touch my soul, Lord, with Your grace to convert me as You did Mary Magdalene. "Do not put off conversion. Now is the day of salvation."*

July 23
St. Bridget, also Birgitta (c. 1303-1373)
Princess, Founder of Order of The Savior,
Patroness of Sweden

Today we honor St. Bridget of Sweden. Bridget was born of the Swedish royal family in 1304. In obedience to her father, she married Prince Ulpho of Sweden, and became the mother of eight children. One of the girls was St. Catherine. (see March 24).

After many years she and her husband separated by mutual consent. He entered the Cistercian Order, and Bridget founded the Order of the Savior in the Abbey of Wastein, Sweden. In 1344 she became a widow and thenceforth received a series of the most sublime revelations. She scrupulously submitted these to her confessor. By the command of our Lord, Bridget went on a pilgrimage to the Holy Land, and amidst the

141

very scenes of the Passion was further instructed in the sacred mysteries. She died in 1373. St. Bridget's example of living helps us to realize that we must always be open to the Lord, and ready to do His will.

— Jane J. Stefancic

TODAY: Happy are those who dwell in Your house. They will praise You always.

July 23
St. Apollinaris (d. c. 75)
First Bishop of Ravenna, Italy

Close to the Apostles, near to the time of Christ, and still unknown, Apollinaris was sent to Ravenna in Italy by St. Peter. It became a famous see, perhaps because its first bishop was a disciple of the Prince of the Apostles.

In the Church in Ravenna where St. Apollinaris is buried there is a mosaic showing him as a bishop surrounded by his flock in a blooming paradise. The words of the Mass are as though coming from him: "Feed the flock that is entrusted to you, taking care of it, not because you must but with sincere interest. . . ." Strictly speaking, the words apply only to bishops. But in a broad sense they apply to all who have charge of others: parents, teachers, those in any authority. We all share the responsibility. Let us share it well, that we may reap the reward.

— Titus Cranny, S.A.

TODAY: Give me the opportunity to persevere in my daily trials and tribulations, that I might offer them up to You, O Lord.

July 24
St. Christina the Astonishing (1150-1224)
Belgian, Virgin, Patron of Epileptics

Day by day we learn more and more about those special saints whose astonishing lives have given much to the Church. Today's saint is all the more "astonishing," as her title reveals. In 1182 she is supposed to have died during an epileptic seizure; it was during her Requiem Mass that Christina "sat up in the coffin, soared to the beams of the roof — like a bird — and there perched herself." With the exception of her sister and the priest celebrant at Mass, the frightened congregation fled the church. Her pastor ordered her to come down from the ceiling. Christina did so, and during the Agnus Dei prayers her soul was restored to her body. She said that she had died . . . "gone down to hell and there recognized many friends; to purgatory, where she had seen many friends, and then to heaven. The astonishing Christina was allowed to return to life in order that she could better pray for the poor souls in purgatory." Because of her levitation and other preternatural occurrences, she was thought to be "mad or full of devils."

> TODAY: Isn't it just as astonishing that Christ our Master and Maker offered himself for us? He "suffered under Pontius Pilate, was crucified, died and buried . . . He arose again from the dead; He ascended into heaven!"

July 25
St. James (d. c. 44)
Apostle, Martyr, Patron of Spain, Patron of Those Afflicted with Rheumatism

James the Apostle is called "the Greater," perhaps because he was called before the other Apostle of the same name. This James is the brother of John, "the beloved disciple." Their mother asked Jesus if He would place her sons, one on His right hand and the other on His left, in His kingdom. Sensing jealousy's presence, Jesus said, "Whoever would be great among you must be your servant" (Matthew 20:26). Service is the key to true greatness. It is not achieved by seeking for oneself. Christian greatness is measured in seeking Christ and serving Him in our neighbor.

This must have been the spirit of the James we honor today. He was the first Apostle to give up his life for Christ. As the Bishop of Jerusalem, he was put to death by the nephew of the Herod who passed the death sentence on Jesus.

— **Rev. Thomas J. Carpender**

> TODAY: Lord, inspire me to serve You in my neighbor and deliver me from the spirit of jealousy. "Seek to serve rather than be served."

July 26
SS. Joachim and Ann (1st century)
Parents of the Blessed Virgin Mary

St. Joachim and his wife, St. Ann, as parents of the Blessed
Virgin Mary, were chosen out of all the world to be the father
and mother of the ever-sinless Mother of our Lord Jesus Christ.
According to apocrypha, angels appeared to both Joachim and
Ann to tell them of the great honor that was to be theirs.

It was St. Ann who chiefly educated our Lady, with the
help of God. Thus St. Ann serves as a model to all Christian
mothers in the holy upbringing of their children. St. Joachim
too provided for his family as the best of fathers. Probably
belonging to the House of David, he would have passed along to
Mary, and through Mary to Jesus, his membership in that family, thus fulfilling many prophecies about the Messiah.

Numerous churches have been dedicated to St. Ann. Her
chief shrines are at Ste. Anne d'Auray in Brittany, and Ste.
Anne de Beaupré in Quebec, where many miracles have occurred. St. Ann is patron of all women in labor.

— **Paul Kocher**

*TODAY: When famiy life is being attacked by so
many forces, it is necessary for parents to provide the
model and set the example for their children. "The example of parents flowers in the child."*

July 27
St. Pantaleon (c. 305)
Martyr, Patron of Physicians

St. Pantaleon is venerated as the patron of physicians and mid-
wives. He is presumed to have been a martyr, but most of his
life is legendary. One point, however, which is consistently referred to is that he himself was a practicing physician but refused payment for his services.

We might draw a strange lesson from the little we know of
this saint. That lesson might well be the deep gratitude we owe
the medical profession. It is commonly known that physicians
as a class are most self-sacrificing and devoted to helping mankind. It is impossible for a physician to treat all his patients

144

without remuneration, but there is many a doctor who has a thick file of uncollectible fees. We should be very conscientious about meeting our doctor bills and very thoughtful of the men and women who come to our rescue in so many distressing crises. — John C. Selner, S.S.

TODAY: Grant, we beseech You, almighty God, that, through the intercession of Your martyr, blessed Pantaleon, we may be free in body from all adversaries, and pure in mind from depraved thoughts, through Christ, our Lord. Amen. —Roman Missal.

July 28
SS. Nazarius and Celsus (1st century)
Early Christian Martyrs

Nazarius was supposed to have been baptized by Pope St. Linus, the immediate successor of St. Peter. And Nazarius in turn baptized a boy named Celsus whom he had instructed in Christian doctrine. Later they both went to Milan, where they spread the Faith of Christ and for that reason they were both beheaded by the prefect Anolinus. Their bodies were discovered by St. Ambrose, Bishop of Milan.

While it is true that we often know only a few facts about the early Christians individually, the accumulation of inspiring details over the first two or three centuries cannot but increase our Faith and make us realize how fortunate we are to know Christ and to have had so many brave forebears in the religion which He left us. — John C. Selner, S.S.

TODAY: It doesn't matter how long we live, but how we live!

July 29
St. Martha (1st century)
Sister of Mary and Lazarus of Bethany; Patron of Cooks

St. Martha is a most intriguing saint, because she dared so much. After the death of her brother Lazarus, she boldly told the Lord that she wanted a miracle. Our Lord complied. Although Lazarus was over three days in the grave, Jesus commanded him to come forth and then presented him back to his sisters. This happened only a few days before the passion and death of Christ, almost a type of His own Resurrection.

Friendship goes to great lengths, and this incident certainly indicates the depth of the friendship that Christ had for the house of Lazarus. Each baptized person is invited into the intimate friendship with Christ. And love dares be bold!

— Msgr. Charles Dollen

TODAY: Lord, let me respect You in everyone who enters my home. By my serving You in my brothers and sisters, may You receive me in Your heavenly home.

July 30
St. Peter Chrysologus (c. 400-450)
Archbishop, Doctor of the Church

Peter, named "Chrysologus" (Golden Word) because of his eloquence, was Archbishop of Ravenna for 18 years. He made it a point to avoid all rhetorical phrases and keep his sermons short so as not to tire the congregation. He urged his people to receive Holy Communion frequently.

In one of his New Year's sermons he coined the famous phrase: "The man who wants to play with the devil will not be able to rejoice with Christ." He ended another sermon with these words: "Clothe yourself with the garment of sanctity: gird yourself with the cincture of chastity: let Christ be the covering of your head; let the cross of Christ be the protection for your face; instill in your breast the sacrament of divine wisdom: let the odor of your prayers always ascend on high."

— Msgr. John J. Duggan

TODAY: Lord, grant that I might imitate the "goldenworded" in my speech and conversation with others.

July 30
St. Julitta (c. 305)
Widow, Martyr

This saint is not commemorated in the breviary or the Mass, but St. Basil the Great, Bishop of Cappadocia, where she lived, gave an account of her martyrdom in one of his sermons.

A strange story: Some powerful crook was trying to despoil her of her property — she was a well-to-do widow — and she resolved to sue him in court. The case was going against him when all of a sudden he changed the course of action by declaring that she had no rights since she was a Christian and refused to adore the gods. The judge ordered an altar brought in and told her to offer incense upon it. "May my body perish rather than deny God, my Creator," she said. She was forthwith condemned to die at the stake, and she responded to the consolation of her friends by exhorting them to suffer for Christ if ever the occasion presented itself. — John C. Selner, S.S.

TODAY: Lord, keep me before Your blood when I am tempted to betray You by sin.

July 31
St. Ignatius of Loyola (1491-1556)
Founder of the Society of Jesus; Patron of Soldiers

This soldier was the son of a Spanish nobleman. During battle the soldier's leg was badly shattered. A long, trying period of hospitalization was necessary before the young man could ever walk again. Time passed slowly, almost as slowly as nature healed the wound. The soldier asked for a novel and was given instead a life of our Lord and several works on the lives of the saints.

What happened to this young soldier as he read about Christ and His saintly followers? A great change took place. He admired Christ and His heroic followers. He was challenged to match their heroism. But most of all he began to hate his past life with all his sins, especially those of the flesh.

This was the turning point in his life. When he recovered he had already adopted a new way of life. He gave up his rich and noble family, his position in the army to become a saint. If that young soldier had read a novel instead of the life of Christ, the world would not know the founder of the Jesuits, Ignatius of Loyola. — Msgr. Harry J. Welp

TODAY: Ignatius teaches us as he did his fellow Jesuits, "Be loyal to Christ and His Church."

AUGUST

August 1
St. Alphonsus Liguori (1696-1787)
*Bishop, Founder of the Redemptorists, Doctor of the
Church, Patron of Confessors and Moralists*

The figure of St. Alphonsus Liguori, calls forth a consideration which bears repeating in this postconciliar age: there must be something for everyone in the Church of God.

St. Alphonsus was, and remains in his writings, one of the great minds of the Church — a brilliant lawyer and a great theologian. Yet it was the advice of St. Alphonsus to his first Redemptorists that they put aside high-flown oratory and theory in their preaching and devote themselves to practical and devotional sermons. It is too obvious to repeat that the Church is made up of faithful of varying ages, degrees of knowledge, temperament and circumstances. But this truth tends to be lost in the mountain of postconciliar writings, produced by authors who are learned and highly specialized in their fields. There is, therefore, the danger that the simple folk, who can experience true spiritual growth by their simple piety, may be forgotten.

— Msgr. James I. Tucek

TODAY: O God, let all the nations praise You. May we add our praise through the saints.

August 2
St. Eusebius of Vercelli (283-370)
Italian Bishop

God's words are like precious gems, but we must not put them in a tiny velour bag to be stored in a vault. We must vest in the diamonds, rubies and emeralds of His teachings, which will reflect God's love and His truth for the world to see. Instead of molding our lives into our own image or the image of others, let us place our spirit and life, like the potter's clay, into God's hands. Our heavenly Father created us. Who, then, is better qualified to shape us or to restore the sculpture of our life into

His image? If the reign of God is like a dragnet for the angels to screen, then we must become a valuable gem glittering with honesty and holiness, not marred by sinfulness, untruthfulness and evil.

Many of the saints, especially, those born within the childhood of Christianity like St. Eusebius, were not only educated in the Christian Faith but were greatly influenced by devout mothers. These mothers mirrored the holiness and piety of Mary, Mother of God.   — Dorothy Travers Zisa

TODAY: Lord, may I, on this summer day, take the opportunity to renew my fidelity to You.

August 3
St. Waltheof (d. 1160)
English, Abbot of Melrose, Also Known as Walther

Waltheof is another one of the noble or royal saints. His father was the Earl of Huntingdon and his mother was of the dukedom of Northumberland. A fascinating story reveals the religious character of this saint. As a child, his brother Simon liked to play soldiers and to build toy castles. On the other hand, Waltheof disliked war and soldier games, and was content to build churches and monasteries of stone and wood. Their mother, Maud, after the death of her husband, remarried King David of Scotland, who is also a saint of the Church, but was never formally canonized. St. Aelred, a member of the Scottish court and master of the royal household, became a close friend and companion of Waltheof.

His daily philosophy is expressed in his own words: "What will this avail me to eternal life?" He entered the Augustinian abbey in Yorkshire and was later elected Prior of Kirkham Abbey. While saying Mass on Christmas day, Waltheof was visited by a miraculous vision — the Christ Child appeared in his hands, rather than the consecrated Host. This spiritual manifestation led to his choosing a stricter religious life at a Cistercian abbey. He was later elected Abbot of Melrose, a monastery founded by his stepfather King David. St. Waltheof died after a long and painful illness.

TODAY: Remember, "What will this avail me to eternal life?"

August 4
St. John Vianney (1786-1859)
Curé of Ars, France; Patron of Parish Priests

St. John Vianney's arrival in Ars in 1815 aroused little enthusiasm in the tiny French parish. The news that he had barely passed through the seminary had gone before him. "Oh, how dull his sermons will be," people said. "And how will this fellow be able to administer the finances of such a poor flock?" Who could have guessed that this humble curé would become the patron of parish priests?

Your pastor is the spiritual guide chosen for you at this time by the wisdom of God. Does he receive all that he has a right to expect from you? Your cooperation in parish activities? Financial support? Respect? Frequent remembrance in your prayers? Even though it may appear that he is a man who has neither tact nor talent, your pastor can still lay claim to your respect for the sole reason that he has persevered in a vocation which is almost as demanding as it is dignified.

— Rev. Francis R. Moeslein

TODAY: More than half of the Curé's day was spent in the confessional healing people of their sins. Do we frequent this powerful Sacrament of Reconciliation? Meditate on the powerful and meaningful words of absolution as we too become healed.

August 5
Dedication of St. Mary Major Basilica (c. 432-440)
First Western Church Dedicated to Blessed Virgin Mary

Before the liturgical calendar was revised, today was the feast of Our Lady of the Snows. Curiosity prompted me to look into the reason. There is an ancient tradition that in the fourth century, our Lady appeared to a Roman patrician named John and declared that she wanted a church built in her honor on a spot she indicated by a miraculous fall of snow in summer. He immediately founded and endowed the church in 352. It was called the Liberian Basilica after the reigning Pope Liberius.

After the Council of Ephesus in 431, when Mary was declared to be Mother of God, Pope Sixtus III enlarged and consecrated the church under the title of the Virgin Mary. It has come to be known as St. Mary Major because it is the first church dedicated to her in the West. On every feast of a dedication of a church, let us praise and thank God for the great dignity bestowed on us by the indwelling of His Spirit in us, and renew our resolve to live lives in keeping with such dignity.

— Sister Lorraine Dennehy, C.S.J.

TODAY: "How lovely is thy dwelling place, O Lord of hosts!" (Psalm 84:1).

August 6
Transfiguration of the Lord (1st century)
Revelation of Christ's Divinity to Peter, James and John on Mount Tabor

The Gospel of St. Matthew (17:1-9) tells us that "... Jesus took with him Peter and James and John his brother, and led them up a high mountain apart. And he was transfigured before them, and his face shone like the sun, and his garments became white as light. And behold, there appeared to them Moses and Elijah, talking with him. And Peter said to Jesus, 'Lord, it is well that we are here; if you wish, I will make three booths here, one for you and one for Moses and one for Elijah. He was still speaking, when lo, a bright cloud overshadowed them, and a voice from the cloud said, 'This is my beloved Son, with whom I am well pleased; listen to him.' When the disciples heard this, they fell on their faces, and were filled with awe. But Jesus came and touched them, saying, 'Rise and have no fear.' And when they lifted up their eyes, they saw no one but Jesus only. ... As they were coming down the mountain, Jesus commanded them, 'Tell no one the vision, until the Son of man is raised from the dead.' "

TODAY: "The Son of man is to come with his angels in the glory of his Father, and then he will repay every man for what he has done" (Matthew 16:27).

August 7
St. Cajetan (1480-1547)
Italian Lawyer, Founder of Theatines

In the same years that Martin Luther at Wittenberg in Saxony was taking action against the scandals within the Church by setting the stage for the Reformation, Cajetan of Tiene was working from one end of Italy to the other to draw the dissolute clergy back to Christ by his good example. It may be true, as modern historians tell us, that Luther was prompted by the highest motivation and had no intention of shattering the unity of Christendom. Yet, who can measure the harm done to souls by his revolt against the authority of the Church?

Cajetan, on the other hand, sought reform through practical charity and holiness of life, beginning with himself and extending it by example to others. In the year 1517, when Luther was posting his 95 theses on the castle door at Wittenberg, Cajetan was founding a hospital at Vicenza for incurables; in the year 1521, when Luther was excommunicated, Cajetan was laying the groundwork to found the Theatine monks to care for the sick. — **Most Rev. Thomas K. Gorman**

TODAY: The life of St. Cajetan teaches that Christ is found in His sick and in our service to them.

August 8
St. Dominic (1170-1221)
Spanish Priest, Founder of Dominican Order

St. Dominic is honored among many other things not only for the religious organization he founded, the Order of Preachers, but for his notable part in the preservation and spread of the Faith at a time it was greatly jeopardized. A particularly repulsive rival religious group, the Albigensians, had overrun great areas of Europe, threatening both Church and state. Against them Dominic set his first forces which soon grew into a strong right arm of the Church in the 13th century.

Significant to us is Dominic's insistence on the priority of self-sanctification and the spread of the Gospel after the fashion of the Apostles. "We must sow the seed, not hoard it," he said as he dispersed his disciples to every part of Europe. His command we must heed as well in the 20th century. Only sanctity and zeal can abort the dangers which assail the modern Church. — **G. Joseph Gustafson, S.S.**

TODAY: When St. Dominic was not praying, he was preaching; when he was not traveling, he was fasting. Here is a model for everyone.

152

August 9
St. Romanus (d. 258)
Roman Martyr

According to early biographical sources, Romanus was a doorkeeper of the Roman Church who also suffered martyrdom with Severinus, a priest, Claudius, a subdeacon, and Crescentius, a reader. In *The Roman Martyrology* we learn that Romanus, along with others, was imprisoned with St. Lawrence the deacon. Romanus, "seeing the joy and constancy with which the holy martyrs suffered persecution, . . . was moved to embrace the Faith, and was instructed and baptized by Deacon Lawrence" while in prison.

When Romanus told of his conversion and baptism, he was condemned to die by beheading — the day before his "guide and master," St. Lawrence.

TODAY: Ponder well these thoughts of St. Thomas More: "It's a new day, Lord. Nothing is going to happen this day that You and I can't handle together."

August 10
St. Lawrence (d. 258)
Roman Deacon, Martyr, Patron of the Poor

The constant image of St. Lawrence in the Church is of his martyrdom by being burned slowly to death on a gridiron. And the pious joke, attributed to St. Ambrose, has St. Lawrence instructing his tormentors to turn him over since he is well done on one side. As the modern Romans say, "Se non e vero, e ben' trovato." That is, "If it isn't true, it is well put."

Very few of us will be called upon to witness our Faith by martyrdom. But all of us are required to apply our living Faith to the daily martyrdom of little trials: hard to get right up when the alarm goes off, difficult to be civil in the first hours of the morning, endless little annoyances and interruptions, difficult people to associate with in our day, discourtesies to bear. It would help to remember the good humor attributed to St. Lawrence as he was dying a painful death. A necessary part of love of neighbor is in being pleasant ourselves.

— Most Rev. Thomas K. Gorman

TODAY: It takes resolute courage to offer ourselves to God as a living sacrifice rather than conform ourselves to the spirit of this age.

August 11
St. Clare (1194-1253)
Founder of the Poor Clares, Patron of Television

St. Francis of Assisi had many followers during his lifetime. One of these was St. Clare, whose feast we celebrate today. She was a young woman from the same town of Assisi. The sincerity of Clare to follow Christ by imitating the way of Francis was undaunted. St. Clare was as intense as was St. Francis in following the suggestion of Jesus to the rich young man in the Gospel to sell all possessions and follow Jesus. St. Clare desired to be a follower of Christ, and in her doing so, her lifestyle was drastically changed.

St. Francis made provisions for St. Clare so that her top priority to live a Gospel life would become a reality. Before she founded the contemplative community of the Poor Clares under the Franciscan rule, she received formative training in another religious community. Do we make the following of Jesus a top priority in our life?

— Sister Mary Maureen, S.S.J.

TODAY: The prayer with which St. Clare died is a good prayer with which to live daily: "May the Lord God be blessed for having created me."

August 12
St. Euplius (d. 304)
Sicilian Deacon, Martyr

During the persecution by Diocletian, a deacon of the Church stood in the governor's hall with a book of Gospels in his hands. Euplius said to Governor Calvesian, "I am a Christian, and shall rejoice to die for the name of Jesus Christ." After days of torment and torture, the deacon was asked to pay homage to the Roman gods. He refused and said, "I adore the Father, the Son, and the Holy Spirit." Euplius pledged his fidelity to the Church with these words, "I worship the Holy Trinity, and there is no other god but my God." Prison guards then hung the book of Gospels around the deacon's neck and led him to the executioner's block, where he was beheaded.

TODAY: Trust in the Lord and have confidence in Him. When He is your friend what can you possibly have to worry about?

August 13
St. Pontian (d. c. 235)
Pope, Spiritual Writer, Martyr
St. Hippolytus (d. c. 235)
Roman Priest, Martyr

We can identify with the saints of the 19th and 20th centuries; however, what of the saints of the second and third centuries? Many of them were martyrs for Christ's Church. Should they be strangers to us?

Exiled by Emperor Maximus to the mines of Sardinia, Pope Pontian was persecuted. He accepted his sufferings and martyrdom with Christ-like dignity and patience. St. Pontian shared his exile with Hippolytus, a priest-theologian who had written a commentary on Scripture and Apostolic Tradition, which contains the earliest known ritual. He preached in Rome; a defender of the Faith, he joined Christ's vicar on earth in death.

— Dorothy Travers Zisa

TODAY: Time is priceless. Each moment is an opportunity to develop Christ-like patience, gentleness and humility, through spiritual reading, meditation and prayer.

August 14
St. Maximilian Kolbe (1894-1941)
Polish Conventual Franciscan, Called "Patron of Our Difficult Century" by Pope Paul VI

Arrested in February 1941 for his anti-Nazi activities, this modern-day martyr was shipped to the Nazi concentration camp at Auschwitz. There, he volunteered to take the place of another prisoner by the name of Franciszek Gajowniczek, who had been condemned to death. Gajowniczek was a married man with a wife and children, and Father Kolbe thought, *Surely this man should be spared . . . I will go in his place.* The priest was starved, injected with carbolic acid (phenol) and then cremated in one of Auschwitz's "ovens of death."

Because of Kolbe's actions, Gajowniczek is alive today. The priest interceded on the prisoner's behalf and in a compassionate manner placed himself between death and Gajowniczek. Our prayers and our actions of intercession place us, like Father Kolbe, in the position of those in need, at the heart of their suffering. Christ, who is in us, stands between them and the pain.

— Julia Dugger

> TODAY: *Lord, let me pray for others and back up these prayers with action. "Greater love has no man than this, that a man lay down his life for his friends" (John 15:13).*

August 15
Assumption of the Blessed Virgin Mary (1st century)
Dogma Proclaimed by Pope Pius XII November 1, 1950

Today is the feast of the Assumption, one of those days in the liturgical year when we honor the Mother of our Lord. The love of Mary is an essential part of our Catholic spirituality, it gives our spiritual life a richness. Catholics are sometimes asked by those who are not Catholics why Catholics honor Mary so much.

God has already honored her beyond any honor we could pay her when He chose her out of all generations to be the Mother of His only-begotten Son. If God honored her so greatly, how could we fail to honor her? She was the Mother of our Lord; she gave Him birth, nurtured Him at her breast, reared Him to manhood and stood beside the cross that day He died. How could we fail to love her? And when we come to her, to ask her intercession, she now, as at Cana, turns us closer to Him.

— Dale Francis

> TODAY: *"At your right hand stands the queen in gold . . ." (Psalm 45:9).*

August 16
St. Stephen of Hungary (975-1038)
King, Apostle of Hungary, Patron of Bricklayers and Stonemasons

Born of convert parents in Hungary in the 10th century, Stephen received a Christian education from the virtuous Italian Count Theodatus and from St. Adalbert, Bishop of Prague. After the death of his father, Stephen succeeded him as Duke of Hungary.

Never aggressive but always persuasive, he established peace with neighboring nations and abolished idolatry from Hungary. At first, his subjects rebelled, for he had uprooted the religion of their ancestors. With only a few men, he diligently prepared for battle showing a determination through fasting, almsgiving and prayer. Generating faith with renowned vigor, he founded monasteries, churches and dioceses, which he dedicated to the Blessed Virgin Mary. In gratitude, his people requested he be given the title of King. Bringing the crown from Rome, Pope Sylvester II anointed and crowned Stephen King of Hungary in the year 1000.

— **Dorothy Travers Zisa**

TODAY: Grant that I may live constantly in God's grace through humility and mortification. Like St. Stephen the King, I too must face the daily battles as one of the troops.

August 17
St. Hyacinth (1185-1257)
Polish Dominican, Patron of Poland

This was a young Polish nobleman. He had studied at Cracow, Prague and Bologna and earned doctorates in law and divinity. He was a priest of the cathedral chapter of Cracow where his uncle was bishop. Accompanying his uncle to Rome, he met St. Dominic, who was then just forming his Order of Friars Preachers. He received the Dominican habit from St. Dominic himself and returned to Poland as a missionary.

What could by all rights have been the life of a young, wealthy and learned man, enjoying the respect of his contemporaries and the comforts of his position, now became one to be spent in poverty as a mendicant, in the ceaseless works of preaching, traveling and founding monasteries. The love of Christ will alter the life of any Christian who is honest about his religion, sending his life in quite another direction than it could by all rights have taken. This is so because the love of Christ, if it is allowed to grow as it will, will drive us to seek nothing purely for ourselves.

— Most Rev. Thomas K. Gorman

TODAY: Dwell on the words of St. John Chrysostom: "He (Hyacinth) has left behind him the feasts of the earth and gone to take part in the celebrations of the angels."

August 18
St. Helena (250-330)
Empress, Mother of Constantine the Great

Do senior citizens have a patron saint? They might adopt St. Helena, who at age 80 journeyed from Rome to Jerusalem in search of the Holy Cross.

We interviewed 24 residents of Golden Valley, the senior housing complex in our Colorado community. Their stories unfolded into word sketches which reflected the strength they inherited from pioneer background: the patient devotion of one husband who sits beside his senile mate in a nursing home each day; the neighborliness these elderly demonstrate in caring for those who are frail among them; the common joy they share living in modern apartments with tiny flower gardens to tend.

At 80 St. Helena found the True Cross. At that same age many of the widowed of Golden Valley are starting a new life. The late Bishop Lawrence Casey of Paterson, N.J., once said: "Growing old gracefully should begin with youth. Ultimately it is not how old we are that matters but how we are old."

— Marion Egan

TODAY: Grant that I may face daily crosses of pain and suffering so that I will grow gracefully in Christ.

August 19
St. John Eudes (1601-1680)
*Founded Sisters of Our Lady of Charity of Refuge
and the Society of Jesus and Mary (Eudist Order)*

Of the seven children born to Isaac Eudes and Marthe Corbin, two became famous. One was surnamed Seigneur de Mezeray and authored the monumental *History of France;* the other, John, became a saint. St. John Eudes, a scholar in his own right, is best remembered as founder of the Society of Jesus and Mary, more popularly known as the Eudists, and author of a little volume on Mary entitled *The True Devotion.* St. John and his brother were writing just on the eve of that age, sparked by Newton, Descartes, Bacon and Locke, which is termed "the Enlightenment." The historian, we may guess, was honored as a serious scholar, while the priest's writings on devotion to the Blessed Mother must have been taken less seriously. In our present thermonuclear age we again find the sacred sciences being either ignored or treated as inferior in the world of learning. Yet the Christian knows that he must not allow himself to become blind. — **Most Rev. Thomas K. Gorman**

TODAY: St. John Eudes, strengthen my devotion to the Sacred Heart of Jesus, whose cause you championed.

August 20
St. Bernard of Clairvaux (c. 1090-1153)
*Abbot, Doctor of the Church, Patron
of Candlemakers and Skiers*

By words and actions, St. Bernard, the famed Abbot of Clairvaux, whose feast we celebrate today, encouraged his monks to practice outstanding virtue. His message of peace and unity and his writings about the Lord Jesus, spirituality, the Scriptures, and the Blessed Mother, although written in the 12th century, are applicable today.

One of his many sermons on the love of God exemplifies this as he tells us: "For when God loves — all He desires is to be loved in return; the sole purpose of His love is to be loved in the knowledge that those who love Him are made happy by their

159

love of Him." How he truly took the words of Matthew's Gospel to heart! "The greatest among you will be the one who serves the rest." By his example let us reflect on how we serve others. Do we use the gifts God has given to each of us to help others come closer to Him or do we keep them hidden, not willing to share our abilities with those we daily come in contact with? — Sister Carol Ann Kenz, C.S.J.

> TODAY: Each one of us will be left free at any given moment to assent or dissent, to say yes or no, to deal with God's graces.

August 21
St. Pius X (1835-1914)
2nd of the 20th-century Popes, "Pope of the Eucharist," Canonized by Pope Pius XII on May 29, 1954

Joseph Sarto was born into a poor family in the little Italian town of Riese in 1835. He was endowed with high intelligence, but he was enabled only by scholarship to pursue priestly studies. It was his simplicity of lifestyle that endeared him to all throughout a long and distinguished career from simple parish priest to Bishop of Mantua, Cardinal-Patriarch of Venice and eventually Pope in 1903.

"To restore all things in Christ," became his motto as Pius X. During his short pontificate he did all in his power to bring this about, first by exhorting bishops to reorganize seminaries and provide the best possible training for the clergy. His second step was to combat ignorance among the people by religious instruction of young and old; he himself shared this task by giving Sunday instruction to the people in one of the Vatican courtyards.

St. Pius X never lost the simple habits he acquired as a poor boy, and he exercised throughout his life a sensitive charity to all in need. Let us imitate his loving kindness in our lives and praise the Lord for so great an intercessor.

— Sister Lorraine Dennehy, C.S.J.

> TODAY: Like this saintly Pontiff, "I was born poor, I have lived poor, and I wish to die poor" — but rich in God's graces.

August 22
Queenship of Mary (1st century)
Queen of Heaven, Angels and Men

The Queenship of Mary was instituted by Pope Pius XII on October 11, 1954, during his Marian Year. The object of the feast is to honor Mary as sovereign of heaven and earth. She deserves this honor because she is inseparably united with Christ the King. Together they have a claim on our homage.

The Queenship of Mary arises not only from the birthright of her royal Son but also by right of conquest. With Christ, Mary is deeply involved in the struggle to free mankind from the captivity of Satan. With this freedom come justice and holiness. Mary shares in the victory. Why should she not wear a crown? She is queen of angels and archangels, queen of martyrs and confessors, queen of virgins and all saints. She is indeed queen of the universe.

— Albert J. Nimeth, O.F.M.

TODAY: Love of Mary is a precious grace. It grows through the years; it is a light to our life, a comfort in sorrow, strength in temptation; it makes our joys double, and gives us peace while serving God.

August 23
St. Rose of Lima (1586-1617)
Dominican Tertiary, Patron of South America

"Come, spouse of Christ, receive the crown prepared for thee from all eternity." St. Rose is important because she is the first saint of the New World to be canonized and is thus a witness to the fact that, amid the injustice and inhumanity inseparably bound up with the Spanish conquest of America, the leaven of Christianity was still at work. Let us ask her today to help us to grow in love and understanding of our Latin American fellow members of Christ.

St. Rose, when still very young, dedicated her whole heart, her whole body and soul to Jesus Christ alone. This is the true meaning of Christian virginity. The modern world does not understand the love of Christ and so does not understand virgin-

161

ity. Far from being negative, religious life is a total consecration of a human being to God himself, as He comes to us in Jesus Christ.

— **Sister M. Charles Borromeo, C.S.C.**

TODAY: Pray to this heavenly Rose to restore peace and goodwill to the revolutionary areas of the Americas.

August 23
St. Philip Benizi (1233-1285)
Servite Friar, Medical Practitioner

St. Philip Benizi was known for his great charity. We may wonder why the saints stressed this good work, and the answer is that Our Lord said He would judge the human race by what they did or failed to do for the "least" of His brethren. The least of His brethren were made in the image and likeness of God, and therefore Jesus said if we don't practice charity for them, then we do not do it for Him. We must always bear in mind that the lowliest human being was made to the image and likeness of God, who cannot like someone who despises His image in his fellow man.

— **Msgr. Joseph B. Lux**

TODAY: O God, grant me the grace to follow the example of blessed Philip and spurn earthly riches in order to strive after the treasures of heaven.

August 24
St. Bartholomew (1st century)
Apostle, Martyr, Patron of Armenia

Today we have another saint noted for his simplicity, one commended by our Lord himself as we hear in the Gospel: "Behold, an Israelite indeed, in whom is no guile" (John 1:47). If the name puzzles you because Jesus is talking to Nathanael, the name Bartholomew signifies son of Tolmai in the same sense that Peter is referred to as Simon bar Jonah. Scripture scholars identify Nathanael with the Bartholomew named in the list of the Apostles.

162

There is little known for certain about Bartholomew, but tradition tells us that he preached the Gospel as far east as India and was probably martyred in Armenia. However, it seems his importance to us as Christians today is that he was singled out by Jesus himself for his single-mindedness and lack of duplicity. Because of Nathanael's simplicity, he was one of those first to proclaim belief in Christ as the Son of God. If we too are characterized by a single-mindedness in our search for truth and a simple-hearted guilelessness in our approach to God, we will be identifiable in these words of Psalm 145:11: "They shall speak of the glory of thy kingdom . . . ."

— Sister Lorraine Dennehy, C.S.J.

TODAY: With the Apostle Bartholomew, let us say: "Rabbi, you are the Son of God! You are the King of Israel!" (John 1:49).

August 25
St. Louis IX (1215-1270)
*King of France, Crusader, Patron
of the Secular Franciscan Order*

St. Louis, the King of France, believed in the essential goodness of man and spent the years of his reign trying to establish an atmosphere in which the goodness of his people could flourish. In all this great king did, never did personal ambition share, for his only motives were the glory of God and the good of his subjects. When he was urged to execute the son of Hugh de la Marche for following his father in rebellion against the crown, Louis refused: "A son cannot refuse to obey his father." For many generations afterward, whenever the people were dissatisfied with their rulers, they demanded that abuses be reformed and justice impartially administered as it was in the reign of St. Louis.

For this, Louis has remained to the present times "beloved of God and men, whose memory is blessed."

— Sebastian V. Ramge, O.C.D.

TODAY: That this saintly peacemaker for Christ may lead me to a life of peaceful coexistence with a warring society.

August 25
St. Patricia (c. 665)
Virgin; Patron of Naples, Italy

Contrary to popular opinion, today's saint is not a *mavourneen* of Irish origin, nor was she any kin to St. Patrick.

According to legend, Patricia was the daughter of a wealthy landowner in Constantinople. While in her 20s, she fled from her family to Italy to escape marriage to a mean-tempered older neighbor, a friend of her father's. Accompanied by her maid Emilia, St. Patricia went to Naples, where she founded homes and shelters for orphaned and abandoned children. A virtuous person, Patricia consecrated herself to God. Some years later she returned to her homeland in order to distribute her estate to the poor. She returned to Italy and her charges — the foundlings and suffering children of the streets. She is buried in the courtyard of St. Marcian's Church in Naples. Like that of another Neapolitan saint (St. Januarius), Patricia's blood periodically undergoes a miraculous liquefaction.

TODAY: St. Patricia could be the harbinger of our modern social services in caring for the wayward, the poor and those "leftover children."

August 26
St. Teresa of Jesus Jornet Ibars (1843-1897)
Spanish Religious; Founded Mothers of the Helpless

Although today's saint lived in the 1800s, she is one of the Church's new saints, having been canonized by Pope Paul VI in 1974.

Teresa was a poor girl in search of a religious life and entered the convent of the Poor Clares. Because of frailty and ill health, she could not stand the rigors of convent life and was forced to leave the order. With her spiritual advisor, Father Saturnino Lopez Novoa, she started a community of Religious to care for the aged in the province of Huesca. This was a new venture in terms of specific care for the physical and spiritual well-being of older citizens. Sister Teresa was the superior general of the new community and later began a convent and motherhouse for the new order in Valencia.

*TODAY: Religious faith cannot run the store, the of-
fice or the government, but it should integrate the lives
and actions of those who do.*

August 27
St. Monica (332-387)
Mother of St. Augustine; Patron of Mothers

St. Monica will be forever remembered as the mother who, by long years of persevering prayer, brought about the conversion of her wayward son. As he went on after her death to become the immortal St. Augustine, one of his chief inspirations was the memory of her holy life.

Son or daughter may go astray through no fault of father or mother. In such instances, parents can draw great consolation from the example of St. Monica. To children who have done serious wrong they may show grief but not anger. Above all, they must not stop praying, for such prayer is particularly pleasing to God. St. Monica teaches all of us that we must pray perseveringly. Often the greater the favor we ask, the more does God try us, and the less prone to respond does He let himself appear. But humble and persevering prayer, we may be sure, He will never refuse.

— **Most Rev. Joseph M. Marling, C.PP.S.**

*TODAY: All parents can learn from St. Monica and
pray unceasingly for their children. As Tennyson
wrote, "More things are wrought by prayer than this
world dreams of."*

August 28
St. Augustine (354-430)
*Bishop, Father and Doctor of the Church;
Patron of Printers*

St. Augustine, a Doctor of the Church, is one of her greatest figures: certainly one of the most interesting in view of his conversion, which he tells of so tenderly in his *Confessions*. In the same terms, he is one of the most human and winning to modern tastes; one of the greatest intellectuals too, in that all following ages are his debtors. Even St. Thomas Aquinas had

165

to turn to him to borrow almost intact the great Augustinian developments in theology.

St. Augustine saw with absolute clarity that only two things are really necessary — in his own words: to know God and to know oneself. Everything else in his crowded life as preacher, teacher, controversialist, bishop and pioneering thinker, was subordinated to this. Thus he could tell his people at Hippo, "I do not wish to be saved without you. Why am I in the world? Only to live in Jesus Christ; but to live in Him with you."

"I wish to know only God and my soul. Nothing more? Absolutely nothing more."(St. Augustine, Soliloquia)

— G. Joseph Gustafson, S.S.

TODAY: Reflect on Augustine's life. It was like praying: "Make me a saint, Lord, but not yet." We must be patient with our powerlessness, and depend on God's omnipotence to bring us to what we are called to be — yes, saints.

August 29
Beheading of St. John the Baptist (1st century)
Martyr, "The Baptizer"; Patron of Blacksmiths

The first Scripture reading in today's Mass, from the Book of Jeremiah (1:19), predicts John's difficult ministry in this manner: "They will fight against you; but they shall not prevail against you, for I am with you, says the Lord, to deliver you." Yes, the Lord offers His companionship and fidelity — the same help He gives to us.

In the Gospel of Mark (6:14-30), we read the dramatic account of John's martyrdom. John was arrested, chained and imprisoned and finally beheaded on account of Herodias, the wife of Herod's brother Philip. John fearlessly said: "It is not lawful for you to have your brother's wife" (6:18). That statement caused John his life. How willing he was to sacrifice all — even life itself — to proclaim the truth. Ask yourself if you are willing to sacrifice all to proclaim the true message of Christ.

— **Sister Carol Ann Kenz, C.S.J.**

TODAY: May St. John intercede for me as I ask him to keep me faithful in my adherence to Church teachings.

166

August 30
St. Margaret Ward (d. 1558)
English, Martyr, Canonized by Pope Paul VI in 1970

Writing for *My Daily Visitor*, Sister Lorraine Dennehy, C.S.J., affords readers this pleasing day-by-day reflection. She writes: "The month of August is replete with memorials of saints of every walk of life: rich and poor; men and women; married and single; cleric and lay. From them we can surely find incentives to grow in the Christian life to which we are called by our baptism."

Such is the memorial of St. Margaret Ward, a maidservant in 16th-century London. She was implicated with John Roche, a friend, in helping a prisoner (Father Richard Watson) escape from prison. When captured by the police, she refused to divulge the priest's hiding place. Queen Elizabeth I ordered the prisoners to be hanged at Tyburn prison.

TODAY: Let us implore St. Margaret's intercession to lead us to a happy death, united with our Maker.

August 31
St. Raymond Nonnatus (1204-1240)
Spanish Mercedarian, Cardinal; Patron of Mothers-to-Be

The greater part of St. Raymond's religious life was spent in begging funds to ransom slaves. It was only toward the end of his life, and then in obedience to the Pope, that he turned to preaching the Crusades. He was a priest of the Mercedarian Order and as such had taken a vow to give himself in ransom for captives, if necessary. In compliance with this vow, he gave himself up to eight months' hard labor to free a captive.

Love of one's neighbor out of love of God is the lesson to be learned from St. Raymond and the many like him who dedicated their lives to the freeing of slaves. Times have changed, but the descendants of the slaves are still with us in our black brothers. Furthermore, the times have not changed the obligation of all who follow Christ to love their neighbor as themselves.   — **Most Rev. Thomas K. Gorman**

TODAY: Pray to Our Lady of Ransom, asking her help in ransoming those souls lost in sin and vice.

SEPTEMBER

September 1
St. Giles (c. 712)
Hermit, Patron of Cripples and Beggars

Giles, or Aegidius, was one of Europe's most popular saints during the later years of the Middle Ages. Yet he proved to be one of the least known, as most accounts of his life were based on popular legends. Giles left the riches and security of family and home to go to France and become a hermit in a woods near the mouth of the Rhô River.

A popular biography notes that Giles is remembered "among the Fourteen Holy Helpers — the only one who is not a martyr." Prior to the Crusades of the 12th century, St. Giles's tomb — located in a town named for him — was a main pilgrimage center. He is especially popular in England and Scotland, as numerous churches invoke him as their namesake.

A 15th-century poet and monk by the name of John Lydgate dedicated this poem to the memory of St. Giles:

Gracious Giles, of poor folk chief patron,
  Medicine to sick in their distress,
To all needy shield and protection,
  Refuge to wretches, their damage to redress,
  Folk that were dead restoring to quickness. . . .

TODAY: St. Giles, I implore your help in making me humble, honorable and worthy of walking with your beggars and cripples.

September 2
St. Brocard (d. 1231)
Superior of Frankish Hermits on Mount Carmel

Brocard succeeded St. Berthold as superior of the hermitage on Palestine's Mount Carmel in 1195. This hermeneutical foundation marked the origin of the Order of Carmelite friars. St. Albert of Vercelli, the Latin patriarch and papal legate in Palestine, provided the hermitage with its first spiritual rules of order. "It bound them to live alone in separate cells, to recite the Divine Office and other prayers, to work with their hands, and to meet together daily for Mass." The hermits were also to "observe perfect poverty, perpetual abstinence and long silences." They pledged themselves to this monastic rule and also promised obedience to Prior Brocard during his life, and afterward to his successors. In the year 1226, Pope Honorius III was going to suppress the hermitage, but "warned by a vision from our Lady, he formally approved of the new spiritual rules of life."

TODAY: If you do not love the world, you cannot really sacrifice it for God. You are seeking a flight, not a dedication!

September 3
St. Gregory the Great (c. 540-604)
Pope, Father and Doctor of the Church,
"Storehouse of Theology"

Gregory the Great ranks with Ambrose, Jerome and Augustine among the great Doctors of the Western Church. His piety was instilled in him by his mother and two aunts. He became a deeply ascetic monk who made his Roman home on the Coelian Hill a noted monastery and founded six monasteries in Sicily. His own wealth and the wealth of the Church were to him the property of the poor and needy.

As Roman Pontiff he ruled the Church with extraordinary prudence, not only winning pagans to Christ but even converting pagan ways to Christian feasts and usages. The liturgy bears the stamp we call Gregorian. His writings, largely moral and ascetical, have deeply influenced the thought and life of the whole Church, so practical and rich is their meaning in its application. Though the most exalted ruler in the Church, he was always the *Servant of the servants of God.* He is a model for the rich, the politically powerful, and also for the simple and humble who delight in the reading of the Scriptures, as Gregory explained the words and works of Jesus. Many churches honor him as their patron.

— Edwin G. Kaiser, C.PP.S.

TODAY: The Holy Bible was the tool with which Pope

169

Gregory I prepared his "Homilies on the Gospel." Pray to St. Gregory to help us become more aware of Christ's teachings in our daily lives.

September 4
St. Boniface I (d. 422)
42nd Pope (418-422)

This remarkable priest, already an old man, succeeded St. Zosimus to the Chair of Peter some 15 weeks after being elected at a conclave. Dissidents had seized the Lateran office and elected Eulalius the Pope. The Emperor Honorius called for a council at Ravenna which ousted Eulalius and named Boniface the true Pope of the Church.

Pope Boniface I sought the return of Illyricum (area including the Balkan peninsula), a patriarchate of the Holy Roman Empire, to the Western Church from Eastern jurisdiction. He also supported St. Augustine's fight against Pelagianism, a heresy that denied the supernatural order of things. (Its theories, involving errors on the nature of original sin and the meaning of grace, were condemned by the Council of Ephesus in the year 431.) Pope St. Boniface I was buried near the grave of St. Felicitas on Rome's Salarian Way.

TODAY: With Rome, "let the great churches, namely Alexandria and Antioch, keep their dignity.... The blessed Apostle Peter received by our Lord's word and commission the care of the whole Church."

September 5
St. Lawrence Justinian (1381-1455)
First Bishop of Venice

Worried about "Keeping up with the Joneses"? Are you a status seeker? Do these drives dominate your life, causing you unhappiness and constant discontentment? If so, then, as always, the Church has just the saint for you. In this instance it is St. Lawrence Justinian, a 14th-century saint who was the first bishop of Venice.

He was a humble man. When he was appointed bishop of the proud Venetians right at a time when Venice was at the height of its glory, prosperity and achievement, he was an object of great suspicion and disappointment to the leaders of Venice. However, after Bishop Lawrence had been there some years, one of the Venetians' most powerful leaders referred to him as "angel, not a man. . . ." His humility and genuine love for God and man had won the day. Venice was at his feet!

— Msgr. James P. Conroy

TODAY: Let us seek a genuine contentment with our position in life.

September 6
St. Eleutherius (c. 590)
Italian Abbot, "The Holy Man — Old Father Eleutherius"

An old monk was asked where he had found his deep sense of contentment. "I think I discovered it by seeking poverty of spirit," he replied. ". . . when I gave way to anger, pride or laziness, I was distressed for days and told myself that it was because I hated sin so. Only after I learned to look squarely at my spiritual ugliness did I discover that I was sorry because I loved myself so inordinately; I found it unbearable that I, the great I, could cut such a bad figure. Contentment came when I learned to accept myself." This reflection by the late Father John J. Considine, M.M., squares with that of today's saint, Eleutherius. An Abbot of St. Mark's Monastery near Spoleto, "The old father" is mentioned in the *Dialogues* of St. Gregory. An entry in *The Roman Martyrology* also credits Eleutherius with raising a dead man to life. The patriarch died at St. Gregory's monastery at Rome, where he had lived for many years.

TODAY: The power to suffer for others through a love of God is the richest accomplishment of man, and the most sublime secret of true happiness for man.

September 7
St. Sozon (c. 304)
Martyr, Shepherd of Cilicia (Southern Turkey)

Day by day we learn more and more about a certain call to greatness among the saints of the Church. Greatness, however, can be defined in many ways, depending on one's personal outlook. For some it means riches, political power or success in business. For St. Sozon, greatness meant, playing his shepherd's pipe "to make music only to God." This youth was also known as Tarasius and took the name Sozon upon his baptism. Legend has the young herdsman attacking pagan temples and destroying "golden idols" with his shepherd's crook. Because he would not venerate the pagan gods and idols, he was arrested, suffered inhuman cruelties and was burned to death.

> TODAY: "For thou hast delivered my soul from death, my eyes from tears, my feet from stumbling. I walk before the Lord in the land of the living" (Psalm 116:8-9).

September 8
Birth of Mary (1st century)
Nativity of the Mother of God

St. Irenaeus, one of the earliest Church Fathers, hailed Mary as the "cause of our salvation" and spoke of her birth as the "dawn of our salvation." Today we celebrate that birth, the birth that brought joy to the whole world.

Like many feasts of Our Blessed Mother, the Nativity came to us from the East, where it had been celebrated since the sixth century. A Syrian Pope, Sergius I, introduced it at Rome in the late seventh century. The Liturgy of St. John Chrysostom greets Mary in these words: "Your nativity, O Mother of God, heralded joy to the universe, for from you rose the Sun of Justice, Christ our God. By delivering us from the curse, He imparted upon us His blessing; by vanquishing death, He gave us eternal life." Mary, to whom we give the title "Mother of the Church," is the archetype of the Church. She is the fulfillment of the New Jerusalem, yet she is one of us. She has gone before us, the first fruit of our redemption. Our task is to imitate her in her perfect cooperation with God's plan for us.

— **Sister Elizabeth Ann Clifford, O.L.V.M.**

> TODAY: Reflect on the virtue of obedience. Mary's awesome "Yes" gave life to the Savior, God the Father's greatest gift to mankind.

September 9
St. Peter Claver (1580-1654)
Spanish Jesuit, Patron of Missions, Also of Colombia

St. Peter Claver, a Spanish Jesuit, spent his life ministering to and healing the African slaves who were treated inhumanly in the South American port of New Cartagena. Today's saint graduated with honors from the University of Barcelona. Peter volunteered for mission work in New Granada when he heard of the plight of the slaves, and determined to make the care of the blacks his life's apostolate.

He brought them food and drink, baptizing the dying, and any newborn baby he could find. A band of seven interpreters helped him teach the slaves the basic truths of the Catholic Faith, preparatory to baptizing them. It is estimated that in 40 years he had converted over 300,000 slaves. In race relations, the love of St. Peter Claver was the loftiest of any saint in modern times.

— **Maurus Fitzgerald, O.F.M.**

TODAY: In our efforts at bringing about civil rights, we must remember that we, like St. Peter Claver, are working for human beings, not merely trying to right a system.

September 10
St. Nicholas Tolentino (1245-1305)
Augustinian Preacher; Patron of Mariners, Poor Souls

Here is one of those saints of the Church about whom it is almost impossible to believe. Living in and around Tolentino for almost 30 years, he was known for his preaching and for the effect he had on the lives of thousands to whom his words went forth. But he would not eat or take care of his health. It seems that the more his health failed the greater the success of his mission.

The Church would not advise us to imitate this kind of thing down to the last letter. Advanced medicine would frown upon it completely — and with some reason. Yet, it is the spirit of this great saint which captivates us. The ability to rely entirely upon the Lord for his strength and effectiveness with others is the important thing about Nicholas. A little — just a little bit of that in our well-calculated, material lives — would lift many of us from the doldrums of mediocrity to real accomplishments for God and man.

— Msgr. James P. Conroy

TODAY: Hear, O Lord, our supplications which we make on the solemnity of Thy Confessor, blessed Nicholas, so that we, who have no confidence in our own justice, may be helped by him who pleased Thee, through Christ, our Lord. Amen. — The Roman Missal

September 11
SS. Protus and Hyacinth (d. 257)
Roman Brothers, Slaves, Martyrs

The Church used to observe this day in honor of St. Protus and St. Hyacinth, but by reason of the new arrangement for the liturgical year this is a ferial day — an open day on the Church calendar. However, we are perfectly free to address ourselves to the intercession of these two saints today. Actually, they were not only saints but martyrs — two slaves who were burned at the stake in the year 257.

Of such is the Church made. Two humble men, ignorant and unlettered and known but to God. Yet the fact of their martyrdom gave new life to the Church, and along with those of other martyrs their death is responsible for the existence of the Church today. No brilliant orators or theologians were they. But in death they were eloquent. They gave witness to Christ and the Church with their blood and thus brought to us today the fruits of the Redemption. May their courage influence us to greater sacrifice for the same Christ for whom they died!

— Msgr. James P. Conroy

TODAY: Reflect on these words of Cardinal John Henry Newman: "God has created me to do Him some definite service; He has committed some work to me. . . . I have my mission. I am a link in a chain, a bond of connection between persons."

September 12
St. Guy (c. 1012)
Belgian Sacristan, "The Poor Man of Anderlecht"

It is said that today's saint belongs to that category of simple, hidden souls, like wanderers or workmen. Guy was born near Brussels, of a poor family, and had no formal education. However, he was schooled in the practices of his holy religion by his parents, who instilled in him the teachings and doctrines of Christ.

The Lives of the Saints relates: "He never ceased to beg of God the grace to love the state of poverty in which Divine Providence had placed him, and to bear all its hardships with joy and in a spirit of penance, without which all the tribulations of this world are of no advantage for Heaven." As sacristan at the Church of Our Lady of Laeken, Belgium, he rejoiced over being employed in one of the humblest offices of the Church.

TODAY: Remember that, like St. Guy, the lowliest of people have all been messengers of Christ.

September 13
St. John Chrysostom (c. 347-407)
Archbishop of Constantinople, Doctor of the Church, Patron of Preachers, Called "Golden-Mouthed"

St. John Chrysostom has been acclaimed the greatest Christian orator of all time. The riches of the Scriptures overflow in his sermons. Tremendous is his explanation of the priesthood. He has been called the Doctor of the Eucharist. With the courage of a John the Baptist, he denounced evil in high places, the abuse of wealth and the neglect of the poor. He seems to have felt that no one can attain to wealth without injustice. Profound was his ascetic and moral depth. He was sent into exile for the proclamation of his moral ideals and his demand of moral standards in the men and women of political power.

We must turn to St. John today as the ideal bishop, the advocate of the poor and needy, of social justice for all. Students for the priesthood should constantly study the sermons of Chrysostom as part of their formation. Christian mothers may read with great encouragement of Chrysostom's mother, Anthusa (his father died when she was but 20), who renounced a second marriage and educated her son in wisdom and piety. In his work on the priesthood John pays her the tribute that she was a great Christian mother.   — Edwin G. Kaiser, C.PP.S.

TODAY: Let me speak no profanities or utter any obscenities. Clean my speech in the manner of today's saint, that I might denounce evil and abuse.

September 14
Triumph of the Cross (326)
Feast Day Commemorating St. Helena's Finding of the Cross on Which Christ Was Crucified

"Christ became obedient for us to death, even to death on a cross. Therefore God also has exalted Him, and has bestowed upon Him the Name that is above every name. . . . Alleluia, alleluia. Sweet the wood, sweet the nails, sweet the load that hangs on the cross. . . ."

On this day in 335 the basilica built by Constantine the Great over both Calvary and the Holy Sepulchre was dedicated. In 615, the King of Persia carried off the relic of the true cross, but 14 years later, in 629, Emperor Heraclius defeated King Chosroes and insisted on the restitution of the true cross. While carrying it into Jerusalem on his own shoulder, he was stopped at the gate of the Holy City by an invisible force, and not until the garb was laid aside was he allowed to proceed. We pray: "By the sign of the holy cross, Lord, protect Your people from the snares of all enemies. . . ."

TODAY: Deliver us from our enemies, O God, by the sign of the cross.

September 15
Our Lady of Sorrows (1st century)
Memorial Recalling the Sorrows Experienced by Mary

Our Lady, Co-Redemptrix — "The Virgin of Sorrows," wrote Pope Pius XI in 1923, "participated with Christ in the work of Redemption."

Men are mistaken who see our Lady merely as the Child-bearer and the caretaker. Mary's life follows a pattern of fiery charity, of spiritual grandeur, with distinctly missionary objective, namely to cooperate in the Incarnation for the saving of mankind and in the Redemption to satisfy for mankind. Mary possesses spiritual loveliness: intelligence that is very pure and keen, a will that has never failed, a soul that is exquisitely sensitive, altogether the quality of admirableness — *Mater Admirabilis*.

Mary is inextricably bound up with Christ the Priest. His great role of Redeemer is a sacerdotal role; hers is to be the Mother, but Co-Redemptrix as well. Mary was not a mere weeper on Calvary — at every Mass there is the same union between her and Jesus for the world's redemption.

— John J. Considine, M.M.

TODAY: Immaculate Heart of Mary, wounded in love by the sins of men — pray for me.

September 16
St. Cornelius (d. 253)
Pope, Regarded as a Martyr
St. Cyprian (d. 258)
African Lawyer, Convert, Bishop, Martyr

The martyrs we honor today were men of lofty and noble stature. Cornelius was a staunch defender of the Church, a Roman pontiff who was sent into exile. Such were his sufferings that his death was declared that of a martyr for the sake of Christ.

Even more distinguished is the patrician Cyprian, born of a noble and rich family. Converted to the Faith, he was consecrated shortly after as Bishop of Carthage. He suffered much opposition even from the Christians. His writings are among the most practical spiritual treasures of that early age. Great was his esteem for virginity. His work on the Habit of the Virgins speaks of dedicated souls as flowers in the garden of the Church. His beautiful work on the unity of the Church holds fast to the unity of Christians with their bishop: one cannot have God for his Father who does not have the Church for his Mother. In the time of pestilence, his concern for the sick and needy was heroically evident. He himself died a martyr in the year 258.

— Edwin G. Kaiser, C.PP.S.

*TODAY: Reflect on Cyprian's letter: "If God does one
of us the favor to die shortly, may our friendship continue in the Lord's presence." Be as close as you can to
your brothers in the Faith.*

September 17
St. Robert Bellarmine (1542-1621)
*Italian Jesuit Archbishop, Doctor of the Church,
Patron of Catechists, Canonized in 1930*

St. Robert Bellarmine wrote a catechism especially directed to
children and simpleminded people. Today everyone seems to be
an authority. In this scientific age we are confronted with complex situations and confusing answers. In his day Robert
Bellarmine was faced with much scandal and corruption within
the Church. It was his simplicity of heart that carried him
through the era, and he emerged with the honor "Doctor of the
Church."

Are we over-complicating our Faith? Christ's message was
entrusted to simpleminded men, fishermen like Peter. Granted,
our Faith has developed across the span of time; however, the
basic concepts given by Christ to Peter and the Apostles has remained unchanged. Burdened with all of our knowledge —
which doubles every 15 years — is it still possible to approach
God with childlike trust and simplicity? The child is direct; the
adult more oblique.   — **Robert G. Lee**

*TODAY: Biting attacks upon others may be adjudged
by some to be a mark of zeal and concern for religious
truth, but usually they are hallmarks of pride.*

September 18
St. Joseph of Cupertino (1603-1663)
*Italian Conventual Franciscan; Patron
of Air Travelers and Pilots*

Today's patron is often called the "flying saint" because of his
manner of levitating to the heights of the chapel while in prayer.
His manner of flight was powered only by the holiness of his
life for God and for His Church.

Joseph Dessa was born in Cupertino, Italy. By coincidence,

he was the son of a carpenter, born in a shed behind a house that was being claimed by creditors. At this stage the coincidental comparison with the Holy Family ends. Joseph was an unhappy and unloved child. His mother looked upon him as a "nuisance and a burden" and treated him badly. He was in and out of the Conventual and Capuchin monasteries so often that biographical accounts are confusing. Because of ignorance, he was found to be "inept" for the Franciscan life. He later was a lay brother of the Capuchin Franciscans and after eight months was dismissed because of "clumsiness and low intelligence." He returned to the Conventual monastery at Grotella. We learn that he had no special pastoral expertise, but his asceticism, miracles, ecstasies, and other supernatural gifts like levitation marked him a phenomenal friar. St. Joseph was fervently devoted to Our Lady of Grotella, whose image was revered in the parish church at Cupertino. He died at Osimo, and the saint's body is enshrined in a glass coffin in the church of his name, cared for by the Conventual Franciscans.

> TODAY: Pray as did St. Joseph Cupertino: "Oh! That my soul were freed from the shackles of my body to be reunited to Jesus Christ."

September 19
St. Januarius (d. 304)
Italian Bishop, Martyr; Patron of Blood Banks,
Also of Campania, Region Around Naples, Italy

The city of Naples honors St. Januarius, bishop and martyr, as its great protector whose blood liquefies — 18 times in the year, as a rule. Though there are similar instances in the case of others saints (see Patricia, August 25), Januarius is by far the most noted. Though on the occasions of liquefaction the crowds are tumultuous, the deep faith is evident from the vast numbers who attend the holy Mass and receive the Eucharist.

The writer witnessed the great event many years ago, seeing the liquefied blood at close range and attending closely to the splendid sermon of the prelate who preached on the Blood of Christ. From this the liquefaction derives all its meaning. We honor the Blood of Christ, the living Blood in heavenly glory, mystically present and shed in the Eucharist, when we honor

179

the martyrs who laid down their lives for Christ. We may say that spiritually they mingle their blood with His.

May the great St. Januarius teach us the deep meaning of living for Christ and dying for Him so as to be united with Him in glory.

— Edwin G. Kaiser, C.PP.S.

TODAY: In this era of disregard and even ridicule of the supernatural, this miracle of liquefaction takes place regularly in spite of all attempts to explain it away.

September 20
St. Vincent Madelgarus (c. 615-677)
Belgian Monk, Husband of St. Waldetrudis

Vincent is the only saint listed for this day in the Roman calendar. He is known under the names of Madelgoire and Mauger. In Flanders, he is also known as Vincent of Soignies. He was of noble parentage — the family of the Count of Hainault. When he was 20 years old he married (St.) Waldetrudis. They had four children, "all venerated as saints, namely Landry, Madelberta, Aldetrudis and Dentelinus."

The saintly family entered a formal religious life, with Vincent becoming a Benedictine monk at Hautmont Abbey. Waldetrudis became a nun in a nearby convent built by the family. Later, Vincent was the Abbot of a monastery on his estate at Saignes, Belgium.

— Felician A. Foy, O.F.M.

TODAY: Lord, we pray that Thy grace may always precede and follow us; and make us continuously intent upon doing good works.

September 21
St. Matthew (1st century)
Apostle, Evangelist, Martyr; Patron of Accountants, Bankers, Bookkeepers, Tax Collectors

Matthew before he was a saint was a tax collector. He was totally involved in serving his own self-interest. When Jesus said to him, "Come follow me," He was calling Matthew to serve others. He responded wholeheartedly, and then he became *St. Matthew.*

We who follow Christ are called to serve others. Our Lord says, "Whoever would be great among you must be your servant" (Mark 10:43). When we serve others, it makes us feel inferior. This is true especially *among those with whom we live.* When we serve outsiders, for instance visiting the sick in the hospital, we don't mind because we realize "how good we are." But, if we have to clean up after someone in our own family, we feel that we are being abused. We might look for opportunities in our own family to be of service, and offer it up.

— **Valerian Schott, O.F.M.**

TODAY: Read the account of Matthew's call to apostleship in the ninth chapter of the Gospel of St. Matthew.

September 22
St. Thomas of Villanova (1488-1555)
Spanish Augustinian, Preacher, Archbishop of Valencia

Spiritual writers often refer to St. Thomas of Villanova as "the glory of the Church in Spain." During his lifetime he was referred to as "the Patron of Bishops," "the Almsgiver," and "the Father of the Poor." Thomas was one of Spain's finest scholars and educators. He was a professor of theology at the University of Alcala when he was only 26. Then he was nominated for the chair of philosophy at the University of Salamanca, a prestigious school, but declined in order to join the monks of the Augustinian Order. In 1553, as the provincial of Castile, he sent the first Augustinian missionaries to the new world of the Americas, where they established missions in Mexico.

Emperor Charles V sought Thomas as a counselor and soon named him Archbishop of Valencia — a seat that had been vacant for 90 years. Thomas was also one of Spain's finest preachers, and biographers write: "His sermons were followed by a wonderful change in the life of the people." One might say, "He was a new apostle or prophet raised by God to reform the people."

TODAY: St. Thomas's charitable disposition was the most valuable part of his parental inheritance.

September 23
St. Linus (d. c. 76)
Native of Tuscany, 2nd Pope, Martyr

St. Linus was the second Pope (67-76), the one who succeeded St. Peter. He was mentioned by St. Paul (2 Timothy 4:21). His name also appears in the Canon of the Mass, a sure sign that the Church wants to preserve his memory. It was Linus who wrote the Acts of Peter and was chief witness of the action which Peter took against Simon Magus (see Acts 8:18). So great was Linus's Faith and holiness that he too is remembered for not only casting out devils, but also raising the dead to life.

Of Linus the Church sings in a special Breviary hymn:
"But sin and pomp of sin foreswore, / Knew all their gall and passed them by / and reached the throne prepared on high."

Linus is here presented to us timid souls as a man of greatness and courage. A martyr at the hands of someone for whom he had performed a miraculous favor, he too was prepared for and accepted the supreme sacrifice. May he intercede for us in our weakness!

— **Msgr. James P. Conroy**

TODAY: Good example and humble service to God gain us God's favor in spite of our weakness. Just so we try!

September 24
Our Lady of Ransom (Universal Feast, 1696)
Vision of the Blessed Virgin Mary in Spain,
Which Led to Founding of the Mercedarians

In *The Roman Martyrology* for today we read: "The feast of Our Lady of Ransom." Her miraculous appearance is noted in the *Martyrology* in the entry of August 10: "In Spain, the Apparition of the Blessed Virgin Mary, under the name of Our Lady of Ransom, foundress of the Order for the Redemption of Captives."

Referring to this Marian feast, Pope Pius XI, said: ". . . We all have recourse to the blessed Mother of God. We may run to her protection, praying for help from heaven, if yet more difficult times come upon the Church, if Faith declines with the growing-cold of charity, if private and public conduct becomes corrupt, if danger threatens the Catholic name and civil society."

The Pontiff reminds us: "So, at last, in the supreme trial of death, when no hope or help can be looked for elsewhere, we may lift up to her our weeping eyes and trembling hands, asking through her for forgiveness from her Son and endless happiness in heaven."

> TODAY: Especially during modern terrorism against people or governments, we plead with Our Lady of Ransom, to intercede for the return of hostages and those missing in wars, and to pray for all victims of terrorism.

September 25
St. Vincent Strambi (1745-1824)
Italian Bishop of Macerata and Tolentino

This popular saint of the 19th century was canonized by Pope Pius XII in 1950. We could likely honor him as a New Year's Day saint, as he was born January 1, 1745, and died on January 1 some 79 years later. While on a spiritual retreat prior to his ordination, Vincent was intrigued with the spirituality of his retreat master, the famed St. Paul of the Cross, who encouraged Vincent to join the Passionist community rather than become a parish priest. He was a professor of theology and sacred eloquence, holding many other offices in the Order. Pope Pius VII appointed Father Vincent Bishop of Macerata and Tolentino. During this disturbing period in Italian history (1808), Bishop Strambi refused any allegiance to Napoleon of France and was expelled from his diocese. He was able to return five years later upon the defeat of Napoleon. In *The Lives of the Saints* we read, "After Napoleon's escape from Elba, (General) Murat with an army of 30,000 made Macerata his headquarters. His troops were defeated by the Austrians, and would have sacked that town . . . had not Bishop Strambi gone out, like another St. Leo, and pleaded with their commander." He later resigned his bishopric to be an advisor to Pope Leo XII, a devoted friend.

TODAY: May the peace of the Lord be with His servants, those bishops and priests who carry His Word to the suffering people in Poland, Northern Ireland, the Near East and Latin America.

September 26
SS. Cosmas and Damian (d. c. 303)
Twin Brothers, Physicians, Martyrs; Patrons of Physicians, Surgeons, Barbers, Druggists

Honored as physicians, these two saints are pictured in one of the grandest of the Roman mosaics. The two are presented to Christ, the Redeemer and Physician of souls, by the Apostles Peter and Paul at the waters of regeneration, the Jordan. For centuries they were venerated in the Canon of the Mass. Though much that is recounted of them is legendary, the story of their generosity in caring physically for the sick and the magnificent mosaic has had an influence on the many pilgrims who pondered the works of art with wonder throughout many centuries.

We should think of them as "saints and martyrs who practiced a noble profession in the love and spirit of Christ." Today all our professional duties must be practiced in love for men through a love of Christ. May the spirit of Cosmas and Damian teach us to value both bodily and spiritual health, and continue unsullied in the gift of regeneration, even though frequently we are harassed by bodily disease. Spiritual health is our greatest concern.   — Edwin G. Kaiser, C.PP.S.

TODAY: With Cosmas and Damian let us turn our attention to the power of God rather than that of men and their electronics.

September 27
St. Vincent de Paul (1581-1660)
French Priest, Founder of Vincentians, Co-founder of Sisters of Charity; Declared Patron of All Charitable Organizations and Works by Pope Leo XIII

Monsieur Vincent, as he was fondly called in his lifetime, is a splendid proof that the saints have quite understood our

Savior's insistence on the love of one's neighbor. It is characteristic of the saints that they attempted and carried off exceedingly difficult tasks, and perhaps that is why they so excelled in the task (it is no less) of loving and serving men without the slightest reference to the attractiveness or merits of men. If I cultivate men for my own sake I am an opportunist. If I assist them for their sake I am a humanitarian. If I serve them for the sake and love of Christ I am a Christian. Only in this event do I purely love my neighbor, and this the saints understood.

The mighty brotherly love of St. Vincent de Paul lives on in the noble religious families that bear his name. A degree of that same fraternal charity ought to live in every Christian heart. Didn't our Lord say that in just that manner we would be recognized as His? — **Vincent P. McCorry, S.J.**

TODAY: Pray to the Lord of the harvest that He send laborers.

September 28
St. Wenceslaus (d. 935)
*Duke of Bohemia, Martyr; Patron
of Bohemia and Czechoslovakia*

An evil-minded pagan mother and a vicious pagan brother reflect the background — the struggle between the dark forces of paganism and the loving faith in Christ — in the life and cruel death of St. Wenceslaus, Duke of Bohemia. His profound faith, his deeply religious soul, decided that Christianity was to triumph: such was the inception of the *Wenceslaus Tradition* in Bohemia. But this was to be only at the cost of his life, for he was murdered on his way to church, giving his life for Christ.

The martyred Wencelaus was canonized and became the heavenly patron of Czechoslovakia. The popular love is expressed in the beautiful Christmas carol, for he was prudent and enlightened in domestic affairs and firm and farsighted in foreign relations. In our own day of violence and strife, partisan bitterness, total disregard of the common good, we should ponder this lesson of Christian history.

— **Edwin G. Kaiser, C.PP.S.**

TODAY: Good King Wenceslaus, pray for us, that we

be enlightened by faith in Christ even though it be at
the price of our life.

September 29
SS. Michael, Gabriel, Raphael (Archangels)
Joint Feast of Three Archangels Instituted in 1970

The word angel means messenger. Angels are messengers of
God. Sacred Scripture refers often to angels, archangels, the
seraphim, cherubim. Only the angels we honor in a special way
today are known to us by name: Michael, Gabriel, Raphael. The
others are referred to in a more general way: The Angel of the
Lord, Angel of Mercy, and other names.

Michael and Gabriel figure in both the Old and New Testa-
ments. We meet Raphael only in the Book of Tobit and Tobiah,
but his story spans eight out of the 14 chapters. Raphael, whose
name means *God has healed*, is invoked for healing and as a
guide for travelers.

The angels see God and glorify Him face to face. The Seer
in the Book of Revelation (7:12) tells us that they cry out day
and night: "Amen! Blessing and glory and wisdom and thanksgiving and honor and power and might be to our God for ever
and ever. Amen." We too with all the choirs of angels in heaven
proclaim God's glory and join in their unending hymn of praise:
Holy, holy, holy. . . .

— Sister Elizabeth Ann Clifford, O.L.V.M.

*TODAY: "In the sight of the angels I will sing your
praises" (Psalm 138:1).*

September 30
St. Jerome (c. 342-420)
*Father and Doctor of the Church, "Father of
Biblical Science," Patron of Librarians*

St. Jerome, priest and Doctor of the Church, ranks with Ambrose, Augustine and Gregory the Great among the Doctors of
the Western Church. He combined the most varied intellectual
gifts. We might rightly call him the greatest Bible scholar of all
times, a great lover of classical literature, with splendor and
beauty of literary style manifested especially in his letters.

In great part the Vulgate, which was the Church's official Latin version of the Bible throughout the Middle Ages and in a sense still is today, is owing to this saint. His extreme ascetical life did not prevent him from guiding and instructing noble and saintly women in learning and piety. He could be suprisingly harsh in his discussions, though his primary object was truth and love for the truth of the inspired Word.

Equally great was his loyalty to the Holy See of Rome. Outstanding was his love for virginity and the virginity of Mary. Almost excessive was his love of study, a perfect model for us. Above all, we learn from Jerome an affection for the inspired Word of the Scripture and for beautiful literature.

— **Edwin G. Kaiser, C.PP.S.**

TODAY: St. Jerome, instill in me your love and devotion for the Word of God.

OCTOBER

St. Thérèse of the Child Jesus (1873-1897)
*French Carmelite Nun, Also Known as Thérèse of Lisieux,
and The Little Flower; Patron of Aviators, Florists,
Foreign Missions, National Patron of France*

The world considers a long life a successful life; on the other hand, it moans with great grief when death takes to itself someone in the flower of youth. St. Thérèse, the Little Flower, breathed her last in in her early 20s. Hers was a hidden life, buried behind the cloistered walls of Carmel in Lisieux. Yet behold her achievement — sanctity, a sainthood which has been the comfort and help of millions since she closed her eyes in death.

The prayer recited at her Mass today should give pause: "May we imitate the *humility* and the *simplicity* of the blessed virgin Thérèse." In humility and simplicity of heart is indeed to be found the secret of peace of soul, after which all seek but so few find. Resolve: To forget ourselves! To watch over our tendency to make life complicated by schemes, plans, interpretations of other's motives, self-seeking. Feel the peace which comes from humility and simplicity of heart!

— Most Rev. John J. Carberry

TODAY: Reflect on the words of the Little Flower: "Sometimes, when I am in such a state of spiritual dryness that not a single thought occurs to me, I say very slowly the 'Our Father' or the 'Hail Mary,' and these prayers suffice to take me out of myself and wonderfully refresh me."

October 2
Feast of Guardian Angels (16th century)
*Commemorates Angels who Protect People from Spiritual
and Physical Dangers and Assist People in Doing Good*

Before the creation of man and of the earth, God created myriads of *spirits*, whom the Bible calls angels. By nature they were immortal, and were destined for everlasting happiness with God. Heaven was to be their *reward* for serving their Creator as free beings. However, Holy Scripture teaches us that many of them refused to render the service demanded of them, and that God showed them no mercy. These angels then became demons, and in punishment of their rebellion hell was created (Isaiah 14:12-19; Luke 10:18; 2 Peter 11:4).

The loyal angels were forthwith rewarded with the vision of God. Holy Scripture mentions nine different choirs or divisions of angels, of whom the Seraphim are the highest. The angels in heaven are guardians of people here on earth (Matthew 18:10); they have often been sent as messengers from heaven to earth, whence the name "angel."

— Most Rev. John F. Noll

TODAY: Learn this prayer: "Angel of God, whom God had appointed to be my protector against all things evil; be always at my side, and keep me aware of your presence as God's messenger to me all the days of my life, for my good. Pray for me this day and every day of my life in this world. Amen."

October 3
St. Froilan (c. 905)
Spanish Benedictine, Bishop of Leon
St. Attilanus (c. 905)
Spanish Benedictine, Bishop of Zamara

Both bishops were hailed for their charity and holiness. They are also regarded as the principal restorers of monasticism in Spain. Saints Froilan and Attilanus were among the greatest intercessors in reconquering Spain from the Moors. They were teenagers spending their days as hermits in the wilderness. Their followers joined them as a Benedictine monastic community at Moreruela, on the Esla River in Old Castile. Abbot Froilan and his prior, Attilanus, were consecrated bishops of the adjoining sees of Leon and Zamara in the year 900.

TODAY: May the Lord bless us all the days of our lives. Happy are you who fear the Lord, who walk in His ways.

October 4
St. Francis of Assisi (1182-1226)
Founder of the Franciscans, Stigmatist; Patron
of Italy, Also of Catholic Action, Ecologists

Turning his back on the commercialism of his day, St. Francis embraced holy poverty. He was a romantic in love with nature. As troubador of the Lord, singing the praises of all God's creatures, he is an appropriate saint for an age of ecology. No doubt he would be a sympathizer of efforts to preserve the various forms of animal life.

Yet how different was his motivation from ours! St. Francis was in love with the Lord. Creatures were the reflection of God's glory. St. Francis understood this because he was one of the little ones to whom Jesus made known the mysteries of the kingdom of heaven. "All things have been delivered to me by my Father; and no one knows the Son except the Father, and no one knows the Father except the Son and anyone to whom the Son chooses to reveal him" (Matthew 11:27). The world of St. Francis was the world redeemed by Christ, not the world in opposition to the Gospel: "Far be it from me to glory except in the cross of our Lord Jesus Christ" (Galatians 6:14). St. Francis, always cheerful, led a life of self-denial in imitation of his Master. He could say with St. Paul, "I bear on my body the marks of Jesus" (Galatians 6:17)

— George M. Buckley, M.M.

TODAY: Lord, make me an instrument of Your peace that I may imitate the charity of St. Francis.

October 5
St. Placid (6th century)
Italian Monk, Martyr

St. Placid was a follower of St. Benedict, and he was sent by the great Benedict to found a monastery in Sicily. With him went several companions, two brothers and his sister. The entire community was massacred by pirates in 541.

Whether in the sixth century or in the 20th, monks play a vital role in the Church. They remind us that prayer is an essential condition for the Christian life. They remind us too that contemplation, whether acquired or infused, can be a normal development of our life with God.

As two people in love can find peace and ecstasy in silent communion, so can the human soul commune with God without words or images. Contemplation does not rely on such phenomena as levitation or bilocation. As the aged man reportedly told the Curé of Ars, "I don't say anything to God. I look at Him and He looks at me." — **Rev. Francis X. Canfield**

TODAY: The love of Christ is the mortar that binds the saints of history together. However, the way that love is expressed often differs from age to age.

October 6
St. Bruno (1030-1101)
German Monk, Founded Carthusians; Theologian,
Patron of Ruthenia, Patron of the Possessed

St. Bruno, the founder of the Carthusians, spent most of his life seeking solitude. Although most of us are not as inclined as Bruno to have a life of complete solitude, nevertheless, we all desire it at one time or another.

It is good and spiritually profitable to be alone occasionally so that we have the opportunity to ask ourselves who we are and where we are going, to examine honestly our motives and drives. Such solitude is not depressing but rather is marvelously refreshing when we return to an active life and communion with others more sure of ourselves and more certain of our capacity to give. — **Rev. John McCarthy**

TODAY: Dwell on the moment of silence, solitude and fasting. What a rebuke to the noise, the gadding about and the overindulgence that characterize my own life.

October 7
Our Lady of the Rosary (1716)
Commemoration of the Blessed Virgin Mary Through
the Mysteries of the Rosary; Feast marking Christian
victory over Mohammedan forces at Lepanto October 7, 1571

If we love Our Lady we will say the Rosary daily, for the Rosary is a test of that love. It is just as simple as that. The

Rosary may seem wearisome, the mind may wander as the Hail Mary is repeated; this is true — but Our Lady understands. The Rosary is strength, it is power, it is a chain of gold which links us to Mary.

Let us think of the beautiful prayers of the Rosary. The Apostles' Creed is a profession of our Faith. The Our Father is the perfect prayer given to us by our Blessed Lord. Heaven and earth combined to give us the beautiful prayer of the Hail Mary. The Glory Be to the Father expresses our praise to the Most Blessed Trinity. In addition, our Faith is strengthened in the daily review of the life of Christ unfolded in the Mysteries of the Rosary.

— Most Rev. John J. Carberry

TODAY: Resolve that nothing will interfere with our daily recitation of the Rosary. Queen of the Most Holy Rosary, pray for us!

October 8
St. Simeon (1st century)
Prophet, Author of the Canticle "Nunc Dimittis"

According to Scripture, Simeon lived in Jerusalem and was a just and devout man. Imbued with the Holy Spirit, Simeon was told that he should not die until he had seen the "Anointed of the Lord." According to custom, Mary and Joseph brought the Child Jesus into the Temple. Simeon took the Child in his arms, blessed Him and praised God. He said: "Lord, now lettest thou thy servant depart in peace, according to thy word; for mine eyes have seen thy salvation which thou hast prepared in the presence of all peoples, a light for revelation to the Gentiles, and for glory to thy people Israel" (Luke 2:29-32). Joseph and Mary were pleased at what was said about the Child. Simeon blessed them and said to Mary: "Behold, this child is set for the fall and rising of many in Israel, and for a sign that is spoken against (and a sword will pierce through your own soul also), that thoughts out of many hearts may be revealed" (Luke 2:34-35).

TODAY: Mary "kept all these things in her heart" (Luke 2:51).

October 9
St. John Leonardi (1550-1609)
Italian Priest, Founded a Religious Order;
Canonized by Pope Pius XI in 1938

Today's feast focuses our attention on the role of the priest as a zealous "minister according to the dispensation of God."

St. John Leonardi directed his ministry especially toward prisoners and the sick in hospitals. He extended his pastoral work by founding the Clerics Regular of the Mother of God and earned from St. Philip Neri the compliment "a true reformer." Both men are sterling examples of the Church in the 16th century, reforming and renewing itself. St. John is also credited with establishing an institute for educating and aiding foreign missionaries in the great age of discovery and exploration. Because of this, he is called the founder of the College for the Propagation of the Faith in Rome.

Do we pray for priests often? Do we realize that they labor under the same human weaknesses that afflict all men? Do we support them not by flattery but by sincere encouragement? Do we recognize our obligation to share in their ministry by whatever means possible for us? — Rev. Francis X. Canfield

TODAY: Include a priest or pastor in your daily prayers. Pray: "Jesus, Eternal Priest, keep this Thy holy one within the shelter of Thy Sacred Heart where none may touch him. Keep unstained his anointed hands which daily touch Thy Sacred Body. Keep unsullied the lips purpled with Thy Precious Blood. Keep pure and unearthly a heart sealed with the sublime mark of Thy glorious priesthood. Let Thy holy love surround him and shield him from the world's contagion. Bless his labors with abundant fruit, and may they to whom he has ministered be here below his joy and consolation, and in heaven his beautiful and everlasting crown. Amen."

October 10
St. Francis Borgia (1510-1572)
Spanish Jesuit, Preacher, Missionary

The name "Borgia" calls up historical scenes of intrigue, murder and duplicity. When a Borgia becomes a saint, then we are

193

convinced that God's grace is indeed a force in human affairs and that a man need not be victimized by heredity or environment. Once married and a duke in the court of Emperor Charles V, Francis entered the young Jesuit community on the death of his wife and became its general. Humility characterized his life, a humility that sees all talent and opportunity as gifts from God.

Whatever our role may be, true humility is an essential condition for the Christian life. Amazingly enough, it springs from a proper love and appreciation of self. If we recognize that whatever God has created is lovable, and that sin comes from our self-will, then we are well on the way to humility. The humble man thinks first of others, their joy, their pain, their problems. — Rev. Francis X. Canfield

TODAY: The humble man gives thanks always for his life, his family, his friends. He knows that all good things — and people — come from God.

October 11
St. Bruno the Great (c. 925-965)
German Statesman, Archbishop of Cologne

Today's Bruno was the youngest son of five children of Emperor Henry the Fowler and his wife St. Matilda. He began school when he was only four years old. When he was 15, St. Bruno became the confidential secretary of the Emperor Otto I, having the title of chancellor. In the year 950 he was ordained a deacon. Bruno accompanied his brother, Emperor Otto I, to Italy as archchancellor of the empire. In 953 Bruno was appointed Archbishop of Cologne.

It is easy to see how political problems could also have a part to play in the spiritual and religious responsibilities of the archbishop as a member of the royal family. St. Bruno, however, was as capable a statesman as he was a religious man. Biographers write, "Recognition of his worth and ability reached its climax in 961 when he was named co-regent of the Empire with his half-brother William, the Archbishop of Mainz."

TODAY: Our leaders are hard-pressed. They ask for our allegiance, our understanding and our prayers. Remember to render to Caesar the things that are Caesar's.

194

October 12
St. Felix, Cyprian and Companions (c. 484)
Bishops, North African Martyrs

One of the entries for today in *The Roman Martyrology* reads: "In Africa, 4,966 holy confessors and martyrs, in the persecution of the Vandals under the Arian King Hunneric. Some of them were bishops, some priests and deacons, with a multitude of the faithful accompanying them, who were driven into a frightful wilderness for the defense of Catholic truth. Many of them were cruelly treated by the Moorish leaders, and with sharp-pointed spears and stones forced to hasten their march, while others, with their feet tied, were dragged like corpses through rough places and mangled in all their limbs. They were finally tortured in a different manner, and won the honor of martyrdom. The principals among them were the Bishops Felix and Cyprian."

The Libyan desert was the staging area for this fifth century holocaust of almost 5,000 servants of Christ.

TODAY: "For the Son of Man also came not to be served but to serve, and to give His life as a ransom for many" (Mark 10:45).

October 13
St. Edward the Confessor (1003-1066)
King of England (1042-1066), Patron of Westminster

Edward was the last of the Saxon kings. He is called "The Confessor" because of his Christian piety: "... one who became a witness to Christ by his holy life." King Edward built St. Peter's Abbey on the site that is now Westminster Abbey in London.

Edward was the son of King Ethelred III and Queen Eman, daughter of Duke Richard I of Normandy. Edward spent 29 years in exile with his mother at Normandy. When he was recalled to England as king in 1042, he was "more Norman than English." He married the daughter of Earl Godwin, his chief minister of state. It was mostly through the efforts of the powerful Godwin that Edward was named King of England. In *The Lives of the Saints*, we read: "His reign of 24 years was one of almost unbroken peace, the country grew prosperous, the revised churches rose under his hand, the weak lived secure, and for ages men spoke with affection of the laws of 'good St. Edward.' "

TODAY: *"The stone which the builders rejected has become the cornerstone" (Psalm 118:22).*

October 14
St. Callistus I (d. 222)
Roman Pope, Martyr

Every day a stream of pilgrims passes in hushed reverence through the catacombs of St. Callistus on the Appian Way. This third-century Pope is identified with the cemetery because he enlarged it and improved it out of respect for the many holy priests and martyrs buried there.

The care of St. Callistus for the dead should stir in us a comparable concern especially for the souls of our relatives and friends. Soon we will commemorate all the faithful departed. But every day we should put them in our prayers. Saints in heaven, souls in purgatory, the living on earth — we all share a supernatural life in the Communion of Saints.

— Rev. Francis X. Canfield

TODAY: *Visit the gravesite of someone near and dear, your family or loved one. Pray to God for mercy in His judgment of the faithful departed.*

October 15
St. Teresa of Avila (1515-1582)
Spanish Carmelite, First Woman Doctor of the Church, Patron of Spain

Today we honor Teresa of Avila, whose books on prayer made her a Doctor of the Church. The passage from St. Paul for the liturgy is on our difficulties in prayer. We have within us the Spirit of God who makes us aware that God is our Father, provided we suffer with Christ — even in prayer. For "we ourselves, who have the first fruits of the Spirit, . . wait for . . . the redemption of our bodies" (Romans 8:23). We look forward in hope to complete union with God, yet there is no way of knowing now what that will be like. We can only wait for it patiently.

Sincere efforts to pray make us conscious of our failures, but we should never lose confidence. In our weakness, the Holy Spirit helps us, "for we do not know how to pray as we ought, but the Spirit himself intercedes for us with sighs too deep for words" (Romans 8:26). How well this fits into our feelings when we don't seem to be getting anywhere! But God understands; it is the Spirit who transcends our weakness and intercedes for us as God wills.

Teresa of Avila developed these ideas of St. Paul in her books on prayer.

— George M. Buckley, M.M.

TODAY: St. Teresa's "Bookmark" is rich in spiritual philosophy. Let us pray. "Let nothing disturb thee,/ Nothing affright thee./ All passes away,/ God only shall stay;/ Patience wins all,/ Who has God/ Lacks nothing,/ For God is his all."

October 16
St. Hedwig (1174-1243)
*Bavarian Noblewoman, Married Duke Henry of Silesia;
Head of Polish Royal Family, Patron of Silesia*

This great saint of the early 13th century is claimed by the Poles. She was a royal personage of Eastern Europe, and her son Henry II was killed in a war against the Tartars. For this remarkable woman — who bore six children, was widowed and then took the veil — the Church uses the Mass formula which contains the magnificent eulogy of the valiant woman to be found in Proverbs 31:10-31.

Here the valiant woman is pictured as the industrious wife, busy with the chores of home and family. She prepares the food and clothing; she manages well her household. She is loyal to her husband: "The heart of her husband trusts in her . . . she does him good, and not harm, all the days of her life."

Her glory is in her virtues: "Strength and dignity are her clothing. . . . She opens her mouth with wisdom, and the teaching of kindness is on her tongue."

— Rev. Francis X. Canfield

TODAY: Physical suffering is the lot of many among

us. By offering it up in reparation for our sins, we can make it eternally profitable for ourselves and others.

October 17
St. Ignatius of Antioch (d. 107)
Bishop, Writer, Martyr

During a persecution at the beginning of the second century, probably in the year 107, Ignatius, Bishop of Antioch, was arrested, sentenced to death and sent over land and sea to Rome to die in the Colosseum. It was a death for which he had apparently long prepared himself, and he was not to be denied martyrdom. On the way, Ignatius learned that the faithful in Rome might try to get a mitigation of his sentence. He at once sent a letter ahead to them. The text of it still remains. In it Ignatius begged his Roman brethren to give up any such idea: "I implore you to spare me untimely kindness. Let me be food for wild beasts, for thus shall I be able to reach God. I am God's wheat, to be ground by animals' teeth into Christ's good bread. . . ."

A martyr like Ignatius is not simply giving his body to beasts; he is giving all that he is and has to God. And he does it gladly; not always without fear, but always without regret. Ignatius was for the growing Church what Stephen had been in its beginnings.   — **Thomas M. Brew, S.J.**

TODAY: The modern Church also suffers persecution: sometimes with the fury of Communist torture, or political imprisonment; sometimes with the sophisticated indifference of prime-time TV.

October 18
St. Luke (1st century)
Apostle, Physician, Author of the Third Gospel and Acts of the Apostles; Patron of Artists, Glassworkers, Notaries, Painters, Physicians

Today is the feast day of St. Luke, one of the Gospel authors. Trained as a physician, he worked with St. Paul in Greece and Rome, and he gave up his life for Christ toward the end of the first century.

We can, however, see his disciplined, educated mind reflected in his Gospel, for he seeks detail with precision. Today's Gospel is his account of Christ sending out the 72 disciples. They are going forth to prepare the way for Christ. "The harvest is great, the workers are few," Christ reminds them. Luke then enshrines Christ's values, "I am sending you as lambs in the midst of wolves." We too are to be humble, gentle as lambs, but wary that we do not become infected with the world's values. Remembered as "the good and gentle physician," Luke gives us a portrait of Christ the relentless missionary.

— Rev. Thomas J. Carpender

TODAY: Lord, help me prepare the way for You. Inspire me to spread Your Gospel by living Your values.

October 19
SS. Isaac Jogues, John de Brébeuf and Companions
(d. 1642-1649)
Jesuit North American Martyrs, Canonized in 1930 by Pope Pius XI

Between 1642 and 1649, eight French Jesuit missionaries became the first servants of God to attain the martyr's crown in North America. Father Isaac Jogues and Brothers John de Lalande and René Goupil were martyred at what is now Auriesville, New York. Father John de Brébeuf, Charles Garnier, Anthony Daniel, Gabriel Lalemont and Noel Chabanel suffered in lower Canada.

The chief difference between the saint and the ordinary Christian is heroism. That martyrs are heroes is plain enough. The hero has nobility of soul; he is generous; fear does not stop him. Suffering does not get him down, nor does death make him flinch. God's hero is tenacious; he does not count the cost of attaining his goal. He will wear himself out doing it, and his strength seems more than a man's.

Only a few are called to the glory of martyrdom. There is a day-by-day heroism that is quiet, unspectacular and often unnoticed, but it takes a courage that is not less fine than the courage of him who gives his life all at once. It is the consistently faithful and cheerful performance each day of the duties of one's state of life. — Thomas M. Brew, S.J.

TODAY: When faith seems to weaken and vocations fall off, we look to St. Isaac and companions for inspiration. God grant that their noble example will strengthen the faltering will of laity and clergy alike.

October 19
St. Paul of the Cross (1694-1775)
Italian Religious, Founder of the Passionists

St. Paul of the Cross, the founder of the Passionist Order, was so devoted to Christ's passion and death that this has become the theme of the Order's preaching. He took after the Apostle Paul, who said that "we preach Christ crucified" (1 Corinthians 1:23). When they preach a mission, the Passionists urge people to make the Way of the Cross.

I am always edified by the number of my parishioners who pray the Stations before and after Mass each day. It seems to me there would be no better thanksgiving after Mass. The Way of the Cross in Jerusalem today is just as it must have been in Christ's day — through narrow alleys lined with small shops, a sort of bazaar crowded with shouting people. You begin to realize the shame that the Master bore for us.

— Msgr. Maurice Cooney

TODAY: Lord, by Your cross and resurrection, You have set us free; You are the Savior of the world.

October 20
St. Bertilla Boscardin (1888-1922)
Italian Religious, Nurse, Canonized by Pope John XXIII in 1961

If mention were made of St. Bertilla Boscardin, one could expect the quick question "Who's she?" Well, she is the humble farm girl who became a nun and attained such heights of sanctity that she has become a canonized saint. And her sanctity was due to her centering her life on a little book called the "catechism," which unfortunately has been getting a bad press in our present day.

St. Bertilla's love for the catechism caused Pope Pius XII to say on the occasion of her beatification in 1952: "This little book (the catechism) has in itself greater value than a bulky encyclopedia; it contains the truths we must believe, the duties we must fulfill, the means to use to sanctify ourselves. What is there of greater importance on this earth? . . . Blessed Bertilla had understood this, and it created her happiness."

Pope John XXIII found in the catechism "the explanations and answers to all questions which harass the consciences of all." — **Msgr. Ralph G. Kutz**

TODAY: A frail peasant maiden, who was thought not too "bright," now shines as a saintly star in heaven.

October 21
St. Hilarion (c. 291-371)
Abbot, Hermit, Ascetic

Hilarion is another of those fascinating desert saints. Much of the biography was written by St. Jerome in 391. Although based on historical fact, some of Hilarion's ventures are embellished with legendary figures. For example: "A serpent of enormous size devoured both cattle and man, and . . . Hilarion, having prayed, induced the creature to come onto a pile of wood . . . then set fire to it so that it was burnt to ashes." (A 14th-century artist, Pietro Lorenzetti, painted a fresco detailing St. Hilarion chasing a dragon.) Is it coincidental that St. George (who lived at the same time) killed a dragon in the city of Sylene in Libya?

Hilarion patterned his life after that of St. Anthony of Egypt (January 17), with whom he stayed for several months. He later returned to Palestine and his home in Gaza, where he began his hermitage. The simplicity and austerity of this desert saint is revealed in his last will and testament, where he bequeathed his riches: ". . .his book of Gospels, a sackcloth shirt, hood and a little cloak."

TODAY: Pray, "O Lord, may these gifts, which we offer to Your majesty, be an aid to our salvation."

October 22
St. Donatus (c. 876)
Bishop of Fiesole in Italy

The story is told of Donatus, an Irish nobleman, who, while journeying through Italy upon his return from a pilgrimage, came to the city of Fiesole. There the clergy and people were in the process of electing a new bishop. Donatus was a little person, and so insignificant that nobody would especially notice him. However, as he entered the cathedral, the church bells began to ring and all lamps and candles were illuminated in a miraculous manner. The people took these events to be signs from heaven that Donatus, the insignificant little stranger, should be their new bishop. Like all Irishmen, Donatus was gifted with tongue and pen. He wrote poetry and also geographical sketches on the Emerald Isle. Although he was a bishop in Italy, St. Donatus is still acclaimed one of Ireland's great saints.

> TODAY: Another Irishman by the name of Patrick leaves us with this thought: "Would that you . . . imitate greater things and do better things that will be to my glory."

October 23
St. John Capistran (1386-1456)
Italian Franciscan, Preacher, Papal Diplomat,
Patron of Military Chaplains

An anonymous contributor to *My Daily Visitor* once wrote that vocations to the priesthood and religious life are essentially an invitation from our Lord to those with the necessary qualifications of good character, health and adequate mental ability. Because they are an invitation — and not a command — they may be accepted or declined.

St. John Capistran, or Capistrano, was a 33-year-old mayor of Perugia and a married man when he received his "invitation" to become a Franciscan. The husband and wife received special marital dispensations that enabled them to enter the religious life. This "invitation" also came about during his imprisonment in one of Italy's regional wars. John was ordained in 1420, and for 30 years he was a popular preacher at parish missions. He was also a confrere of St. Bernardine of Siena in strengthening the Franciscan Order. Father John Capistran personally commanded the left wing of the Christian army of Janos Hunyady in Hungary's defeat of the Turks at the Battle of Belgrade in 1456. This military victory saved Europe from a Turkish onslaught, and it also provided members of the Chaplain's Corps with a heavenly intercessor.

TODAY: The beauty of our Christian Faith is that the path to religious vocation can never be overgrown or obliterated, unless we choose not to seek it.

October 24
St. Anthony Mary Claret (1807-1870)
Spanish Priest, Founder of the Claretians,
Archbishop of Santiago, Cuba

Anthony's middle name of Mary is a rather unusual baptismal name for a male. The only other saints also having Mary for a middle name are St. Anthony Mary Zaccaria, founder of the Barnabites (July 5), and Clement Mary Hofbauer, the famed Redemptorist missionary (see March 15).

It is interesting to read that Mary played a very active role in his life. As a young seminarian, Anthony was miraculously saved from drowning through Mary's intercession. As Spain's most popular preacher, his theme was repeatedly "devotion to the Eucharist, and to the Immaculate Heart of Mary." Is it any wonder, then, that his religious congregation of preachers is known as the Sons of the Immaculate Heart of Mary, or Claretians?

Father Anthony became the Archbishop of Santiago, Cuba, in 1850. He set about reorganizing the seminary training of his clergy. He also lashed out against the vices and immorality of the islanders. He helped the poor farmers by introducing credit unions to the island. Pope Pius IX, in 1867, sent the archbishop to Spain as the confessor to Queen Isabella II. While there, he began printing and publishing religious pamphlets. He is said to have preached over 10,000 sermons and to have published 200 books and pamphlets. He was exiled to France during the revolution of 1868, and died at a Cistercian monastery near Narbonne.

TODAY: Pray that our Blessed Mother Mary becomes a part of my name, my life and my dedication to God.

October 25
SS. Chrysanthus and Daria (d. 283)
Roman Martyrs

Others listed in the Roman Calendar for today are: Saints Crispin & Crispinian, martyrs (c. 285); Saints Fronto & George, bishops of the fourth century, and St. Gaudentius, Bishop of Brescia (c. 410).

Information about these saints is mostly legendary, but stories of Chrysanthus and Daria are factual because of their popularity and the veneration of the two at Rome. Chrysanthus was born in Egypt and brought to Rome by his father, Polemius, a nobleman. The youth was baptized and received into the Church against his father's wishes. His father tried to entrap him into sin and consequent loss of his religion — to no avail. Chrysanthus married a Greek maiden, Daria, a priestess of Minerva. She soon converted to the Faith, and the two lived in conjugal chastity. Chrysanthus was arrested and tortured for his beliefs, and through his example, the judge and his wife along with 70 soldiers were baptized. These were all slain. While her husband was in prison, Daria was placed in a brothel, where it is said she was protected by a lion. Saints Chrysanthus and Daria were later stoned to death and buried in a sand pit near Rome.

TODAY: Modesty is a forgotten gift in the life of the world. What example do we set, as Christians, to counterattack public exhibitionism?

October 26
St. Evaristus (d. 105)
Pope, Martyr, First Pontiff to Divide Rome into Parishes

St. Evaristus was the fifth Pope. Like most of the early Pontiffs, he suffered martyrdom and was buried at the Vatican. History tells of his dividing Rome into parishes and legislating for the greater good of the Church.

The Universal Church has grown until today when the Holy Father shoulders the responsibility for 500 million Catholics throughout the world. The inevitable problems of administering a church of such vast magnitude spread over the entire world staggers the imagination. In all things it is the spiritual values that must take precedence.

During Mass, at the Liturgy of the Eucharist, we pray each day for Pope John Paul II and for our own bishop. Do we pause a moment to consider the awesome offices they fill, the unremitting pressures of hourly demands on their energy and talent? They deserve our unfailing prayers and reverence.

— Rev. Francis X. Canfield

TODAY: Lord, teach me to carry my cross with patience.

October 27
St. Otteran (d. 563)
British Benedictine, Abbot of Meath

The feast day of St. Otteran is one of popular festivity in Ireland today. The Irish monks also referred to him as St. Odhran. Historians likened him as "noble and without sin." He was said to be a Briton, one of the 12 missionaries who sailed with St. Columba from Loch Foyle and landed at Iona (an island off the coast of Scotland).

Abbot Otteran predicted his own death soon after they landed on the isle. It is recorded: "I would be the first to die under the covenant of the kingdom of God in this place." St. Columban said to Otteran: "I will give you that kingdom . . . and moreover . . . whoever makes a request at my burial place shall not get it until he prays to you as well."

TODAY: I am weary, broken and bent . . . until You enter the islands with me to help me along the paths to holiness.

October 28
SS. Simon and Jude (1st century)
Apostles, Martyrs: Simon, Patron of Tanners; Jude (Thaddeus), Patron of Desperate Situations, Hospitals

History records that Saints Simon and Jude devoted their lives to preaching the Gospel. Both died as martyrs. Despite their being among the 12 Apostles, devotion to either or both of them did not become exceptional until recent years when intercessory prayers to St. Jude brought favorable results in desperate and well-nigh hopeless cases.

Many are the secular newspapers that day after day, week after week, carry paid classified advertisements in thanksgiving to St. Jude for favors received. Each advertisement undoubtedly increases the numbers seeking his intercessory favors from Almighty God. St. Simon has his clientele too.

St. Jude, in his one epistle, advises us: "Build yourselves up on your most holy faith; pray in the Holy Spirit; keep yourselves in the love of God; wait for the mercy of our Lord Jesus Christ unto eternal life" (1:20-21). Our Lord's mercy is most assuredly channeled to devotees of Saints Simon and Jude.

— Msgr. Ralph G. Kutz

> *TODAY: O God, who called Thy blessed Apostles Simon and Jude to the knowledge of Thy name, allow us to celebrate their everlasting glory by growing in holiness, as well as to grow in holiness by celebrating it, through Christ, our Lord. Amen.*

October 29
St. Narcissus (c.120-220)
Greek Bishop of Jerusalem

Shortly after his ordination, Father Timothy Delaney penned a reflection for *My Daily Visitor* in which he wrote, "A priest is a man called to serve; to suffer with a suffering people; to rejoice with those in joy."

Today's saint was a priest and bishop who lived more than 100 years. St. Narcissus headed the Church at Jerusalem, and his coadjutor bishop was St. Alexander. Bishop Narcissus presided at a council in Caesarea and decreed that the feast of Easter should always be celebrated on Sunday, not along with the Jewish passover as had been the custom of Christians in Asia Minor. He also miraculously changed water into oil for the lamps to burn during the Easter liturgy.

Father Delaney emphasized this beautiful prayer of priests in our daily Mass: "Through him/ with him,/ in him,/ in the Unity of the Holy Spirit,/ all glory and honor/ is yours,/ Almighty Father,/ forever and ever!" Amen.

TODAY: Peace is offered to us by the Holy Spirit when our hearts and minds are secure in knowing that God's will is truly our own.

October 30
St. Alphonsus Rodriguez (1533-1617)
Spanish Jesuit Brother

Upon the death of his father, Diego, the younger son Alphonsus returned from school in Alcalá to manage the family wool and cloth business in Segovia. His mother left him in charge of the mercantile shops, and he married when he was 23. Over a short time his daughter, wife, mother, and his only son died. "This succession of misfortunes and losses made Alphonsus give very serious thought to what God was calling him to do."

Alphonsus was about 50 years old when he tried to join the Society of Jesus, and only by a special ruling from the prefect was he accepted into the order as a brother. He was sent from Spain to the island of Majorca, where he was to be a porter at Montesia College there. Brother Alphonsus carried out the duties of the lowly office for 24 years. One bright spot in his life was the fact that Peter Claver (also a saint) was a pupil under the brother's care. Peter himself sought the spiritual guidance of the venerable brother. Alphonsus died of rheumatoid fever when he was 84 years old. It is interesting to note that Brother Alphonsus, the mentor, was joined with Peter Claver, the pupil, when they were named saints of the Church in 1888.

TODAY: "I call upon thee, for thou wilt answer me, O God; incline thine ear to me, hear my words. . . . Keep me as the apple of the eye; hide me in the shadow of thy wings" (Psalm 17:6-8).

October 31
St. Wolfgang (c. 930-994)
Benedictine, Bishop of Ratisbon in West Germany

Day by day we learn more about God's friends, the saints. Some of their names sound strange and exotic. They seem to come from faraway places and times distant from our own. Today's patron is one of these.

Wolfgang was a master teacher in the cathedral school at Trier, Germany. In 964 he entered the Benedictine monastery at Einsiedeln, and soon was director of the monastery school. When he was ordained in 971, he was assigned as a missionary to the Magyars in Hungary. The next year he was consecrated Bishop of Ratisbon (Regensburg). Biographers write: "He never quitted the monastic habit, and practiced all the austerities of a religious life when in the episcopal dignity." He was known for clergy reforms and the enforcement of all monastic rules in his diocese, in addition to helping the poor and downtrodden. As a preacher, "he had the art of looking at the hearts of his hearers."

> TODAY: *The saints, in fact, were simply God's friends, those who took His friendship seriously. This is within the reach of us all.*

NOVEMBER

November 1
All Saints (4th century)
*Feast Honors All the Saints
of Every Time and Place*

T oday, at the end of her annual review of Christ's mysteries, the Church reminds us of His crowning achievement by celebrating the Feast of All Saints — for all sanctity is the work of Christ, our Savior. Holiness is the triumph of Christ's grace — one might even say Christ's life — in the soul of the sanctified. The Christian vocation was summed up perfectly by the great prophet St. John the Baptist when he said: "He (Christ) must increase, but I must decrease" (John 3:30). "It is no longer I who live, but Christ who lives in me" — St. Paul (Galatians 2:20).

It was in order to come to live in each one of us, and to sanctify us and all we do by sharing each one of our actions, that Christ became man, and He became our Food in Holy Communion. He reaches out through His sacraments from Palestine to share all human activity. But since He is dedicated to doing the will of His Father, He can only share those actions that are in harmony with that divine will. All, however, that is His Father's will, He shares with eagerness begotten of love for His Father and for us.

— Eugene Boylan, O.C.S.O.

TODAY: It is comforting to know that the saints we honor on this day must surely include people we have known.

November 2
All Souls (10th century)
Feast Commemorates All the Faithful Departed

T he Church asks us to remember the dead. The dogma, vitalizing our loving devotion to these souls, is that there is a purgatory in the next world. Through our prayers these souls can be helped to enter the gates of heaven. In purgatory, all souls are completing the atonement due for their sins. Job tells us they ask of us: "Have pity on me, have pity on me, O you my friends" (Job 19:21).

Devotion to the Poor Souls in Purgatory is one of the most beautiful practices of Christian charity. Our prayers and good deeds can alleviate their suffering. We can help them enter heaven. St. Leonard said: "If you deliver one soul from purgatory you can say with confidence, 'Heaven is mine.' " Let us pray for all souls on their day. "Eternal rest grant unto them, O Lord, and let the perpetual light shine upon them. May they rest in peace."

— Marie Layne

> TODAY: Pope Paul VI reminded us: "We believe in the communion of all the faithful of Christ, those who are pilgrims on earth, the dead who are attaining their purification, and the blessed in heaven, all together forming one Church; and we believe that in this communion the merciful love of God and His saints is ever listening to our prayers..." (Creed of the People of God, June 20, 1968).

November 3
St. Martin de Porres (1579-1639)
Dominican Lay Brother, Patron of Interracial Justice,
Canonized by Pope John XXIII in 1969

No civil rights bill need be written for the Community (or Communion) of Saints. St. Paul told us that fact when he said: "We are all one in Christ." Martin de Porres was black, son of a Spanish knight and a black freed-woman from Panama. But when Mass is said in his honor today the priest must vest in white. There never was, nor will there ever be, need for integration among the true children of God; for they realize they are more closely related than are brothers and sisters; they are as closely knit as are members to members of the one same body.

This mulatto boy became a lay brother in the Dominican Order at Lima, Peru, but soon was extending his services not only to the poor, sick, orphaned and outraged of the city and country, but became a one-man SPCA, because even vermin, rats and mice were creatures of God. Prelates and noblemen vied for the honor of carrying the body of this black man to the grave. The only color line to recognize is that which separates sanctity from us.　　　　　　　　　　— M. Raymond, O.C.S.O.

TODAY: Martin was nicknamed "Saint of the Broom" by his confreres. This humble man would say: "We are all of the same Heavenly Father, and all are entitled to the same dignity."

November 4
St. Charles Borromeo (1538-1584)
Italian Cardinal, Patron of Catechists, Seminarians

St. Charles Borromeo, the Cardinal-Archbishop of Milan in the latter half of the 16th century, is renowned for his reforming zeal, following upon the initiative of the Council of Trent, which occurred during his youth. He sought interior renewal through his own prayer and self-discipline and reform of the Church by his unceasing zeal. He even went so far as to sell his own furniture, including his bed, to help the sick and needy when the plague struck the city of Milan.

Our zeal and our patience, our quest for spiritual understanding should be enhanced by the example of men such as St. Charles Borromeo. Lord Jesus, make us willing to be dedicated to Yourself and Your service.　　　— Gary Lauenstein, C.SS.R.

TODAY: May you "lead a life worthy of the Lord, fully pleasing to him, bearing fruit in every good work and increasing in the knowledge of God" (Colossians 1:10).

November 5
St. Bertilla (c. 705)
French Benedictine Nun, Abbess of Ghelles

A spiritual writer once asked this question: "Who are your guides in life?" This is a very good question because everyone needs a guide and we become like those we follow. "We are our ideals," the old adage tells us. We naturally imitate the people we look up to and admire. Another proverb reads, "Tell me who your friends are — and I will tell you who you are!" If your friends are the saints, then you're okay. If you don't admire anyone — you are in trouble!

St. Bertilla could be your guide and friend. She was born of an illustrious family at Soisson, France. She became a Benedictine nun at the monastery of Jouarre and soon was known as the community's "best friend." Her kindness to strangers, her care of the sick, her teaching and guidance of the young were all noteworthy traits. She became the first Abbess of Chelles Abbey. Biographers write: "The holy abbess, who saw two queens (Hereswitha and Bathildis) every day at her feet, seemed the most humble and the most fervent among her sisters."

> *TODAY: Sister Bertilla demonstrated by her conduct that old adage, "No one commands well who has not first learned and is not always ready to obey well."*

November 6
St. Demetrian (c. 835-912)
Bishop of Khytri, or Kyrka, in Cyprus

Demetrian is hailed as one of the greatest bishops and saints of Cyprus. He is especially honored for his purity and power of healing. The aged bishop was also a fighter and a brave man as the legend relates. "Near the end of an episcopate of some 25 years, Cyprus was ravaged by the Saracens and many Christians were carried off in slavery." Bishop Demetrian is said to have followed them and interceded with the invaders to release the Christian captives.

> *TODAY: ". . .Whatever you ask in prayer, believe that you receive it, and you will" (Mark 11:24).*

November 7
St. Willibrord (c. 658-739)
"Apostle of the Frisians," Founded Echternach Monastery in Luxembourg

The missionary works for God and His people. His life is often in danger in faraway lands, where the people do not yet know of the existence of God. St. Willibrord was such a missionary. He set sail from Heligoland in the North Sea and landed in The Netherlands. At Walcheren he was attacked by a pagan who tried to kill him with a sword. The missionary had entered a pagan temple and pushed over and partially destroyed an idol. Willibrord miraculously escaped death and returned in safety to Utrecht. In 719 Willibrord was joined in his missionary apostolate by St. Boniface, who worked in Friesland for three years before going to Germany. Through the efforts and zeal of Bishop Willibrord, the Faith was planted in many parts of Holland, Zeeland and The Netherlands. The Apostle of the Frisians died at his beloved monastery of Echternach in his 81st year.

> TODAY: The missionary, to win souls for Christ, still spends long, tireless hours under the poorest of conditions without complaining. What are we doing to win souls for Jesus Christ?

November 8
St. Godfrey (1065-1115)
Bishop of Amiens in France

The saints are at one in revealing the note of joy in life, even in suffering. Many of them suffered a great deal, much more than we are called upon to endure. Indeed, we might say that the real test of all followers of Christ is our attitude toward the cross and suffering.

Abbot Godfrey, of Nogent Abbey in Champagne, was 25 years old when he turned this seemingly neglected and dilapidated monastery into a flourishing spiritual community. When he was named Bishop of Amiens, he entered the city barefoot and lived in simple, austere fashion. "When he thought the cook was treating him too well, he took the best food from the kitchen and gave it to the poor and sick." However, in his episcopal capacity, Bishop Godfrey "was unbending, severe, and inflexibly just."

> TODAY: God, the Creator of all mankind, help me to forgive those who offend or irritate me.

November 9
Dedication of St. John Lateran (324)
Commemorates the Consecration of the Basilica
of the Most Holy Savior in Rome

When St. Francis of Assisi received God's message to rebuild His Church, he immediately set out to restore physically the run-down chapel of San Damiano. It was natural for him to interpret the command that way.

Churches have been important centers of Christian life from the time of the Edict of Milan in 313, when church building became widespread. Before that time, Christians met in private homes for the celebration of the Eucharist, or in the catacombs, because of persecution.

The feast of the Dedication of St. John Lateran commemorates the first public consecration of a church on November 9, 324, by Pope St. Sylvester I. The church was a gift of the Emperor Constantine and was known as the Basilica of the Most Holy Savior until the 12th century when it received its present title in honor of St. John the Baptist. The basilica, which was rebuilt, reconsecrated and enlarged over the years, is regarded as the church of highest dignity in Rome and throughout the Roman Rite.

— Rose M. Avato

TODAY: "I have chosen and consecrated this house
that My name may be there forever. . ." said the Lord.

November 10
St. Leo I, the Great (400-461)
Pope, Doctor of the Church

Back in the middle 400s, St. Leo the Great, Pope of Rome, wrote 96 sermons which stressed the virtues of almsgiving, fasting and prayer. He earned the title "Great" because of his exposition of Christian doctrine. The theological problems of his times were entirely different from ours. Out beyond the dissensions of the Church — particularly in the East — was the oncoming invasion of Christian Europe by Attila the Hun.

When we analyze all the manifold crises through which the

214

Church has already passed in nearly 2,000 years of existence, it becomes clear that each generation is a link to cope with the particular problems of its time in a kind of kaleidoscopic evolution of growth. New generations will accept or reject what we are struggling to produce today in the light of their needs and environments.

— Anne Tansey

TODAY: Study recent writings by the Pope and our bishops dealing with the Church in modern times. We will learn of the problems and changes occurring in the living Church.

November 10
St. Andrew Avellino (1521-1608)
Italian Civil and Canon Lawyer, Theatine Priest

Lancelot is a name associated with knighthood and chivalry. But the chivalry and knighthood of literature are nothing compared to the knightly chivalry shown in the life of Andrew Avellino, who was named Lancelot at baptism.

He was a lawyer who once caught himself in a lie as he pleaded a case. That evening, reading Scripture, he came across the line: "The mouth that lies kills the soul." He gave up law and dedicated his life to the care of souls. He became a Theatine and changed his name to Andrew. He vowed "ever to turn away from self and to ever draw nearer the Sovereign God." He kept that vow. His greatest chivalry toward God was shown in his constant efforts to form a better priesthood. He died as he was beginning to celebrate Mass. Consequently, he is honored as a protector against sudden and unprovided death. Let death be sudden so long as it is not unprovided. It will never be unprovided for, if we live chivalrously toward God.

— M. Raymond, O.C.S.O.

TODAY: Reflect on these words of Scripture that radically changed the life of St. Andrew Avellino: "The mouth that lies kills the soul."

215

November 11
St. Martin of Tours (316-397)
Bishop, Pioneer of Western Monasticism, Patron
of Soldiers; First Non-Martyr Venerated

"Truly, I say to you, as you did it to one of the least of these my brethren, you did it to me" (Matthew 25:40).

El Greco's painting of St. Martin has immortalized him in our day as the young soldier who split his own cloak in half to share it with a beggar. It is based on the legend which told how Martin did this charitable deed and was rewarded by a vision of Christ clothed in Martin's half-cloak. The lesson to be learned is the type of charity for all which made Martin of Tours a saint. Even on his agonizing deathbed, he prayed that if his labors were necessary for the Church he be allowed to live on: it was an offer of service to his brothers, not a selfish request.

We can find occasion of service to others, especially in our ordinary line of work, household chores or studies. Do we use them to manifest Christ's charity? Lord Jesus, make us love our brothers and sisters.

— Gary Lauenstein, C.SS.R.

TODAY: Lord, open my heart and my mind to see You in all the small and undramatic people, those who surround me.

November 12
St. Josaphat (1584-1623)
Polish Basilian Monk, Martyr

St. Josaphat Kuncevyc has been called a martyr of Christian union. He was born about 1584 in Vladimir, Poland, and became a Basilian monk at the monastery of Vilna, Lithuania, in 1604. Ordained a priest of the Byzantine Rite in 1609, he became a leading advocate for the reunion of dissident Easterners with Rome. In 1617 he was named Bishop of Vitebsk and a few months later became Archbishop of Polotsk. He put into effect much-needed reforms in the archdiocese and also began a reform of the Basilian Order.

Josaphat's success in reuniting dissidents aroused the anger of those opposed to union. He was attacked and martyred by an angry mob of schismatics in Vitebsk in 1623. He was canonized in 1867. Josaphat's "work of reform and renewed fidelity to the Apostolic See" cost him his life, Pope John Paul declared in a 1982 letter to the superior general of the Basilian Order of St. Josaphat.

— Rose M. Avato

TODAY: *The Church of silence still needs our prayers and assistance, now as much as ever.*

November 13
St. Frances Xavier Cabrini (1850-1917)
American Founder, Missionary Sisters of Sacred Heart;
First U.S. Citizen Canonized, 1946; Patron of Immigrants

As a young girl in Italy, Frances Xavier Cabrini was refused admittance to many convents. Why? She appeared to be undernourished, not able to do much work. So she taught catechism to children every place she could.

Pope Leo XIII heard of her catechetical work. In a short audience, the Holy Father told her, "Go to America and teach catechism to the neglected people. If no one accepts you in any convent, start an Order of your own." She came to America in 1889. Mother Cabrini taught, started an Order of her own and everything went on smoothly. She had little difficulty in establishing schools, convents, hospitals in the Americas and even back in Europe.

At 67 years of age, Mother Cabrini had established 67 institutions, each worth a million. When asked, "How did you do it?" She replied, "I did not do it. I just witnessed it. Our Lord did it." Did not our Lord say that "all things are possible with God" (Mark 10:27)?

— Tom Martin, S.J.

TODAY: *We too are missionaries bringing the example of Christ to those we come in contact with at home, in the office, school, supermarket and neighborhood. Remember: "Nothing will be impossible to you" (Matthew 17:21).*

November 13
St. Stanislaus Kostka (1550-1568)
Polish Jesuit, Patron of Poland

$\mathbf{A}$ young boy — a brother of ours "in Christ Jesus" — proves that teenagers can live up to their dignity, do their duty and achieve their destiny.

Stanislaus Kostka was the son of a Polish senator who opposed his son's desire to become a Jesuit. Stanislaus is said to have been told by the Blessed Virgin that it was God's will for him to enter the Society of Jesus. That was enough for the boy. He walked 350 miles to present himself to St. Peter Canisius, provincial of Upper Germany. This saint sent him to Rome, where another saint, Francis Borgia, general of the Society, received him and accepted him as candidate. After nine months as a novice, Stanislaus fell ill, and died on the Feast of our Lady's Assumption. One month later his brother arrived in Rome with orders from his father to bring Stanislaus back at all costs. Some teenagers have to learn that they must obey their heavenly Father rather than follow their earthly father when he is in opposition to heaven. — **M. Raymond, O.C.S.O.**

TODAY: Recall these words of St. Stanislaus, "I was not born for the good things of this earth; what my heart alone desires are the good things of eternity."

November 14
St. Lawrence (Lorcan) O'Toole (1128-1180)
Irish Peacemaker, Archbishop of Dublin

"$\mathbf{T}$he Fighting Irish" is the name given New York's 69th Regiment in World War I. But the name fitted other Sons of St. Patrick centuries before America was discovered. Yet saints flourished amid all the strife. One such was Lawrence O'Toole, Abbot of Glendalough when only 25 years old, and Archbishop of Dublin before he was 33.

During his lifetime "the Irish Problem" began when King Dermot McMurrogh asked the help of Henry II of England to regain his position in Ireland. For the next 10 years Lawrence O'Toole was the peacemaker between the various warring parties in Ireland, as well as between Henry II and Rory

O'Connor, the high king of Ireland. He suffered from both sides, and for both sides, and thus won success. When about to die, Lawrence was urged to make a will. His answer was a smile and the words: "God knows I have not a penny in the world." But who can gauge his riches in the other world?

— M. Raymond, O.C.S.O.

TODAY: Pray to this peacemaker to heal the discord of a partitioned Ireland.

November 15
St. Albert the Great (c. 1200-1280)
German Dominican, Bishop, Doctor (Universalis et Expertus) of the Church, Canonized in 1931; Patron of Natural Sciences, Medical Technologists

Wisdom is "a breath of the power of God and a pure emanation of the glory of the Almighty; . . in every generation she passes into holy souls and makes them friends of God and prophets" (Wisdom 7:25-27).

Some of these friends of God were the Doctors of the Church — men and women ecclesiastical writers of eminent learning and sanctity. Among the Doctors of the Church is St. Albert the Great, whose feast day is commemorated today. He was born in Germany about 1200; joined the Dominicans in 1223; taught at Cologne and Paris. Albert wrote extensively on logic, natural sciences, ethics, metaphysics, Scripture, systematic theology. He contributed to the development of scholastic theology and was a teacher of St. Thomas Aquinas. For a brief period (1260-62) Albert was Bishop of Regensburg. In 1931 he was canonized and proclaimed a Doctor of the Church.

— Rose M. Avato

TODAY: Seek the intercession of Albertus Magnus in all medical research for a cure of cancer and our nation's other ills.

November 16
St. Margaret (1045-1093)
Queen and Patron of Scotland

The Queen of Scotland instructed her children, and what a spiritual heritage she left them. She taught the children:

- To die a thousand deaths rather than commit one mortal sin.

- To give honor and adoration to the Most Holy Trinity; and to have particular respect and veneration for the Blessed Virgin, the Mother of God.

- To be charitable to the poor, to protect orphans and provide them with their necessities.

- To abhor all obscene language and uncleanness of spirit.

- To converse with persons of blameless life and to follow their judgment and counsel.

- To be firm, constant and unchangeable in caring for the Catholic Faith.

> TODAY: *Queen Margaret used her power for the glory of God, the progress of the Church, the good of her subjects and for the sanctification of her family.*

November 17
St. Elizabeth of Hungary (1207-1231)
Queen; Patron of Secular Franciscan Order, Also of Bakers, Nursing and Nursing Services, Tertiaries

Elizabeth died at age 24 after six years of romantic marriage with Louis of Thuringia. She was 20 when Louis died, away on the Crusades. Left with three children, Duchess Elizabeth soon felt the bitterness of her in-laws. Cast out of Wartburg Castle, Elizabeth entered the Franciscan Third Order and became wife and mother to the poor and sick.

Queen Elizabeth idealizes woman's role on earth. Through her faith and love, she led Louis to God. Woman deals so intimately with the mysterious, with the divine. Man thirsts for beauty and ideals, but naturally is earthbound and material-minded. Usually a woman leads him to beauty and love . . . and finally to God, who is Beauty and Love personified.

Blessed Mary even physically brought God to man. Through the Holy Spirit, she wrought in herself the union of God with man. To some extent every woman and mother must do precisely this — lead man to union with God.

— Rev. Robert L. Wilken

> TODAY: *The most difficult gift to give is oneself. It is*

much easier to donate money to help the poor and elder-
ly than to go out and actually assist them ourselves.
Learn to give of yourself freely to help others.

November 18
Dedication of the Churches of SS. Peter and Paul
Commemorating Greatest Apostles of the Early Church

The Basilica of St. Peter, as we see it today, was consecrated by Pope Urban VIII on November 18, 1626. The relics of St. Peter rest in the tomb beneath the church's high altar.

St. Paul was martyred at Tre Fontane on the Ossian Way, seven miles from the site of Peter's martyrdom. The great church of St. Paul-Outside-the-Walls is credited to Emperor Theodosius I and Pope St. Leo the Great (440-461). In 1823 the church was destroyed by fire. The "whole world, non-Christian as well as non-Catholic contributed funds to rebuild the edifice." The new basilica was consecrated by Pope Pius IX on December 10, 1854.

St. Augustine writes: ". . .We do not build churches to martyrs as to gods, but as memorials to those departed from this life, whose souls live with God." He also provides this thought: "Nor do we erect altars to sacrifice on them to the martyrs, but to their God and our God."

> *TODAY: When we enter a church, we genuflect, make a sign of the cross with holy water and pray that God will cleanse our souls that we may come before Him spotless in His holy house.*

November 19
St. Barlaam (4th century)
Martyr of Antioch

In *The Roman Martyrology* we read: ". . . St. Barlaam, martyr, who though unpolished and ignorant, yet armed with the wisdom of Christ, overcame the tyrant, and by the constancy of his faith subdued fire itself."

An entry for today in *The Lives of the Saints* tells us that Barlaam's profession of faith in the name of Christ provoked the persecutors in the city of Antioch. When he was taken to

221

trial "the judge laughed at his uncouth language and appearance, but was forced to admire his virtue and constancy." Barlaam was tortured and eventually died of martyrdom by fire. He would not give sacrifices to the pagan gods and was forced to hold a handful of incense over flames. The judge thought that when the flames began to sear the flesh, Barlaam would shake the grains from his hand as if "sacrificing to the gods." The saint, however, clenched his hand until he was "consumed by fire."

> *TODAY: In prayer, we say, "May the Lord accept the sacrifices of your hands for the praise and glory of His name, for our good, and the good of all His Church."*

November 20
St. Felix of Valois (1127-1212)
French Confessor, Co-Founder of the Trinitarians

Felix was born of the royal family of Valois and spent the greater part of his life as a hermit, or recluse, "living only to his Creator." When he was 70 years old he was joined by St. John Matha in forming a religious order for the redemption of captives from the warring Moors. The formation of such as the Order of the Most Holy Trinity was uppermost in the mind of Father Matha ever since he said his first Mass. The order was approved by the Holy See in 1198.

Biographers write that St. John worked with the slaves of Spain and the Barbary Coast, while St. Felix worked in Italy and France in promoting the order. While in France, St. Felix founded the convent of St. Maturinus in Paris. While in Rome, St. Felix looked after the French province of the Trinitarians from the motherhouse at Cerfroid.

> *TODAY: Happy are those who help others live together, and happy are those who forgive.*

November 21
Presentation of Mary
Commemorates the Dedication of the Church of St. Mary Near the Temple of Jerusalem (543)

The child Mary was presented to God in the Temple at Jerusalem. The young virgin, accompanied by her parents, Ann and

Joachim, was following a centuries-old Jewish custom. "Mary was in the Temple of the Lord as if she were a dove that dwelt there." We are given special insight into what constitutes holiness in today's Mass honoring our Blessed Mother. The Gospel tells of the woman who cried out to our Lord, "Blessed is the womb that bore you, and the breasts you sucked." His quick reply was, "Blessed rather are those who hear the word of God and keep it" (Luke 11:27-28).

Surely Mary was given a unique and unfathomable privilege in being chosen for the role of Mother of God. Her acceptance is the foundation for all her other titles. But it should be comforting to us to be told by our Lord himself that Mary is blessed primarily because she heard God's Word and kept it. It means that by living out our everyday lives in a spirit of love, generosity and selflessness — trying our best to live out God's Word in action — we will be called "Blessed."

— **William J. Neidhart, C.S.C.**

TODAY: The Blessed Virgin Mary is our chief intercessor with her Son. She is all grace and smiling light. She is not like earthly beauty but bright and pure like the morning star.

November 22
St. Cecilia (2nd or 3rd century)
Roman Virgin, Martyr, Patron of Musicians, Singers, Organ Builders, Poets

All that we know officially of St. Cecilia is that she was a martyr under the Roman Emperor Alexander Severus around 230. Yet, legends of her have enriched and instructed Christendom down through the ages. She is considered the patron of musicians because, legend says, her husband happened in upon her on their wedding night while she was at prayer and he found her prayers accompanied by the singing of angels.

According to the legend, this led to the conversion of her husband, his brother also, their arrest and the conversion of the jailer, and finally martyrdom. If we had enough faith, our way of life would prove a great contribution to the lives of others, no matter how insignificant it might seem to us. Bless us in this, Jesus.

— Gary Lauenstein, C.SS.R.

TODAY: "O sing to the Lord a new song, for he has done marvelous things!" (Psalm 98:1).

November 23
St. Clement I (c. 97)
Roman Martyr, 4th Pope of the Church (88-97)

At the Propers for the Saints at Mass today, we pray: "All-powerful and ever-loving God,/ we praise your power and glory/ revealed to us in the lives of all Your saints./ Give us joy on this feast of St. Clement,/ the priest and martyr/ who bore witness with his blood to the love he proclaimed/ and the gospel he preached./ We ask this through our Lord Jesus Christ, Your Son, who lives and reigns with you and the Holy spirit, one God, for ever and ever."

St. Clement was a Roman, baptized by St. Peter, and was martyred for the faith in Crimea by Emperor Trajan.

TODAY: Pope Clement I teaches us that the lowliest (persons) in the Church may be the greatest (persons) before God, if they are more faithful in the practice of their duties.

November 23
St. Columban (545-615)
Irish Monk, Scholar; Founded Monasteries in England and Brittany; Patron of Ireland

Ireland has always been a prolific missionary-sending country. One of its earliest missionaries was St. Columban, whose feast may also be observed today.

St. Columban was born about 545, entered a monastery and taught for about 30 years before he received permission to do missionary work on the continent of Europe. He settled in Burgundy, where he founded three monasteries; the most famous was Luxeuil. From these centers his followers spread all over Europe. Columban was expelled from the kingdom because of opposition to his Celtic usages and his censure of the king for immoral practices. Columban eventually went to Italy. There he founded the famous monastery of Bobbio, which became a center of culture and learning. Columban died there in 615, leaving behind a monastic rule, letters and poetry.

— Rose M. Avato

TODAY: Let us pray. Lord, teach me self-control to bear the little inconveniences and nuisances, that I may bear my cross with patience.

November 24
St. Chrysogonus (c. 304)
Roman Official, Martyr

"In union with the whole Church we honor this day. . ." are among the beginning words in Eucharistic Prayer I. Among the saints so honored is Chrysogonus. Although this saint is invoked in daily Mass, he is one of the "lesser knowns," as biographical details are sketchy.

He was a Roman official, and because of his faith was imprisoned by the Emperor Diocletian. He was beheaded at Aquileia, Italy, and his body was thrown into the sea. The titular Church of St. Chrysogonus in Rome's Trastevere quarter was mentioned in the year 499.

TODAY: Lord, accept the gifts we offer in memory of the martyr Chrysogonus. May they be pleasing to You as was the shedding of his blood for the Faith. Grant this through Christ, our Lord.

November 25
St. Catherine of Alexandria (c. 310)
Virgin, Martyr, Patron of Maidens, Women Students, Philosophers, Preachers, Millers and Wheelrights

The first entry in *The Roman Martyrology* for today reads: "The birthday of St. Catherine, virgin and martyr, under the Emperor Maximus. For the confession of the Christian faith, she was cast into prison at Alexandria, and afterward endured a long scourging with whips garnished with metal, and finally ended her martyrdom by being decapitated. Her body was miraculously conveyed by angels to Mount Sinai. . . ."

Catherine is marked as one of the 14 Holy Helpers. She is said to have appeared with our Lady to St. Dominic. The Dominicans claim her as their protector. Her voice is reportedly one of those "heavenly voices" heard by St. Joan of Arc in the 1400s.

TODAY: *The real Christ-follower has the wisdom of Christ and not the philosophy of expediency in the world.*

November 26
St. Leonard of Port Maurice (1676-1751)
Italian Franciscan, Spiritual Writer,
Patron of Parish Missions

This aging missionary had difficulty in offering his daily Mass. He practiced the axiom that "a single Mass is worth more than all the wealth in the world." St. Leonard also mentioned in his book *Resolutions*: "Holy Mass is the most precious thing we have on earth." He also wrote: "The choir is the place of 'my delight.'" His *Resolutions* contained many spiritual reflections, lectures, sermons and devotional tracts. The popular Franciscan preacher called the Way of the Cross his "devotional weapon." He preached on the Sacred Heart of Jesus, and also the Immaculate Conception. He sought this Marian declaration as "an artist of faith."

Today's patron was baptized Paul Jerome Casanova in the parish church at Porto Maurizio. When he entered the Franciscans of the Strict Observance he took the name of Leonard in gratitude to Leonard Ponzetti, a relative who took him in as a youth when he was abandoned by an uncle.

TODAY: *In the words of St. Leonard, we pray, "If you deliver one soul from purgatory you can say with confidence, 'Heaven is mine.'"*

November 27
St. Secundinus (c. 375-447)
Irish Bishop of Dunslaughlin, Auxiliary of Armagh

Today's saint is also known as Sechnall, or Seachnall. He was a disciple of St. Patrick, joining the Irish missionaries following his ordination in Gaul. A reference study of the saints reveals the fact that "his great claim to remembrance is as a hymn-writer." He wrote *Audites, omnes, amantes Deum,* in honor of St. Patrick. This is the earliest known Latin hymn written in Ireland. He was also the composer of *Sancti, Venite, Christi Corpus Sumite,* a beautiful hymn often referred to as "the hymn when the priests communicate."

> TODAY: *With the psalmist, we say:* "O *sing to the Lord a new song; sing to the Lord, all the earth!" (Psalm 96:1.)*

November 28
St. Catherine Labouré (1806-1876)
French Mystic, Daughter of Charity of St. Vincent de Paul; Inaugurated Devotion to the Miraculous Medal

Father Joseph I. Dirwin, a Vincentian priest, in his biography of St. Catherine Labouré, writes: "The Miraculous Medal is known and worn throughout the world. . . . Less well known, however, is the saint to whom the Medal was manifested in 1830, when she was a novice in the Sisters of Charity of St. Vincent de Paul." The convent was located in the Rue du Bac in Paris. Like other saints of the 19th century, Catherine Labouré led a life of complete anonymity. At her canonization in 1947, Pope Pius XII was heard to say, "Hers is one of heaven's best kept secrets."

Father Dirvin writes: "Not until a few months before her death — and then only because of extreme urgency — did Catherine reveal to her superior that she was the mysterious Sister to whom the Blessed Virgin had manifested the design of the Miraculous Medal 46 years before. For all those long years she had preserved her wonderful secret so well that not even the other Sisters in the Community knew that quiet, self-effacing Sister Catherine was the one to whom Mary Immaculate had appeared."

> TODAY: *Wear the Miraculous Medal of the Immaculate Heart, and pray:* "O *Mary, conceived without sin, pray for us who have recourse to thee."*

November 29
St. Saturninus (c. 257)
Martyr, First Bishop of Toulouse

Also known as Sernin, the missionary was sent from Rome by Pope Fabian in 250 to preach the Faith in Gaul. He became the first Bishop of Toulouse, and he converted many idolators through his preaching and miracles. He was seized by a pagan priest at a temple where they wanted Saturninus to sacrifice to the "offended" deities. The bishop refused, saying, "I worship only one God, and to Him I am ready to offer a sacrifice of praise. Your gods are evil and are more pleased with the sacrifice of your souls than with those of your bullocks. How can I fear them who, as you acknowledge, tremble before a Christian?"

This enraged the pagans, who tied the bishop's feet to a bull, and the animal was driven from the temple, dragging the body through the streets until the bishop was dead.

> *TODAY: God our Father, source of all holiness, the work of Your hands is manifest in Your saints; the beauty of Your truth is reflected in their Faith.*

November 30
St. Andrew (c. 70)
First Apostle, Fisherman, Martyr, Patron of Fishermen

"Come and see," Jesus said to the two disciples of John the Baptist who were following Him. They were curious about where Jesus stayed, especially after they heard John the Baptist refer to Him as the "Lamb of God." One of the disciples was Andrew. The first thing Andrew did was to search out his brother Simon Peter and tell him, "We have found the Messiah" (John 1:35-41).

Andrew heeded the call to follow Jesus and had already become a missionary. According to tradition, he preached the Gospel in northern Greece, Epirus and Scythia. His martyrdom is believed to have occurred about 70 at Patras. Andrew is represented in art with an X-shaped cross, called St. Andrew's cross, believed to have been the instrument of his martyrdom. He is also the patron of Russia and Scotland.

— Rose M. Avato

TODAY: Andrew's journey of faith and witness began with an invitation from Jesus to "come and see." This invitation is for all of us.

DECEMBER

December 1
St. Eligius (c. 590-660)
Frankish Official, Bishop of Noyon and Tournai

The name of Eligius was popularized in the '80s through a TV series entitled "St. Elsewhere." It was about a hospital by the name of St. Eligius and was centered in Boston. One would think that the hospital was named after some saintly doctor, medic, nurse or hospitaler. Not so, write the biographers. St. Eligius is rather the patron of goldsmiths, jewelers, metalsmiths and metalworkers.

King Clotaire I of Paris named Eligius (or Eloi) master of the mint. He was highly favored by the king and his son Dagobert, who appointed Eligius his chief counselor in 629. During this time the saint was noted for his generosity, charity and ransoming of slaves. He also built churches and hospices, founded a monastery at Solignac, and converted a house in Paris (a gift from Dagobert) into a convent. He named St. Aurea as spiritual director of the community. Eligius was named Bishop of Noyon and Tournai in 640. He brought the Gospel to Flanders and converted many at Antwerp and Ghent. He was acclaimed as one of France's most popular saints.

TODAY: Alleluia! The Spirit of the Lord is upon me; He sent me to bring the Good News to the poor.

December 2
St. Vivian (4th century)
Roman Virgin, Martyr, Also Known as Bibiana

A persecution of cyclonic proportions burst over the infant Church. But how sturdy was that babe! It would grow up to supplant the mighty pagan empire of Rome. The Church found refuge in the catacombs. Only after three centuries of indestructible faith, heroic patience and persistent prayer could it come forth into daylight.

St. Vivian's father, mother and sister were slain; her family wealth sequestered. Flattering marriages, tempting pleasures and a hundred other seductive devices, plus starvation and even scourging, could not lure or drive her to adore pagan gods. She was loyal to the teachings of her divinely noble parents. May modern parents learn the lesson. Christ was Vivian's Lover. That love blinded her to all other blandishments and kept her supremely happy. — **Joseph A. Vaughan, S.J.**

TODAY: O Jesus, Lover of mankind, take us all into Your Arms, especially the youth of this 20th century.

December 3
St. Francis Xavier (1506-1552)
Spanish Jesuit, Missionary to the Far East,
Patron of the East Indies, Also Japan

While studying in Paris, St. Francis Xavier met Ignatius Loyola, who convinced him that he should dedicate himself to God. With five others, he took vows in 1534 which not only included the customary ones of poverty and chastity but also a vow to help the Holy Father in propagating the Faith.

Francis was ordained in 1537 and three years later went to India, where he baptized 10,000 persons a month and established three colleges. In 1549 he sailed to Japan. After a year and a half he had to return to India to settle some difficulties. He again departed for China but died on Sancian (Shangchwan) Island in 1552, within sight of the land he had hoped to convert. He is a patron saint of the foreign missions, and is hailed as "Apostle of the Indies," and "Apostle of Japan."
— **John M. Martin, M.M.**

TODAY: It is well to ask ourselves if we are making a regular sacrifice of our prayers and money to help the work which was so close to the heart of this saint.

December 4
St. John Damascene (c. 675-749)
Syrian Monk, Writer, Preacher, Doctor of the Church,
Also Called the "Golden Speaker"

St. John Damascene was born in Damascus of a well-respected and influential Christian family. He worked as a revenue officer

231

and counselor in the Moslem court. When the Arab leader Caliph Abdul Melek, however, turned against the Christians with bitter persecution, John resigned his office and moved near Jerusalem, where he became a monk. He devoted his life to making known the thought of Christians as it had developed in their writings for seven centuries, and to preaching. John Damascene is noted for his three-part study *Fountain of Wisdom*, containing a study of heresies and Christian philosophy. He also wrote Marian homilies and biblical commentaries.

— Gary Lauenstein, C.SS.R.

TODAY: Lord Jesus, You wish that all men of every nation should have the joy of praising God as their Father. Make this our first concern.

December 4
St. Barbara (4th century)
Virgin, Martyr; Patron of Architects, Artillerymen, Builders, Dying, Fire Prevention, Gunners, Miners, Prisoners, Stonemasons

St. Barbara, like St. Vivian, chose Christ for her beloved. Like true lovers on earth, she ignored all others. But Christ is infinite. His love extends to all, and He loved St. Barbara just as He loved St. Vivian. Barbara, not blessed in childhood like Vivian, had a pagan father, a man determined to stifle her divine love. Again, promises of flattering marriage, threats, physical violence and finally death could not separate her from her true Lover.

Centuries later, St. Stanislaus Kostka, a 16-year-old Polish lad, hiking from Warsaw to Rome, set on becoming a Jesuit, was captured by his brother and locked in a room without his clothes. The next morning he lay in bed weeping. He could not receive Holy Communion. Suddenly St. Barbara appeared carrying the sacred ciborium to give him Holy Communion. For centuries she has been the patron of Communion for the sick.

— Joseph A. Vaughan, S.J.

TODAY: Heavenly patron St. Barbara, pray for those who will die as a result of arson, fires and explosions.

December 5
St. John Almond (1577-1612)
English Priest, Martyr of Tyburn

Biographers called him a "Lancashire man, born at Allerton, near Liverpool, England." John Almond was ordained a priest in 1598. He was a courageous man and "ready to suffer for Christ who had suffered for him." The priest was arrested for his beliefs and imprisoned in 1608. Four years later he was arrested again for treason after he had refused to take an Oath of Supremacy to King James I.

Father John did swear: "I do bear in my heart and soul so much allegiance to King James (whom I pray God to bless now and evermore) as he, as any Christian king, could expect by the law of nature, the law of God, or the positive law of the true Church, be it which it will, ours or yours." This "oath" was unacceptable to the court, and Father John was taken to Newgate prison. There he was tried for high treason "as a priest," and sentenced to death. His final act at the gallows was the emptying of his pockets and scattering silver coins among the gallery. St. John Almond was canonized by Pope Paul VI in 1970.

TODAY: Alleluia! I am the servant of the Lord; may His will for me be done.

December 6
St. Nicholas (4th century)
Bishop, Patron of Greece, Russia; Also Bakers, Brides, Children, Coopers, Merchants, Pawnbrokers, Travelers

St. Nicholas of Myra in Lycia, southern Asia, was born in the fourth century. In 1807 his body was moved to Bari in southern Italy. There are many legends about this saint, who is said to be represented in Christian art more times than any other saint except the Virgin Mary.

There are several legends about him which have come down through the centuries. The best known tells about three children who were murdered and put in salt brine. He brought them back to life. He was supposed to provide, secretly, dowries for poor girls who could not afford to get married. From these two tales came the origin of the present-day Santa Claus, origi-

nated by Dutch Protestants who moved to Christmas the custom of giving children gifts. They changed the saint's name to
Santa Claus.

Parents should pray to St. Nicholas to bestow graces upon
their children as a preparation for the birthday of the Christ
Child.   — John M. Martin, M.M.

*TODAY: St. Nicholas, glorious confessor of Christ, as-
sist me in thy loving kindness.*

December 7
St. Ambrose (340-397)
*Bishop, Father and Doctor of the Church;
Patron of Candlemakers, Learning*

By fourth-century standards, St. Ambrose lived a long life,
from 340 until April 4, 397. On December 7, 374, he was ordained as Bishop of Milan, so there is a special reason for celebrating his feast on this day.

Ambrose also has both titles of Father and Doctor of the
Church. Many of his writings, especially his sermons, have
been preserved and are very effective. In writing to a new bishop, he said, "The Church of the Lord is built upon the rock of
the Apostles among so many dangers in the world; it therefore
remains unmoved." Among his most famous converts was St.
Augustine. That was quite a treasure to leave to the Church. After St. Paul, perhaps the three most brilliant men that God ever
gave the Church were Augustine, Bernard and Thomas
Aquinas.   — Msgr. Charles Dollen

*TODAY: We may not possess the brilliant intelligence
of St. Ambrose, but we surely can strive to imitate his
eagerness for truth.*

December 8
Immaculate Conception
*Mary Born Without Original Sin; Dogma of Immaculate
Conception Proclaimed by Pope Piux IX in 1854;
Patron of Brazil, Corsica, Portugal, United States*

On this glorious feast of Mary we reflect on Mary's sin-
lessness and obedience. We hear her beautiful response to the

angel: "Behold, I am the handmaid of the Lord; let it be to me according to your word." Not knowing exactly what God wanted of her as His Mother, she willingly said yes to all. Mary as our Mother and Mother of the Church gives us the perfect example of obedience.

Mary, from her earliest years serving in the Temple, responded completely and totally to the call of God. Mary submitted to what she did not fully understand, for God's love and goodness in her radiated beyond her understanding. The angel did not completely answer her question but addressed her faith in God's power and goodness. Mary is a truly loving mother who watches over all her children on earth, caring for them and interceding to her Son for their needs. Let us reactivate today our personal devotion to her.

— Sister Carol Ann Kenz, C.S.J.

TODAY: Pray for us, O holy Mother of God, that we may be made worthy of the promises of Christ.

December 9
Seven Martyrs of Samosata (c. 311)
Died by Crucifixion

We know these martyrs by their names. There were Hipparchus and Philotheus, magistrates in the ancient Syrian city of Samosata. They were joined in martyrdom by these younger friends whom they had converted: James, Paragrus, Abibus, Romanus and Lollianus.

During a festival in the city, Emperor Maximinus was informed that the local magistrates had not attended the affair which included the sacrificing to pagan gods. In fact, Hipparchus and Philotheus had not taken part in the pagan festival for three years. The seven were arrested at the same time and put in prison, where they were beaten and tortured for several months. Their Faith withstood all physical punishment and so the emperor ordered seven crosses to be erected near the city gates. The battered saints were lashed to the crosses and left to die.

TODAY: During Advent we are reminded of the prayer, "Those who follow You, Lord, will have the light of life."

December 10
St. Melchiades (d. 314)
African Pope, Martyr

Pope Melchiades, who was called by St. Augustine an excellent man, a true son of peace, and a true Father of Christians, suffered severe persecution under Maximinian. He survived, however, to see Constantine establish toleration of Christianity in 313, and died peacefully on this day in 314. In a broad sense he was a martyr for the Faith. He was a native of Africa. At first his remains were in the catacombs of St. Callixtus; now they repose in the Church of St. Sylvester *in capite* in Rome. There are also some of his relics in the church of St. Praxedes.

The champions of Christ suffered in every way and labored for peace. The peace of the Church is the fruit of the sacrifices of the faithful and of their pastors.

— Msgr. Thomas J. Tobin

TODAY: We should ask this patron to obtain for us the grace to desire the greater glory of God, even though it may cost us suffering and humiliation.

December 11
St. Damasus I (d. 384)
Pope; Commissioned St. Jerome to Work on Bible Translation; Developed the Roman Liturgy

Born in Spain at the beginning of the fourth century, Damasus grew up in Rome, where he was ordained to the priesthood. In 366 he became the Pope and ruled the Church until 384.

The years of his reign were troubled, as he had to fight heresies and schisms. The Church had only recently survived the age of the catacombs, and along with rapid growth, there was a great deal of theological speculation and dissension. Pope Damasus I was noteworthy for his devotion to the martyrs. He restored many of their tombs and built churches in their honor. The martyrs are the great heroes of the Church, and we should venerate them with great love. They prove how powerful the grace of God is at work in our souls.   — Msgr. Charles Dollen

TODAY: It is our task to bring the Good News to all men, to spread the joy of Christian love.

December 12
St. Jane Frances de Chantal (1572-1641)
French Widow; Founded Order of Visitation

It is a common boast of circuses and newspapers that "there is something for everyone." The same could be said of the lists of the saints which the Church offers us for imitation.

Jane Frances Fremyot was just short of 40, a widow for 10 years and the mother of four children born during eight years of happy married life, when she founded an Order of nuns. But her holiness began long before she entered the convent. As the Baroness de Chantal, she was a devoted mother, and she gave generously of her time and means to help the unfortunate.

There is the tendency to think of the saints as special creatures in distant times and places. The fact is, though, that they are men and women exactly like ourselves, with the same problems, the same temptations, the same graces. There is no age, no circumstance of life in which any of us find ourselves that cannot be matched among those who have achieved great holiness in the sight of God. To put it simply — why not I? why not you?
— **Most Rev. Thomas K. Gorman**

> *TODAY: Reflect on the words of St. Jane Frances: "Believe me, God will be your guide in all things if you keep yourself humble and lowly in His presence, supporting your neighbor with the utmost gentleness. This is the chief, the great point. . . ."*

December 12
Our Lady of Guadalupe (1531)
Four Apparitions of the Blessed Virgin in Mexico;
Patron of Latin America, "Mother of the Americas"

In early December, 1531, Juan Diego, a poor simple Indian only one generation removed from paganism, was traveling the barren plains on a three-day hike to Mass in Mexico City. Suddenly at Tepeyac the Blessed Mother appeared to him and asked that a shrine be built on the spot in her honor. Later, to convince the skeptical bishop, she had Juan gather roses, rare in the wintertime, into his rough blanket. When the bishop opened the blanket, all saw the miraculous image of Mary, the same image that still hangs in the great Basilica of Guadalupe near Mexico City.

Mary was named patron of all Spanish America, including vast sections of our own southwest. To Juan Diego she was his personal patron, and the poor humble Indian, enriched by the attention of Mary, must have pondered: Why does she choose me, why does she love me?

— Joseph A. Vaughan, S.J.

TODAY: Reflect on the miraculous painting of Our Lady. That image still hangs with motherly serenity in the beautiful new Basilica of Guadalupe in Mexico City. Pray in thanksgiving to Our Lady, patron of the Americas.

December 13
St. Lucy (d. 304)
Virgin, Martyr, Patron of Syracuse, Sicily;
Patron of Those with Eye Troubles

St. Lucy, a virgin and martyr, died about 304, betrayed by a pagan whom she refused to marry. She is invoked against blindness, probably because her name is similar to the Latin *lucis* meaning "of light." An attempt to set her on fire failed and she was slain by a sword. On her feast we ask for light that we may know God's way. We also ask for guidance should we become physically blind, as well as for protection from a spiritual loss of vision. Today we are tempted on all sides by the slogans of the materialists, who say: "Be practical; don't be fooled by the promise of 'pie in the sky.' Get down to earth; take advantage of today, here and now. You won't live forever."

St. Lucy should be invoked to help us keep our eyes on the important goals of life so that we may not be distracted by evil temptations. She can guide us on the road to eternal success.

— John M. Martin, M.M.

TODAY: St. Lucy, pray that my soul may always be brilliant with grace. That God may always love me!

December 14
St. John of the Cross (1542-1591)
Spanish Theologian; Founded Discalced Carmelites;
Named Doctor of Mystical Theology by Pope Pius XI

Born in Spain, St. John of the Cross worked with St. Teresa of Avila reforming the Carmelite priests and sisters. Their new rule included total abstinence from meat and also long fasts and a contemplative life. His consuming desire to suffer for Christ was fulfilled when the unreformed Carmelites carried him off and imprisoned him for nine months as a disobedient monk. However, he made a rope by shredding a blanket, and escaped.

While imprisoned he wrote, among other treatises, *The Dark Night of the Soul*, which became a classic. He died in 1591 and was canonized in 1726. He was declared a Doctor of the Church in 1926, for his teachings are as timely today as they were in the 1500s. St. John had a great love of the Cross, for he understood the value of suffering as taught by his Master, who sanctified suffering as a means of real success in the things that count.

— **John M. Martin, M.M.**

TODAY: As we travel the road to perfection, let us beg St. John of the Cross to intercede for us that we may possess a true love of the Lord.

December 15
St. Mary di Rosa (1813-1855)
Italian Virgin, Founded Handmaids of Charity of Brescia

Mary di Rosa, a signorina of Brescian society, later became Mother Maria Crocifissa. In 1840 she was named the first superior of a new religious society of women dedicated to caring for the sick.

As a teenager, she was a school dropout and remained at home to tend house for her widowed father. In her spare time she would visit with girls who worked in her father's textile mill. By the time she was 23 she was already supervising hospital wards, ministering to cholera victims during the epidemic of 1836. Maria's compassion was spent on the abandoned girls of the streets, and she built a house for them. She also started a school for the deaf and mute handicapped. Her society is known as the Handmaids of Charity. These religious women and nurses cared for wounded soldiers on the battlefields of northern Italy during the fighting of 1849. St. Mary di Rosa was canonized by Pope Pius XII in 1954.

> *TODAY: During Advent we especially pray, "Blessed is every one who fears the Lord, who walks in His ways!" (Psalm 128:1).*

December 16
St. Adelaide (931-999)
Widow, Empress of Germany

It is unusual that a political treaty between Rudolph II of Upper Burgundy and Hugh of Provence would be a warrant of marriage for a lass who was only two years old at that time. Such was the case of St. Adelaide, who fulfilled that contract at 16 when she married King Lothaire of Italy. When her husband died in 950, Adelaide was imprisoned. A year later she was freed by King Otto of Germany, and later married him. Pope Agapitus II was responsible for the German invasion of Italy to stop the troubles in Italy's north sector. Otto the Great was crowned emperor at Rome in 962. He died in 973 and was succeeded by their son Otto II. The Queen mother also saw the death of her son and the succession of a grandson, Otto III, on the throne. Adelaide was 60 years old when she returned as regent of the court. She founded monasteries, restored convents and worked for the conversion of the Slavic people. She died at a monastery which she had founded along the Rhine River near Strasburg.

> *TODAY: In Scripture we read: "The Lord honored the father above the children, and he confirmed the right of the mother over her sons" (Sirach 3:2).*

December 17
St. Olympias (c. 361-408)
Widow, Deaconess in Asia Minor

St. Gregory Nazianzen called St. Olympias "the glory of widows in the Eastern Church." Olympias was born of a wealthy family in Constantinople. She had inherited a vast fortune and was considered attractive in person and character. She married Nebridius, a prefect of Constantinople and treasurer of Emperor Theodosius the Great. She was widowed soon after and refused any offers of remarriage.

When St. John Chrysostom succeeded Nectarius as Patriarch of Constantinople in 398, he took St. Olympias and her disciples under his protection. "Her benefactions were spread to all parts of the empire." She built a hospital and orphanages, and also housed and fed the expelled monks of Nutria. Her listing of friends reads like a litany of saints; and the writer Palladius of Helenopolis referred to her as "a wonderful woman — like a precious vase filled with the Holy Spirit." When Chrysostom was banished in 404, Olympias too shared in the persecution that followed. She died at Nicomedia in 408.

> TODAY: St. John Chrysostom writes to Olympias: "I cannot cease to call you blessed. . . . The charity which has made you throw a veil over the malice of your persecutors has won a glory and reward which hereafter will make all your sufferings seem light and passing in the presence of eternal joy."

December 18
St. Flannan (7th century)
Irish, First Bishop of Killaloe

Flannan was the son of Turlough, a chieftain of Thomond. He was educated by a monk who taught him not only letters, but also "to plow, sow, reap, grind, winnow and bake for the monks." He was consecrated a bishop by Pope John IV, at Rome, during the saint's pilgrimage there. He returned to Killaloe as its first bishop. In *The Lives of the Saints* we learn that "the exhortations and teaching of Bishop Flannan caused his father Turlough to become a monk under St. Colman at Lismore."

> TODAY: During Advent we pray, "Rejoice in the Lord always; again I will say, Rejoice. . . . The Lord is at hand" (Philippians 4:4-5).

241

December 19
St. Anastasius I (d. 401)
Roman, 39th Pope (399-401)

Pope Anastasius I succeeded Pope Siricius as Supreme Pontiff of the Church upon election on November 27, 399. During his short pontificate, he was remembered for his condemnation of the philosophy of Origen, "which had become of importance in the West owing to the controversy between St. Jerome and Rufinus." He urged African Christians to continue their opposition to the Donatist heresy. St. Jerome, in his writings, said of him: "St. Anastasius was a man of most extreme poverty and apostolic solicitude. . . ." Other friends and advisors to the Pontiff were St. Paulinus of Nola and St. Augustine. Some disciplinary and liturgical provisions are attributed to him by the *Liber Pontificalis.*

> *TODAY: During Advent we pray, "Father in heaven, the day draws near when the glory of Your Son will make radiant the night of the waiting world."*

December 20
St. Dominic of Silos (1000-1073)
*Spanish Benedictine, Abbot of San
Sebastian; Patron of Shepherds*

As a boy he was a shepherd caring for his father's sheep in the foothills of the Cantabrian Mountains at Canas, Spain. Dominic became a Benedictine monk and later was the prior of the monastery of San Millan de Cogolla. The monks were driven from the monastery when it was claimed by the throne to be on sovereign property. Dominic was then named abbot of the monastery of St. Sebastian at Silos, and made it one of Spain's most famous religious communities. Its library was one of the greatest in the country. A biographer noted that "many miracles were recorded of St. Dominic in the course of his work, and it was said that there were no diseases known to man which had not been cured by his prayers." St. Dominic of Silos is especially honored by Dominicans of the Order of Preachers.

> *TODAY: During Advent we pray, "Prepare the way of the Lord, make straight his paths . . . and all flesh shall see the salvation of God" (Luke 3:4-6).*

December 21
St. Peter Canisius (1521-1597)
Dutch Jesuit, Doctor of the Church,
Patron of Germany

Called "the hammer of heretics," Peter Canisius was born in Holland and worked in Germany in post-Reformation times. As a Jesuit priest he was a learned adversary of Reformation theology.

His most famous work was a *Catechism* which formed the basis of Catholic apologetics for centuries. He realized that basic religious education is the starting point for all spiritual growth. He impressed me as a real "no nonsense" saint. His devotion to the Catholic Church was deep and all-pervasive, and his loyalty to the Pope almost made him a legend in his own time. St. Peter Canisius died at Fribourg, Switzerland, in 1597. He was canonized and proclaimed a Doctor of the Church by Pope Pius XI in 1925. — **Msgr. Charles Dollen**

TODAY: St. Peter Canisius, guide me in the use of my material blessings.

December 22
SS. Chaeremon, Ischyrion and Others (d. 250)
Egyptian Martyrs

Today's entry in *The Roman Martyrology* reads, "In Egypt, St. Chaeremon, Bishop of Nilopolis, and many others martyred. Some of them fled while the persecution of Decius was raging and, wandering in different directions, were killed by wild beasts; others perished by famine, cold and sickness; others again were murdered by barbarians and robbers, and all were crowned with a glorious martyrdom."

St. Dionysius of Alexandria mentions that Ischyrion was procurator for a magistrate in Alexandria. These saints knew how to deal with matters of the world and still remain servants of God alone.

TODAY: During Advent we pray: "Lord God, may we, Your people, who look forward to the birthday of Christ, experience the joy of salvation and celebrate the feast with love and thanksgiving."

243

December 23
St. John Kanty (1395-1473)
Polish Priest, Theologian, Patron of Poland and Lithuania

John Cantius was named after his birthplace, the city of Kanti in Poland. His home was near Oswiecin, known to readers of today as Auschwitz, site of a Nazi concentration camp during World War II.

John studied at the University of Cracow and received his degrees there. After he was ordained to the priesthood he became a lecturer at the school. We read that "John's success as a preacher and teacher raised up envy against him, and his rivals managed to get him removed and sent as a parish priest to Olkusz." He later returned to the university as a professor of Sacred Scripture, a chair he occupied until his death on Christmas Eve in 1473, at the age of 78.

> *TODAY: This venerable theologian taught his pupils: "Fight all false opinions, but let your weapons be patience, sweetness and love. Roughness is bad for your own soul and spoils the best cause."*

December 24
SS. Tharsilla and Emiliana (c. 550)
Roman Virgins, Ascetics

Today's saints were aunts of Pope Gregory the Great. Tharsilla, the eldest, her sisters Emiliana and Gordiana lived in the home of Gordian — father of Gregory the Great. The sisters Tharsilla and Emiliana lived an ascetic life of prayer and spirituality. The youngest sister joined them in prayer but later married.

St. Gregory tells us that Tharsilla was visited one night by a vision of her great-grandfather, Pope St. Felix III, who showed a place prepared for her in heaven and said, "Come; I will receive you into the habitation of light." She died on the vigil of Christmas. Emiliana also received a heavenly call from her sister and joined her in death several days later.

> *TODAY: Lord, in the Sacrament of the Eucharist we receive the promise of salvation; as Christmas draws*

near, make us grow in faith and love to celebrate the coming of Christ our Savior, who is Lord for ever and ever. Amen.

December 25
Christmas (1st century)
Commemorates the Birth of Our Lord Jesus Christ

Christ the Savior is born! Today we must rejoice in His presence by approaching Christ through our Christmas Mass and Communion. The Eucharist is the sacramental sign of Christ's total gift of himself to each one of us. Because He loves us so, He came down to us one silent, starry night in Bethlehem. The same love keeps Him with us, dwelling in our midst through the Eucharist.

Out of love springs life. The Eucharist is the pledge of life presently vibrating within the Christian community, and stretching through time until that moment when Christ will come again to make all things new.

Little wonder, then, that today we reach out to one another in more kindness and tolerance. We suddenly sense that to be happy together we must be one with one another. Our Christmas Communion, the consummation of our share in the Sacrifice, is an act of Faith in the life, love and wholeness that only Christ can bring.

— Msgr. Francis J. Tournier

TODAY: "This day you shall know — that the Lord will come, and save us: and in the morning you shall see His glory" (Vigil of Christmas).

December 26
St. Stephen (d. 33)
First Christian Martyr, First of the Seven Deacons; Patron of Bricklayers, Also of Stonemasons

An account of the death of St. Stephen, the first of the martyrs, is found in the Acts of the Apostles (7:55-60). Speaking before the Sanhedrin, Stephen recalled the guidance of God through Israel's history, as well as Israel's idolatry and disobedience. He also told them: "You stiff-necked people . . . you al-

245

ways resist the Holy Spirit. As your fathers did, so do you"(7:51).

The speech angered the crowd, and they dragged him out of the city and stoned him to death. One of the witnesses to his death was Saul, the future Apostle Paul. Stephen died as Jesus did: falsely accused, brought to unjust condemnation because he spoke the truth fearlessly. He died with his eyes trustfully fixed on God, and with a prayer of forgiveness on his lips. Whether we die as quietly as Joseph or as violently as Stephen, the happy death we pray for embraces the spirit of Stephen's death: courage, total trust and forgiving love.

— Thomas M. Brew, S.J.

TODAY: As Stephen faced a shower of deadly missiles, he prayed, "Lord Jesus, receive my spirit" — and kneeling among the stones, he asked God to forgive them: "Lord, do not hold this sin against them."

December 27
St. John the Evangelist (d. c. 100)
Apostle, Evangelist, Called "Beloved Disciple";
Author of Fourth Gospel, Three Epistles and Book
of Revelation; Patron of Asia Minor

St. John the Evangelist is called "the disciple whom Jesus loved." That love is shown by the special honors that Our Lord conferred upon him. He prepared the Last Supper; he leaned on the breast of the Master as they reclined at table, and John stood beneath the cross at Calvary. The Scripture says, "When Jesus saw his mother, and the disciple whom he loved standing near, he said to his mother, 'Woman, behold your son!' Then he said to the disciple, 'Behold, your mother.' And from that hour the disciple took her to his own home (John 19:26-27)." He also was at the tomb on Easter morning with Peter. He lived to be 94, far more years than any of the other Apostles.

We ought to pray to St. John for that great but simple love which he had for his Master and ask him to help us to increase our love for Mary, who was his mother by divine appointment.

— John M. Martin, M.M.

TODAY: Reflect on the words from the Gospel of John

(21:24): "This is the disciple who is bearing witness to these things, and who has written these things, and we know that his testimony is true."

December 28
Holy Innocents (1st century)
Commemorates Infant Boys Slain by Herod's Soldiers While Seeking to Kill the Infant Jesus; Feast Observed Since 5th Century; Patrons of Foundlings

The death of a child has its own quality of sadness, and if it is accomplished by cruel and violent means, it takes on the character of a needless tragedy, a wanton outrage, that rouses our deepest indignation.

So must we think of the slaughter of the innocent babies by command of Herod. Hardly anything could reveal so clearly the kind of monster that he was. His trick of making sure that he would do away with the Infant Jesus, the newborn King, by killing all the children, is a further refinement of degradation.

But our reflection on this bloody event must not end here. There are two ways to heaven, the way of innocence and the way of repentance. There can be no question as to which is the quicker and surer way. The sorrow that is supported by faith and hope cannot fail to bring consolation, even to the mothers of the Holy Innocents.

— **Most Rev. Leo A. Pursley**

TODAY: Make this our prayer: "Let the children come to me [Jesus], and do not hinder them; for to such belongs the kingdom of God" (Luke 18:16).

December 29
St. Thomas Becket (1118-1170)
English Martyr, Archbishop of Canterbury, Chancellor Under King Henry II

Thomas Becket is honored by the Church today and is given us as a model. He heard the Word of the Lord and followed what he heard willingly to attest to his love for God by surrendering his life. We hear the exact same teachings of Jesus in St. John's letter that Thomas Becket heard and pondered. Our martyrdom will probably be bloodless, but the call "to give all" is still ours. It is exciting to think that Jesus himself prayed over the same psalms and prophetic words of Jeremiah, Ezekiel and Isaiah. Let us ask for His spirit of quiet meditation and the grace to be open to hearing how God's Word is to be applied in our lives this moment.

Tradition tells us that St. John was asked why he so frequently wrote about the new commandment: "Love as God loves." His answer was that everything else we need to know and do is contained in it.

— Sister Theresa Molphy, C.S.J.

TODAY: Remember these lines — "Iron chains are not strong enough to bind us to duty, only the slender threads of love." Those slender threads of love, rather than iron nails, bound Christ to the Cross. Those same slender threads bound St. Thomas Becket to his God.

December 30
St. Anysia (c. 304)
Martyr of Thessalonica

Today's saint was a Christian girl living in Thessalonica. She received a wealthy estate left to her by deceased parents. She used much of the money taking care of the poor and needy members of the community.

During the reign of Maximian Galerius, all Christians secretly gathered for worship, as they were subject to punishment and death by civil authorities. Anysia was on her way to an "assembly of the faithful," when she was stopped by one of the emperor's guards. She immediately made the sign of the cross on her forehead. She professed her faith in Christ. The angry guard tore the veil off her face and in a struggle stabbed her with his sword.

TODAY: Let us pray: Father, help us to live as the holy family, united in respect and love. Bring us to the joy and peace of Your eternal home. We ask this through Christ, our Lord. Amen.

December 31
St. Sylvester I (d. 335)
Pope, Convoked First Ecumenical Council, Nicaea, 325

The last day of the year presents us with a very interesting saint. Because of the great feast of Christmas, and some of the major feasts during Christmas week, St. Sylvester is most often overlooked. The fact that it is New Year's Eve may also have something to do with it.

Sylvester presided over the Church during the reign of Constantine the Great, when the Church finally began to enjoy freedom. From the death of Christ until the beginning of the fourth century, Christianity had been on trial. The catacombs were always close at hand. Then came freedom. It was almost too much to take, and the Pope found that one set of troubles had given way to another. Now the trials were theological, but Pope St. Sylvester proved worthy of the task — handing on the true Faith in the divinity of Christ. Now it is our turn to live the Good News, and pass it on.

— Msgr. Charles Dollen

TODAY: It is the time for a "new song," a new theme, a new path, a new response, as we begin a new year of Our Lord.

Bibliography

Attwater, Donald. *The Avenel Dictionary of Saints*. New York: Crown Books, 1965.

Butler, Rev. Alban. *The Lives of the Saints*, ed. Herbert Thurston, S.J., and Donald Attwater, Vols. I-IV, VII-XII, New York: P.J. Kenedy & Sons, 1938.

Butler, Rev. Alban. *The Lives of the Saints for Every Day in the Year*. New York: Thomas Kelly Publisher, 1881.

Butler's Lives of the Saints, ed. Herbert Thurston, S.J., and Donald Attwater, Vol. II (April, May, June), New York: P.J. Kenedy & Sons, 1956.

Delaney, John J., *Dictionary of Saints*. Garden City, New York: Doubleday & Co., Inc., 1980.

Dirvin, Joseph I., C.M. *Saint Catherine Laboure of the Miraculous Medal*. New York: Farrar, Straus & Cudahy, Inc., 1958.

Dollen, Rev. Charles. *Prayer Book of the Saints*. Huntington, Indiana: Our Sunday Visitor Publishing, 1984.

Foy, Felician A., O.F.M., and Rose M. Avato. *A Concise Guide to the Catholic Church*. Huntington, Indiana: Our Sunday Visitor Publishing, 1984.

Foy, Felician A., O.F.M., and Rose M. Avato. *1985 Catholic Almanac*. Huntington, Indiana: Our Sunday Visitor Publishing, 1984.

Mould, Daphne D.C. Pochin. *The Celtic Saints*. New York: The Macmillan Co., 1956.

New Catholic Encyclopedia, Catholic University of America, New York: McGraw-Hill Co., 1967.

Pictorial Lives of the Saints, ed. John Gilmary Shea, New York: Benziger Brothers, 1889.

Index of Saints

Turibius de Mongrovejo/ March 23/ 59

V

Valentine/ Feb. 14/ 32
Venantius/ May 18/ 98
Victor/ Feb. 26/ 39
Vincent/ Jan. 22/ 15
Vincent de Paul/ Sept. 27/ 184
Vincent Ferrer/ April 5/ 68
Vincent Madelgarus/ Sept. 20/ 180
Vincent Strambi/ Sept. 25/ 183
Vincentia Gerosa/ June 4/ 110
Visitation/ May 31/ 107
Vitus/ June 15/ 116
Vivian/ Dec. 2/ 230

W

Walburga/ Feb. 25/ 39
Waltheof/ Aug. 3/ 149
Walther/ Aug. 3/ 149
Wenceslaus/ Sept. 28/ 185
William/ Jan. 10/ 7
William/ May 29/ 106
William of Vercelli/ June 25/ 123
Willibrord/ Nov. 7/ 212
Winfrid/ June 5/ 110
Wolfgang/ Oct. 31/ 207
Wulfric/ Feb. 20/ 36

Z

Zeno/ April 12/ 73
Zita/ April 27/ 83

Index of Authors

A

AVATO, Rose M./ 214, 217, 219, 225, 229

B

BARBARA ANNE, Sister M., F.M.S.C./ 24, 32, 37
BOLAND, Paschal, O.S.B./ 25, 32, 33, 34, 76, 119
BORROMEO, Sister M. Charles, C.S.C./ 162
BOYLAN, Eugene, O.C.S.O./ 209
BREW, Thomas M., S.J./ 1, 61, 88, 198, 199, 246
BUCKLEY, George M., M.M./ 190, 197

C

CANFIELD, Rev. Francis X./ 191, 193, 194, 196, 197, 205
CARBERRY, Most Rev. John J./ 188, 192
CARPENDER, Rev. Thomas J./ 12, 18, 141, 143, 199
CLIFFORD, Sister Elizabeth Ann, O.L.V.M./ 172, 186
COLIN, Ricardo, M.G.H./ 70, 104
COONEY, Msgr. Maurice/ 200
CONROY, Msgr. James P./ 171, 173, 174, 182

CONSIDINE, John J., M.M./ 171, 177
COSTELLO, Donald/ 93, 100, 104, 107
COUGHLAN, Msgr. Peter/ 108, 125
CRANNY, Titus, S.A./ 134, 142
CROWHURST, Donald/ 27, 37

D

DAGEFORDE, Jeanne/ 49
DELANEY, Rev. Timothy/ 206
DENNEHY, Sister Lorraine, C.S.J./ 56, 151, 160, 163, 167
DIRVIN, Joseph I, C.M./ 227
DOLLEN, Msgr. Charles/ 4, 14, 29, 35, 67, 102, 135, 146, 234, 236, 243, 249
DUGGAN, Msgr. John J./ 105, 128, 136, 146
DUGGER, Julia/ 156
DWYER, Most Rev. Robert J./ 55, 85, 86

E

EGAN, Marion/ 158

F

FITZGERALD, Maurus, O.F.M./ 173
FOY, Felician A., O.F.M./ 116, 124, 180
FRANCIS, Dale/ 156

256